To

Edward

with best wishes

[illegible]

IN AT THE FINISH

J. G. SMITH

MINERVA PRESS
MONTREUX LONDON WASHINGTON

IN AT THE FINISH

ISBN 1 85863 516 0

First published 1995 by
MINERVA PRESS
1, Cromwell Place,
London SW7 2JE.

Printed in Great Britain by
B.W.D. Ltd., Northolt, Middlesex

In at the Finish

ABOUT THE AUTHOR

John Smith was born at Smarden, Kent, in 1925. From Ashford Grammar School he went straight into the army in 1943. He obtained early release in 1946 to take up a place at the then University College, Exeter, where he gained a degree in Economics. On leaving college he joined International Aeradio Ltd and made a career in civil aviation industrial relations in that company, and, finally in the parent organisation, British Airways. On retirement from BA he returned home to Kent, to Romney Marsh.

He is married with two grown-up sons. He and his wife divide their time between maintenance of a 16th century farmhouse, a small flock of sheep, two dogs, and being grandparents.

DEDICATION

To my wife, Kate.
She has always said that I won the war.
Now, having read this, she is not quite so sure.

PREFACE

What follows is a worm's-eye view of the campaign in North West Europe of 1944/45 in which I played a minor part. I did not keep a diary but the definitive draft of this account was written while I was still in the army and could check locations and events with my comrades.

In preparing this account 50 years later, revisions to the original have been minimal. I have retained the expressions of a somewhat naive and unsophisticated outlook which I had at the time and have not made amendments in the light of hindsight and experience. Such snippets of dialogue as are included are near enough to the actual exchanges as to be the best way I could find to convey the urgency and/or confusion that obtained at a particular juncture. For the narrative, I hope I have balanced my youthful prejudice and irresponsibility by self-criticism of my conduct which was often unsoldierly and certainly never heroic.

One bit of hindsight that I can express, however, is that I was lucky when a lot of others were not.

Ex-14435355, Trooper Smith J., C Squadron, 141st Regiment.,
RAC (The Buffs)
Ivychurch, Kent, 1994.

ACKNOWLEDGEMENT

At our briefings we were given details of the operation and the other units involved but we did not take notes of these. For accurate information on these points I relied on "The Story of the 79th Armoured Division," privately printed in Hamburg in 1945 and which many of us bought, for, I think 10 Marks a copy.

CHAPTER 1

ARRIVAL IN NORMANDY - 2 JULY 1944

I awoke and bumped my head on the bunk above as I sat up suddenly, for my sleep had been deep enough to dispel all recollection of my surroundings. The dark hold of the landing craft[1] stank of sea water, rust and sickness and when I made my way to the tiny lavatory at the end I almost added my contribution to the foul atmosphere. I had no idea of the time but I knew that I should have a job getting into all my equipment and the grey light from the hatchway showed that day was dawning. Some of my companions, members of various armoured units, were also astir and fumbling with their straps and buckles.

I dragged my pack from beneath the bunk. The green blanco was smeared with rust and the webbing stiff from lying in a pool of water. I was inordinately pleased about this - it was tangible evidence that I had finished with the petty annoyances of training and that at long last the condition of one's packs and straps had ceased to be of primary importance.

Naturally, I had slept in my clothes. I should have been able to calculate from the low speed of the landing craft when we were likely to be off the beaches but it had not occurred to me to do this. So I had spent an unnecessarily uncomfortable night. My uniform was crumpled, my hair matted beneath my beret and my feet were hot and seemed swollen inside my boots. The rubber life belt I had put under

---

1 Landing craft. A whole family of landing craft had been developed for amphibious operations, ranging from small assault boats to Landing Ship, Tanks (LST). I went over in one of the smaller boats, a Landing Craft, Infantry (LCI).

my tunic and blown up before going to bed was now flat and clammy against my chest.

With all the equipment finally assembled and in place it was a struggle to climb the vertical ladder to the deck but once there, in the fresh air, I felt less depressed and confident that I was now ready to do whatever I was told.

It was a cold, dull morning. The other holds had given up their occupants and the deck was crowded, so it was with difficulty that I made my way forward, where there was a raised platform for the AA guns. These were still sheeted as they had been in Newhaven harbour the night before - evidently the German air force was no longer to be feared.

The six landing craft were moving in a wide circle and Jock Martin, who had elected to remain on deck all night, said that this had been going on for the last two hours. I wished I had risen earlier, for the invasion fleet was an imposing sight in the half light. The grey sea heaved gently and merged into the overcast sky and cruisers, destroyers and landing craft, all at anchor, loomed out of the mist as we moved slowly on. Save for the muffled beat of our engine and the occasional lap of a wave against the hull there was no sound and the silence made the scene all the more impressive.

The low coastline of Normandy stretched dark but increasingly interesting as we neared the shore. On our right it faded away unbroken but on our left, in the distance, there was a church spire and a cluster of buildings which someone who had studied the newspaper maps more than I had identified as Courseulles. Over all floated the barrage balloons, secured invisibly to lighters and other small craft. There was no wind and they just hung there, numberless great bulbous shapes.

The flotilla had ceased to circle. Ours was the leading ship and now headed straight for the shore. The decks of the rest of the invasion fleet seemed deserted, even that of a cumbersome square-bowed vessel that threshed across ahead of us, 'LCT238' in black on the side of the hull and below her bridge. Our boat paused to let her pass. Then our engines regained their even beat and we approached what had been a channel steamer, 'Isle of Thanet' on a board slung below the concrete protected bridge.

She was the command ship and as we drew level with her, the loudhailer spoke: "Landing Craft One Six Four, land your men on King Beach. One Six Four, land your men on King Beach."

As we passed across her bows I heard the craft behind us receiving the same instructions. On board our own the crew became active and began to unsheet the windlass for lowering the landing ramps. I felt excited and abandoned my position for one on the welldeck near the gangway. I was anxious to be off.

A pontoon had been built from the beach, running perhaps 150 yards out to sea. Another section, with two engines mounted on the deck, tossed in the swell near the end. One engine was running all right but three men were gathered round the other and one of them was winding furiously at the starting handle. As we drifted down upon them the engine fired and they made off towards the beach.

The ramps were lowered. They were like those of a chicken house, very steep and with slats every yard. As they went down two sailors clambered out to the end, ready to drag them into position and then help us off.

The craft checked, the hull grated on the beach, the end of the ramp dropped neatly on to the pontoon. No one gave any orders, but the first soldiers started to go down, treading very gingerly. Astern, the second LCI stood waiting her turn with her passengers crowding the rail to watch.

I was getting near the gangway when the ramp slipped from the pontoon and we drifted slowly back. The engines throbbed spasmodically and the ramp was dragged back into position. I took my turn, clinging to the wire rope that fenced one side. It was terribly steep and the sea looked very deep and wet. Then the sailors swung me off and a sea swept over the pontoon wetting me to the knees. There was another man hard behind me and I scuttled towards land as hard as I could go, my boots clanking on the iron decking.

A wide stretch of sand and the wreckage of landing craft in varying stages of decay. One lay with its back broken, stern under water and bow rearing high in the air. The path led under the bow, between lines of barbed wire. There was barbed wire everywhere, hidden by nettles and ferns and all the debris of the invasion while telephone wires of all colours were looped across the path and straggled across the sand.

A road ran parallel to the sea, in quite good condition considering all the use being made of it. Our track crossed it to join another road that led over the brow of the hill. There was a sign:

"VER-SUR-MER ¾ KILOMETRE"

and another:

"DRIVERS KEEP TO THE RIGHT HAND SIDE OF THE ROAD"

which I had not expected but of course made sense. Only the rules of civilian traffic looked out of place in that setting.

Then another sign:

"REINFORCEMENTS"

with an arrow, ushered us into a field. It was next to the road and dust had settled thickly upon the elderberry bushes and nettles that formed the principal vegetation. There was one great pile of discarded vomit bags and another of life belts but I could not remove mine as it was beneath all my equipment. It was making me sweat, although by now the promise of the dawn had been fulfilled and it was raining hard. There were some partially dug foxholes under the elderberry hedge farthest inland and those who took notice of the weather took shelter there.

Jock Martin and I were far too busy to bother about a little rain. At the Holding Unit we had been given two 24-hour packs: a tin of emergency chocolate that was supposed to supply enough energy for a further twenty-four hours, a packet of very hard biscuits, twenty cigarettes, a portable 'Tommy Cooker' and two tins of solidified methylated spirit as fuel. We made tea with the tea-sugar-milk cubes from the packs - not very successfully but at least it was hot and wet. The mess tins, upon the polishing of which I had spent so much time in the Training Regiment, became beautifully dirty. I was dirty. I had a pleasant irresponsible feeling - I was caught up in the machine and I had not got to think for myself or worry about what I had to do. All that was necessary was to drink my tea and sit around and wait and others would make the decisions for me. I was enjoying myself more than ever before in the army.

When we got moving again our route lay over the hill to Ver-sur-Mer. I was still carrying the pick given me in the Holding Unit. It was a lovely tool and when it was issued it had made the war seem much nearer - I had felt my life might depend on its use. My companions had not been so impressed for the majority of them had either left them on board or thrown them over the side. I saw now that I was not likely to need to use it for some time but I thought I might as well stick to it as long as I could and maybe I would get a chance to take it home to my father.

We were strung out in a long line at the side of the road and commenced climbing the hill. There was still a lot of barbed wire and a sign:

"ACHTUNG MINEN! ATTENTION DES MINES!"

surmounted by a skull and crossbones. An anti-tank ditch. Some vehicles had crossed it by means of fascines - a huge cylinder made up of bundles of fencing posts and dropped into the ditch. A Bren Gun Carrier[2] had not crossed and remained with its tail in the air. There

---

2 Bren Gun Carrier. The tracked maid-of-all-work for the infantry. Open topped, armoured against rifle fire and carrying a Bren Gun, it had room to carry a section of infantry although they seemed mainly used for carrying stores. Unusually for a t racked vehicle, it was steered with a wheel.

was a broken Tommy Gun lying in a crater. Atop the hill was a pillbox of grey concrete. Also a few battered houses away to our left towards La Riviere. From one, the least damaged, a signal lamp winked seawards.

Over the hill, down the other side and we entered the village. There did not seem to be any shops, only old grey stone houses surrounded by high walls with little gates giving glimpses of dirty uncultivated gardens and muddy yards. Heaps of rubble overflowed into the rutted, muddy road. A few craters had been carelessly filled. A few villagers were standing about and they were disappointing. I did not expect to be greeted with flowers - after all, they had been liberated some time - but I did feel we merited some sort of welcome. But they stood glum and unsmiling.

It was tiring, thirsty work, plodding through the mud under the weight of big pack, small pack, water bottle, pistol and pick, and when we halted I tried my French on a native for the first time. It worked. The old lady whom I had chosen as the least forbidding of her family filled my water bottle. There were quite a few of us slaking our thirst when some know-all said that it was not safe to drink French water because of typhoid and put the wind up us. Tainted or no, the old lady got a good price for her water for we were very generous with our cigarettes and boiled sweets. It was not until later that we learnt the true value of the cigarette.

We marched on, through more villages. Everything was dirty - the road, the houses, the villagers, ourselves. Everything was wet. Presently we left the road and by-passed a village by following a path along a tall hedge. Then, after resting on the bank for ten minutes, we followed a track cutting across a field of standing corn. A farm labourer passed us on a cart horse, uninterested. We were soon right out in the open fields with no shelter from the driving rain. I could feel the earth squelching like a bog beneath the semblance of a surface given by the trodden straw. Planted poles, wagons and farm implements standing about to prevent aircraft landing were just the same as in England, but it seemed queer that the Germans had done the same as us, although, again, it was something that could have been expected.

Our way led by a landing strip where Typhoons[3] and Flying Jeeps[4] were scattered about. Nearby was a marquee and a lorry in a field and a black mass of men lining up in the rain with mugs. This was evidently the end of the road and we settled down to wait.

There were four of us who had chummed up for the crossing - Jock Martin and myself from the 58th Training Regiment, Bert Wilde from Manchester and the 51st, whom I had known at the PTW[5] and Taffy from the 13/18th Hussars, the 'Three & Eights'. We excavated a partially-dug foxhole and crouched in it covered by our anti-gas capes and although the rain drove in and we were cold and wet at least we had a place of our own and an impression of privacy that was welcome. Jock and Taffy queued and got half a mug each of tepid tea while someone in a neighbouring foxhole threw me a tin of bully beef to go with our biscuits. The only trouble was that there was a distinct taste of wet earth about everything.

The weather cleared up early in the afternoon and the sun shone and we could throw off our gas capes and look around us. We were on a rise overlooking a thickly wooded valley and down among the trees was a large village, grey roofs clustered around a church spire. Someone who seemed to know said it was Creully, which left me none the wiser.

I made some porridge. It was a queer taste as I could not waste drinking water to wash the tea stains from my mess tin and there was a long queue at the water truck. Jock ate his cake of porridge without cooking and said it tasted better thus.

---

3 Typhoon. The Hawker Typhoon, the standard RAF ground attack fighter at this stage of the war. Armed with four 20 mm. cannon and carrying eight rockets on r ails under the wings. These latter were its main weapon against tanks and all forms of transport and were fairly lethal.

4 Flying Jeep. Our name for the Auster artillery spotting light aircraft, the standard machine for this task.

5 PTW. Primary Training Wing. The first six weeks in the army was spent here, probably the worst part of my military career. Here we were broken in to discipline, drill, PT etc., before being passed on to the Training Regiment.

Although we had been told - or rather, the rumour had gone round, since it seemed to be no one's business to tell us anything - that trucks would arrive during the evening to take us to the Reinforcement Holding Unit, we decided to stretch our legs and have a look at a few houses standing just beyond our field. This proved to be another small village with the name, Tierceville, on a battered sign and 'Calvados' in small letters. All the French villages were well equipped with signs.

The sun was really hot now to make up for previous neglect but among the high stone walls of the village it was cool and would have been pleasant but for the dust which had reasserted itself with the cessation of the rain. Several houses had been knocked down and there were huge craters. As usual, there were no shops save a café with the notice "FERMÉ" stuck on the door.

A number of children were playing in the yard of one of the houses. They were very dirty and happy and more interested in bouncing their ball against the wall than in us but we managed to attract their attention long enough to learn that the Allied Military Money[6] was 'bon'. We had feared that it was only 'bon pour NAAFI'.[7] Our last pay-day in England had been in francs at the rate of 200 to the pound and it was gratifying to know that we could spend the money - if there was anything to buy. My own fortune now only amounted to 145 francs as I had evaded the censorship by getting a civilian friend to send a five-franc note to my father as an indication as to where I was bound.

In passing, I noted that the children showed a great interest in our money - far more than would have been the case with an English child

---

6 Allied Military Money. This was printed in England for use in France as it was expected that all forms of French administration would have broken down. I was given a week's pay before sailing. At that time my pay was 3 shillings a day. One hilling per week was deducted for laundry (of all things) and I allotted 5 shillings a week to my father. So my issue was 15 shillings, or 150 French francs at 200 to the pound.

7 NAAFI. Navy, Army and Air Force Institute. The major provider of canteen and other comforts for the troops during the war. At this stage there was a free issue 'NAAFI ration' of cigarettes, etc.

of comparable age. Continental youth seemed to become worldly-wise more quickly than the English.

Farther along the lane we met two farm workers. They seemed quite willing to stop and talk but we did not get on very fast until a chaplain came along and offered us all cigarettes. We should have done this - it was another lesson in the value of this currency. This chaplain was a big, breezy man and he spoke French well. Well enough, anyway, to be able to talk about foxes and fox hunting, which was out of my grasp. So we thought it time to move on and get back to our field.

A Utility Van had arrived with an officer in search of information. At the Training Regiment we had been asked to state our preference for field units and I had picked the 141st Regiment of the Royal Armoured Corps, which was the armoured battalion of my county regiment, the Buffs. My father had been an infantryman in this regiment in World War I. I had been trained on Cromwells[8] and the Buffs had Churchills[9] but that was a minor point, then. Now it appeared rather more important and I risked being sent to a cavalry unit which was the last thing I wanted. Although the cavalry regiments, equipped with Cromwells and Shermans,[10] figured

---

8 Cromwell. The best British cruiser tank with a 75 mm. gun, good speed and reasonable armour. It was the main tank of the 7th. Armoured Division, the Polish Armoured Division and the Armoured Reconnaissance (Recce) Regiments of other Divisions.

9 Churchill. The text covers the flame equipment of the Mark VII Crocodile and some of the specialised equipment of the Marks III and IV AVRE. Basic details of the Churchills used in Europe were:-
Marks III and IV AVRE: weight 39 tons, armed with spigot mortar, max. armour 4 ½", speed 15½ mph.
Mark V: as Mark IV but armed with a 95 mm. howitzer.
Mark VI: as Mark IV but armed with a 75 mm.
Mark VII: weight 40 tons, armed with a 75 mm., max. armour 6", speed 12 ½ mph.

10 Sherman. This American M4 tank was the main battle tank of the Allies. About 30 tons, it mounted a 75 mm. gun and two .300 machine guns. It was fast, manoeuvrable and reliable, its main drawbacks being a relatively high silhouette and inadequate armour when faced with anti-tank guns like the German 75 mm and 88 mm. It had a reputation for catching fire easily after being hit and the story was that you only had five seconds to get out - which was not long enough. Our Churchills were supposed to give us 15 seconds - which was reckoned to be long enough. Fortunately, I never had to test the truth of this. However, the Sherman

glamorously in the newspapers, they appeared too heavily officered with professional soldiers to allow a comfortable existence for the men. After six months of the 58th I was fed up with 'bullshit'.

"Number? Name? Trade?"

"Driver-operator, Cromwell," I answered to the last query.

"Unit?"

"141 RAC."

"But that's a Churchill mob."

"I know."

"OK. Next."

It was as easy as that.

Soon after this the lorries arrived, we all piled in and I managed to get to the front so that I could cling to the cab. This was always the point of vantage in open army trucks. If they were closed the post of honour was at the back. It was good to get moving again. It was getting dark but was still pleasantly warm and there was a heavy scent of clover and meadowsweet in the air. The lorries wound along lanes, through woods and round the edges of fields. I noted one village, Villers-le-Sec, because of a park of wrecked tanks nearby but after that it was too dark. After a bit we began to halt every few minutes during which we could stop clinging to the cab and wonder what was happening to us.

Then we came to a field bordered with trees and under the trees was a row of tents. There was no light to see by but as I had only one blanket the process of making down my bed was not complicated. I was fortunate, for my end of the tent was free from cow pats but the others were still swearing when I dropped off to sleep.

* * *

The morning was sunny and breakfast was tinned boiled bacon which was very good. The RHU consisted of rows of tents, a marquee for the officers, another as an office and store and a separate tent for the cooks. One of the officers - they had come over with us, apparently, but it was the first I had seen of them - assembled us

---

was available in quantity and, in addition to being the standard gun tank, was the basis for a number of specialised adaptations (q.v.).

outside the office and told us that we were going to be sorted. I was worried again but need not have been for my statement that I belonged to the Buffs had been accepted and my interview was short. There was nothing more to do but move my kit to the tent occupied by four other members of that regiment and wait for transport.

Jock and Bert had been with me, on and off, since we joined the army, but had trained on Shermans. They found that the Sherman units were crying out for men and were posted straight away, the one to the Northamptonshire Yeomanry, the other to the Sherwood Rangers. I heard later that Jock had been killed and Bert wrote to me from hospital in England. His tank was knocked out when crossing the Albert Canal.

A large proportion of the draft, including Jock and Bert, left immediately. A short while afterwards the remainder paraded again to hear a few words from one of the officers. I expected some sort of advice to soldiers landing in a foreign country - remember these people are your friends and all that sort of thing. However, this was not the occasion for a pep talk of that sort, for all the officer wanted to do was to attack our personal appearance. Some of us had not shaved. Some had not even washed. No brasses had been polished.

His speech was resented very much. It could almost be said that the meeting broke up in disorder. The NCO's were the loudest in their complaints, the burden of which was that they only took orders from officers of their own regiments. The discontent must have been obvious to the officer and the threatened inspection in half-an-hour never took place.

During the afternoon the draft continued to break up as and when unit transport arrived. I got to know my new comrades but they did not seem very interested in talking about the regiment so I concluded I should have to contain my eagerness to see something of it. There were some cows in the field and during the evening two French girls came to milk them. I should not have fancied the milk, for they were filthy, but I had a long talk with them which was good for my French.

In the morning we five Buffs were the only troops left in the camp and were so fed up with doing nothing that we welcomed the suggestion of the camp commandant, a Norwegian captain, that we should dig a hole to drain the ablution enclosure. This lasted us until lunch, which was the usual messy meal of such units and then we decided to risk missing our transport and go into the nearby village of Ryes.

It was a short walk down the road in the heat and we were glad to get into the cool, stone-paved kitchen of a house that was half farm and half café, where there was cider for sale. They had French bread, too, which was more to my taste than the rough liquid they served up to us. We learned later that troops were strictly forbidden to purchase bread but the villagers seemed anxious to sell it to us. Presumably we paid well over the odds.

Like all Norman villages, Ryes had the appearance of being very old. If there were any modern buildings they had been put out of sight. The street was more like a farmyard than a thoroughfare. The only damage suffered was to the church, the spire of which had been knocked down. My companions suggested it had harboured snipers.

From Ryes we walked across country and found a searchlight crew tucked away out of sight in the shade of a hedge, their instrument standing in the middle of the field. They were dividing their NAAFI ration as we came up and having completed this satisfactorily they invited us to share a brew. We admitted that this was only our third day in France, whereupon we received a lot of useful advice, especially regarding the state of the roads. The sergeant seemed to be labouring under a sense of injustice on this point and we gathered that breaking down was a crime punishable by about a dozen charges.

On the way back to the RHU we stopped to examine a 20 mm. AA gun left by the Germans, which impressed us as a beautiful piece of machinery. When we reached camp we were told that in all probability our transport would arrive on the morrow.

Surprisingly enough, it did. Or rather, there was a sergeant who told us that the truck was waiting on another road and we should have to slog across the fields to get to it. It was very hot. I was sweating and all the way seemed uphill and across ploughed fields. Despite much chaffing I had clung to my pick but now it proved the last straw and I flung it into a ditch. We were glad to reach that truck.

Ryes had been a backwater and we could now get a good idea of the tremendous effort being made by the invasion forces. The roads were choked with vehicles and each field held its quota of tents, tanks, trucks, AA guns and searchlights. At last we came to Villers-le-Sec and then turned off through Creully. Just beyond there we turned off the road and followed a dirt track downhill into an apple orchard.

One of my companions pointed out to me a huge armoured trailer on two heavy wheels that was upended at the gate into the orchard. There were a lot of trucks under the trees, a line of Honey[11] tanks and some Crusader[12] AA tanks. We passed through to the field below where several Churchills were standing along the hedge, each with a trailer attached. This was D Squadron, which was a reserve of tanks and men from which the three fighting squadrons could draw as needed. While waiting, new arrivals were trained on the flame equipment with which the Churchills were fitted. Also, my companions said, the AA and Recce Troops were being disbanded as the regiment was not fighting as a single unit and the crews were to be trained with the rest of us.

The field was split into two parts by a raised path bordered by trees and bushes amidst which were placed the squadron latrines. This path led down to a piece of marshy ground bordering the River Seulles. On the upper, or eastern, side of the field the tanks were parked, beneath the overhang of the typical high, bushy, bocage hedge. Bivouacs had been built beside each tank and in a corner of the field was the office and Tech. Stores. Near the office marquee was another bivvy, a single tank sheet over a deep hole. The sergeant

---

11 Honey tanks. Our name for the American Stuart light tank, a very fast but lightly armoured vehicle, usually armed with a 37 mm. gun. The most common Recce tank.

12 Crusader AA tanks. A cruiser tank much used in the Western Desert but obsolete at this stage of the war, its role being taken over by the Cromwell. Those used in France had been converted to AA tanks but all were disposed of soon after D-Day as German aircraft no longer posed a significant threat to tanks.

was another bivvy, a single tank sheet over a deep hole. The sergeant explained that 'Duggie' (Captain William Douglas-Home, the Squadron Commander) always liked to sleep in a hole and the first thing his batman did on reaching a new harbour was to dig one for him, to be on the safe side.

I reported to the office. The clerk, who was a lank, weary-looking man who could not be expected to be interested in anything, commented on my cap badge, which I had put up at the RHU. The infantry Buffs had a brass dragon badge but the 141 had them nickel plated. As this was an internal process they were not on sale in the shops so where Jock Martin got mine was a mystery. When he gave it to me I assumed that he had bought it.

After having puzzled the clerk he told me to find myself some blankets and a place to sleep. One of the tank crews generously provided me with these and invited me to bed down under the nose of their tank. No one took any more notice of me so I concluded I was at liberty to follow my inclinations and get some sleep.

CHAPTER 2

D SQUADRON AND B SQUADRON

I never heard any Normans complain about the Germans. They had been very 'correct' towards the country people, very smart, and there had not been too many of them. The innkeeper at Creully, who was a Parisian, said that the railway trucks were invariably labelled 'Paris' as a salve to the Norman conscience. Only luxuries such as cigarettes and soap were in short supply so, probably, the Norman farmer was not best pleased when we landed and he and his village were bombed, his corn crushed or burnt and his cattle shot to lie bloated in the fields. I got the impression that the Normans were glad to see us liberating France but sorry that we had chosen to start with Normandy. A constant grievance was that British troops augmented their compo rations by digging potatoes. Orders were posted to stop this, threatening severe disciplinary action, but no one took any notice.

In the Normandy of that summer the most striking thing was, of course, the dust. Eighth Army men said it was worse than the Western Desert. It lay inches deep on the roads and verges and bushes and trees were bent beneath the weight. There was no tarry road with grass borders and green hedges, only dust and dust-covered mounds, a dust pall shrouding every moving vehicle, dust that blotted out the view behind any form of transport. In the forward areas all traffic was reduced to a snail's pace. There were graves by the roadside marked:

"HE WAS DOING MORE THAN 10 MPH!"

These may have been effective but no one could escape the dust in Normandy.

The inhabitants seemed to exist upon brown bread, eggs, cider and sardines. Our compo packs, which contained food for 14 men for one day (in our case, for five men for three days), usually contained sardines, which were unpopular and were swapped for eggs and butter. When I landed the Normans were getting sick of sardines, or else were running short of eggs and butter, because prices were going up. As I could speak sufficient French my services were often required as interpreter in these transactions, which were vaguely supposed to be illegal.

We could never persuade them to exchange anything for biscuits. Not until the middle of July did we get bread, at first one slice a day issued at teatime, which issue was gradually increased. The difference was made up in biscuits and of these there was always a surfeit. We could not use the universally accepted currency, the cigarette, because we had not enough for ourselves. The ration in D Squadron was seven a day, which was one after every meal, one at each break and two for the evening. The non-smokers were lucky men. Still, it was a free issue and forced me, for one, to go for a breakfast that otherwise was not inviting.

* * *

As I have said, when I reached the 141 the Headquarters Squadron was being reduced to a bare minimum by the break-up of the AA and Recce Troops, who lost their tanks and were transferred to D Squadron for training on the Crocodile Flame-throwers. Tactical HQ was detached, trying to keep some check on the activities of the three fighting squadrons which were scattered all over the British sector. These squadrons were attached to successive units as needed, usually operating in half-squadrons or single Troops.

Our tanks were the much-maligned Churchills. While, I was given to understand, there was a considerable amount of truth in the criticism when applied to the Marks IV, V and VI, with which ordinary tank battalions were equipped, these faults had been largely eliminated from our Mark VIIs. At this stage all Mark VIIs on the Continent were sent to us. The reason lay in its armour being about twice as thick as that of the earlier marks. This was necessary as our work entailed very close support of the infantry and reduction in manoeuvrability due to the trailer. Speed, also, fell from 19 to 13.5 mph. In general, the regiment was satisfied with the Mark VII. It had its faults, notably concerning the hydraulic throttle and brake controls, but it was reliable and probably the best tank possessed by the Allies in France at this time.

The Flame Gun, our speciality, was mounted in the forward machine gun position and operated by the co-driver, dignified by the title of Flame-gunner. The weapon was still very hush-hush and we were supposed to take elaborate precautions to prevent it or its fuel from falling into enemy hands.

At this time no one understood the fitting of the Flame Gun save ourselves and we were merely supplied with the gun tank to which the necessary modifications were made by our Light Aid Detachment of REME.[13] Experience was continually demanding alterations in use and maintenance and we could also improve the tank. When I arrived the REME were busy strengthening the floor plates following the mining of a tank which had resulted in driver and co-driver losing their legs. Later, the tanks arrived with flame equipment installed and all our modifications embodied.

Fuel for the Flame Gun - 400 gallons - was contained in an armoured trailer weighing seven tons that could be jettisoned if it caught fire by turning a switch in the turret. At least, such was the theory although I never saw it done. The fuel was put under pressure by opening five gas bottles in the trailer and this forced it through a very complicated link into the belly-pipe which ran under the tank and reached the gun through the floor of the driving compartment.

The fuel was the most secret part of the whole contraption and we did not know what it contained. In appearance it was a congealed milky-white jelly. The Germans used Diesel oil but our fuel had the great advantage of remaining a compact 'rod' and thus reducing the amount burnt up in flight. Its consistency was such that the flame

---

13 REME. Royal Electrical and Mechanical Engineers. A new corps, the 'garage mechanics' of the army. A very competent and professional organisation.

could be 'rolled' along the ground into slit trenches or bounced round corners. In addition, it stuck to the target.

Flame was still something of an unknown weapon and not greatly liked by our infantry who seemed afraid that we should attack the wrong side. In spite of this suspicion we aroused great interest and I spent one whole afternoon at the village of Brecy, standing in pouring rain and ankle deep in mud, waiting for a general to arrive so that he would have someone to salute him and show him the cleanest gateway. As the campaign wore on our value was recognised and at the end a whole brigade was insufficient to cope with the demands made on it.

In the turret of the Churchill there was a Besa 7.92 mm. machine gun mounted co-axially with a 75 mm. that fired high explosive, armour piercing and smoke shells. The Seventy-five ammunition, save for the smoke, was American and had to be handled gently as the cases were made of very soft brass. The HE was very efficient but the muzzle velocity of the AP was too low for good anti-tank work.

As defensive armament there was a 2-inch Bomb-thrower to provide smoke and dischargers at the rear of the tank to give 'tail smoke'. Against aircraft there was a Bren Gun[14] but it was so stowed as to provide a footrest for the tank commander when entering the turret and thus the barrel inevitably became clogged with dirt. Also, there were never any facilities for winding up the ammunition drums.

The personal weapons of the crew were Sten[15] guns for driver and co-driver and pistols for the remainder. These were usually in worse condition than was the Bren.

On the whole, to sum up, the regiment was pleased with its equipment and had confidence in it, which was the main thing.

---

14 Bren Gun. The standard infantry light machine gun, in their case using a 32-round magazine of .303 ammunition. Issued to us for use against aircraft, with a drum of ammunition rather than a magazine.

15 Sten. Standard British sub-machine gun, a rather shoddy weapon with a 28-round magazine of 9 mm. ammunition. It was alleged to have a tendency to go off of its own accord.

* * *

In normal times Creully must be a very sleepy little place. It is tucked away in a valley among the woods and the main Caen - Bayeux road passes to the south while that to Bayeux from the coast passes on the north. However, when I was there Caen had not fallen and traffic and dust jammed the narrow street. The ruts at the sharp corners grew deeper and dust blew continually about the market square.

The village was a compact mass of buildings huddled round the square and the roads leading to it. Only the war memorial at the corner and the Calvary on the outskirts were of recent date. All the rest was old, grey stone. There were farms right inside the village but only the back door led into the fields. The farmhouses fronted on the street and were indistinguishable from the houses on either side.

There was little choice in the shops. We often bought milk, although repeatedly warned not to do so and, of course, butter and eggs. I once bought some Camembert cheese but was puzzled by the mould on top, not knowing whether or not it should be there. In the end I compromised by scraping off the mould and eating the rest.

The main attraction was the Hotel St. Martin, which stood at one side of the square. A petrol pump riddled with bullet holes stood outside. The Calvados[16] there was the best I ever drank in Normandy. The farmhouses sold a terribly raw spirit but at the hotel the landlord said his stock was ten years old which, I presume, made it good. There was also Denise, the prettiest girl I ever saw in Normandy. She always looked clean and neat, which was unusual in a country where the majority of the population looked as if their most pressing need was a good scrub. However, I never got further than talking to her.

The lack of money enforced moderation which was a good thing as I discovered early that I had not a strong head. The curfew was not

[16] Calvados. A spirit distilled from cider and named after the Department of Normandy in which it is made. Otherwise known as 'apple brandy'.

until eleven o'clock but we all had to stand to our tanks at 2200 hours. Even if it was a job to stand.

Apart from the excursion into Creully there was little to do in the evenings. Some went swimming in the River Seulles. Occasionally there was a film show at Viller-le-Sec but this entailed a mile walk across the fields and in any case the weather was too nice to make a stuffy marquee agreeable.

During the day most of my time was spent on the flame course. It took ten days, mostly devoted to the mechanics of the weapon and the attendant drills but eventually we all had our turn in sending a jet of flame eighty yards to cascade from a pile of old oil drums. Lastly there was a written test. The pupils had been three officers, one captain and two lieutenants, myself and two other men. Obviously the sergeant instructor knew his business because when the results were announced the captain was top, the two lieutenants second and third and then the three other ranks. Not that it mattered.

The village of Brecy, whither we moved from Creully, consisted of a church, three farmhouses and a chateau which had been requisitioned following its abandonment by the Germans. I had finished my tuition on the Flame Gun so with two other wireless operators who also had nothing to do I moved into the chateau for a refresher course on the No. 19 Set[17] and morse. This was not necessary as we had all had recent instruction but it was better than doing nothing. One afternoon we borrowed two scout cars from HQ Squadron and had a practice run out to the coast near La Delivrande. After a fortnight we all had a test and having passed that were sent back to the tanks.

These had to be taken up to a fighting squadron at a moment's notice. The first task, on their arrival from the Delivery Squadron,

17 No. 19 Set. The standard tank wireless set and my particular responsibility. Details are given in the text. Considering the treatment it usually got and the lack of technical knowledge of most wireless operators, it gave remarkably good service. The training period in the 58th Training Regiment was 6 weeks, much of which was concerned with message procedures and morse (which was never used). I did, however, get a useful mnemonic for Ohm's Law: 'Women Are Virgins, Virgins Are Rare', which I have used frequently in subsequent life.

was to stock them with ammunition. This is productive work. The sunlight glistens on the brass rounds, piled on the track guards ready to be handed into the turret where someone has a hammer trying to open the locker doors. Another man is halfway through the pannier stowing the green smoke rounds. Another sits by himself in the shade and primes grenades. Around the tank is a litter of wood, wire and cardboard, a tin box containing smoke bombs, cylinders that have housed the HE rounds, bits of yellow and white adhesive tape, paper torn from the Besa boxes, spilt Sten ammo shining in the grass. The temporary tank commander sits under the rear of the vehicle trying to force the tailsmoke charges into position. Then there is a shout of "Mail up!" and one man goes to collect it while the others break off for a smoke.

Mail took about a week to cross at that time. When I first landed the address of the British Army in Europe was 'BWEF', or 'Burma When Europe's Finished'. This was soon changed to the more dramatic 'BLA' which, in turn, became 'Burma Looms Ahead' or 'Bugger Liberating Anybody'.[18] I spent a lot of time writing letters, and the period before I began to get replies was very trying.

By the time we had the tank ammoed up, the engine cleaned and fuelled, the trailer charged and all the miscellaneous kit checked and stowed there was usually a demand for a tank from one of the squadrons and we had to go through the whole routine again. I hated to see a tank go. I wanted to get up to one of the squadrons and on one occasion tried to exchange with another man who had been posted to B but whose friends were in A. The office said that such action was impossible as it would complicate their records. D Squadron was comfortable enough and had I been older I should have been sensible and tried to stay there safely until the end of the war. As it was I wanted to feel settled and knew this would not be the case until I had a tank of my own and a position in its crew and the standing that went with it.

A second reason for disliking to lose a tank was that the bivvies went with it. After losing two in this way I made my own private

[18] BWEF & BLA. These initials actually stood for 'British Western Expeditionary Force' and 'British Liberation Army'.

dwelling out of empty flame fuel drums, jerricans[19] and discarded gas capes. I built this in a corner of the hedge out of sight of the office tent and avoided many fatigues by being asleep at the right time.

We were supposed to parade for odd jobs after dinner and on one occasion there was a sudden demand to produce pistols for inspection. By this time I had mated up with a man named 'Shag'[20] Taylor, who was about my own age and we were caught napping as we had been trying to shoot partridges the previous evening. At least, we had gone out in the fields to see if there was anything worth picking up and a covey got up before us, tempting the use even of the erratic .38s. Between our bivvies and the parade we managed to get the barrels clean but the chambers were another matter and we spent that evening washing dixies in the cookhouse.

The squadron moved from Brecy to Bretteville-sur-Odon. I was disappointed in my hope to go on the tanks as I was detailed to proceed by commonplace truck to the Faubourg de Vaucelles - the western suburb of Caen - where Tactical HQ[21] was in need of latrines and said to be too busy to dig them. At this period Tac. HQ actually was in close touch with the squadrons although its role appeared to be purely passive as directions for the use of the flame-throwers were issued by the unit to which the squadron happened to be attached.

It was interesting to see Caen although it was largely in ruins, especially about the railway station, which was a mass of rubble and twisted girders about the wreckage of a dozen engines and a lot of trucks. The cathedral seemed unscathed as did several other large public buildings but for the most part the place was a shambles and a heavy grey dust shrouded the streets that remained. The shops and

---

19 Jerrican. The standard robust petrol container, holding 4½ gallons.

20 Nicknames. I never knew why my particular friend was nicknamed 'Shag' as, by tradition, a Taylor should have been 'Spud'. I, of course, was 'Smudger' or 'Smudge', 'Dusty' Miller was our Flame Gunner and we had a 'Chalky' White in another Troop. However, the CO's wireless operator was Charlie Clark when he should have been 'Nobby', so there was a certain lack of consistency. The most apt nicknames were probably 'Jinx' Brown, our gunner when I joined the 'Sandwich' crew and 'Chung' Murray, who looked rather Chinese although, from his surname, he was probably Scottish.

21 Tactical HQ . This was the only time this organisation entered my life. I imagine it was disbanded when the front opened out and our squadrons were spread around.

cafés were shuttered and the few civilians that were visible stood aimlessly at street corners watching the endless procession of trucks.

The Faubourg, typically suburban, was in rather better state. Tac. HQ had a street to itself and occupied three houses which, of course, had no water and hence the need for latrines. The day was very hot and the ground hard and it took us a long time to dig holes in the garden while the skilled members of the party erected a screen of sacking and made seats from empty compo boxes. However, the job was finished at last and we scattered to look for vegetables and valuables, without any success. I returned to the lorry to hear a dusty DR[22] who had arrived in our absence talking about A Squadron echelon which, it appeared, had been bombed by our own planes the previous evening.

I went to the scene the next day, one of a salvage party. The echelon[23] had been harboured in a copse south of Caen, together with a Polish AA battery and a troop of 17-pounder anti-tank guns. We had lost three men, the Poles fourteen, while the casualties of the RA[24] were not reported although all their guns and quads[25] were wrecked. In fact, the whole wood, covering several acres, was gutted. Trees and undergrowth had crumbled to ashes which still smoked as we scuffed through to find our lorries. These were twisted wrecks of brown and red metal smelling strongly of burnt rubber. Some of the gas bottles had blown open but the real messes were the ammo trucks which had simply been blown apart. The Poles had already marked some graves but how they found any bodies left after that holocaust was a wonder. The blame had now been shifted from the RAF to the USAAF[26] but in any case it had been thorough and we returned to Bretteville empty-handed.

The German Air Force was not very active during the daytime and whenever an enemy aeroplane did appear it was attended by a flock of

---

[22] DR. Despatch Rider, a motor-cyclist.

[23] Echelon. The name for the team of 'soft-skinned' trucks which supplied the fighting vehicles. Sometimes divided into 'forward' (petrol, ammo, flame fuel, etc.) and 'rear' (squadron office, quartermaster, etc.).

[24] RA. Royal Artillery.

[25] Quad. The squat, four-wheeled 'tractor' for the 25-pounder gun.

[26] USAAF. United States Army Air Force.

Spitfires. The flak[27] batteries were also very keen. One FW190 I saw, beset by four Spitfires, dived right through an intense barrage in an attempt to lure its opponents to their destruction. On this occasion we had a perfect view of the kill, the German climbing steadily and steeply, the Spitfires creeping up behind. Then the victim slid backward in slow motion, the nose flopped down, a parachute opened and the stricken machine dived straight into the ground while the Spitfires whirled around doing victory rolls.

More often there would only be the scream of engines, a brief glimpse of two streaking shapes over the trees, a flurry of gunfire, a big bang and a plume of smoke. One man told me that just before I joined the regiment the Germans had sent over a formation of captured Spitfires and when he saw one Spit chasing another with guns going he thought some RAF bod had gone mad. There were about half-a-dozen of the Germans and he said the fight was the most vicious he had ever seen - one of ours following a smoking German right down to the ground, blasting away long after it was necessary. He supposed the RAF felt bad about the deception.

Nevertheless, during the night the Luftwaffe kept our AA gunners busy, flak being our principal weapon at night. AA guns were rarely to be seen in the daytime but they were everywhere after dark. The drone of the aeroplane was smothered by bursts in the distance. If we were dressed we would crawl under the tank. If we were in bed someone would say that the canvas bivvy could withstand the shrapnel. It could be heard pattering through the branches of the apple trees while the sky glowed red with balls of tracer from countless Bofors,[28] the rosy spray of an Oerlikon[29] adding to the confusion. No bursts to be seen - just the lazy curving tracer vanishing at its apex. If we were on guard Shag and I would go round

27 Flak. The German abbreviation for anti-aircraft fire, adopted into the English language and still current 50 years later. Also used for someone in trouble, e.g. 'getting a lot of flak'.

28 Bofors. The standard 40 mm. quick-firing AA gun, often mounted on a trailer but always very mobile. Rounds were loaded in clips and theoretical rate of fire was 90 per minute.

29 Oerlikon. The standard 20 mm. quick-firing AA gun. It produced a stream of tracer and, at a distance at night, rather resembled a Roman candle.

to the officers' marquee and throw apples on the roof to make them believe shrapnel was hitting it.

Our own aircraft held the sky in daytime. The Americans who had always specialised in day bombing were now joined by our Lancasters and Halifaxes. The Americans flew in close formation, the sun gleaming on silver fuselages and wings as they toiled steadily in amongst the bursting flak. The black bombers of the RAF affected no special formation but flew in a long procession at varying heights just as I imagine they did on their night raids. We had a grandstand view of the thousand bomber raid on Caen and the surrounding area, when the sky was covered with aircraft appearing in the distance over the sea, passing leisurely overhead and wheeling majestically over the town. Only one Messerschmidt[30] that I saw tried to interfere and he was shot down and after that the Germans left it to the flak.

Inevitably, there were some casualties. Behind a tightly packed formation of Liberators a little black speck would appear and then the parachute opened. Then another and another. The stricken machine gradually lagged from the formation, a thin plume of smoke streaming from an engine, dropping steadily, holding to its course until the fire reached some vital part and brought it twisting to earth.

Or a Lancaster, to all appearances untroubled, would turn suddenly on to its back and scream down to hit the sea beyond our vision while we counted the parachutes anxiously.

I was returning from Creully one evening when a shattering whine sent me diving into the ditch and a Mosquito spun out of the blue sky in which a single parachute drifted. The plane tore itself apart before it hit the ground in a ball of flame with fabric spinning like feathers in its wake. I heard later that two soldiers had the bad luck to be crossing the field in which most of the wreckage crashed and perished with the pilot.

Then there was the sudden burst of gunfire at midday that brought us out of our bivvies to watch a Liberator circling low while half a dozen Spitfires tried to shoot it down. I suppose the crew had set the

[30] Messerschmidt. The Me109, the most common German fighter plane.

automatic pilot before bailing out. It was a lovely clear day and the distance gave the scene the appearance of being enacted in slow motion. The huge bomber rose and fell, now climbing almost vertically, sliding backwards, dropping and turning in wide sweeps, exactly like a fish playing in a glass bowl. We heard a tearing crash as it hit the ground but it rose again, only to turn and fall and a black pillar of smoke rose above the trees.

* * *

The squadron was harboured in an orchard to the west of Bretteville and the green apples which had been knocked down and crushed, the latrines and the refuse from the cookhouse, attracted a myriad of flies. We blamed all these in turn for an attack of the trots that laid most of the squadron low. My own experience was slight and I was able to laugh at the flapping shirttails, for some were so bad that they hardly dare wear trousers. The wood adjoining the orchard held convenient, and soon reeking, foxholes, and was swarming with every kind of insect. Work was suspended for several days, during which we lived on biscuits and tablets distributed by 'Aspro Joe', the MO.[31]

The majority had recovered when four men were needed in B Squadron to replace four who were coming back to D for courses. Shag and I were detailed to go and although it was only a temporary posting we were very pleased as it might lead to something permanent.

The truck arrived very early in the morning and we loaded our kit and bedding. We both had more than we could carry, my principal encumbrance being a 2-inch smoke bomb box in which I kept my best serge, some fishing lines and assorted souvenirs. There were several permanent postings as well so the truck was uncomfortably crowded but at least it was an open one so we should not have to stifle under canvas all the way.

31 MO. Medical Officer.

We passed through Caen and out along the main road towards Lisieux. The dust was very bad and when we turned on to side roads it was absolutely choking, while ruts and holes threw us from one side of the lorry to the other. It was impossible to sit on the wooden let-down seats that were fixed to each side and we had to cram together at the front and cling to the cab.

At length we reached St. Pierre-sur-Dives which once must have been a pretty place but had been fought over several times, and then started to go round in circles. This was usual and lasted for about an hour. Finally we located St. Julien-le-Faucon and B Squadron was in harbour nearby. It was, of course, an apple orchard but a cleaner one than usual as the invasion forces now had more room to move and could pick and choose a bit. Our driver said that the people in the neighbouring farmhouse were very hospitable and had plenty of Calvados. The atmosphere in the squadron was distinctly convivial.

We had no chance to sample it for we had hardly unloaded our kit when the squadron got the order to move and we had to put it all back again. At the first halt, however, one of the drivers shouted out for me and said that I was to be co-driver on his petrol wagon. The rest of the day passed with short moves and long halts.

Our army was moving up to the Seine and B Squadron was constantly on call as opposition was expected but failed to materialise. In consequence there was a move every day and sometimes two.

So the petrol wagons were busy while Shag, who was co-driver on a flame fuel truck, had an easy time. My main job was to read the map and camouflage the lorry when we halted. Every evening we were working late reloading the lorry at the nearest petrol dump. I got on very well with my driver, Harry Salt, who was a rough, good-tempered sort of chap. I probably worked a lot harder than was necessary owing to my lack of experience of field unit life - I wished I had been with the regiment in England for I knew no one apart from Shag and had no idea of what was expected of me. So I was in constant fear of doing something silly or out of order while I was still a stranger.

The squadron had left narrow lanes and bad roads, passed through L'Hotellerie and La Bosquetterie, where the first dead German I ever saw was sitting in the ditch with the top of his head blown off, and entered Lisieux. On along the main road through Thiberville, Brionne and Bourgtheroulde and our moves became shorter. I wrote home proudly that I was sleeping in a hayloft in which German soldiers had been posted the night before. At length we reached Bourg Achard and the squadron assembled to hear the major explain that the Germans were fording the Seine and we were going to try and stop them. This was the only time we had an appreciation of the military position as distinct from an operation briefing. B Squadron was not going into action but it seemed to the major a good idea to let us know what was going on.

After this Shag and I went into the town, looked at a captured Panther tank on a transporter and bought some bread. When we got back to the harbour we were told that we four temporary members of B Squadron had been posted to C and that we were to start as soon as transport could be found.

CHAPTER 3

C SQUADRON

The same evening the major's staff car took us to HQ Squadron at Louviers. We had asked the major to be allowed to stay with B Squadron but he had told us that our posting was a firm one and could not be altered. Although we could apply to be sent back to B after we got to C. We knew how popular this would make us with the commanding officer of C Squadron and how much chance we would stand, so that was that.

HQ was anxious to get rid of us and had a lorry available. Now C Squadron was at Bretteville where, after a breakneck journey, we arrived at three a.m. Not a very good time to arrive in a strange unit.

Fortunately there was moonlight so we could see our way around. The guard commander, tin-hatted for some reason, showed us where the cooks kept their bread in order that we should be able to make toast at a smouldering fire in the farmyard. Then, with the advice to find an empty lorry and sleep in the back of it, he left us to our own devices. The toast was excellent and I wondered that the cooks left their stores in such an accessible position.

In the morning the squadron clerk took our names and numbers and the major had a look at us but our future was undecided. Shag and I attached ourselves to a lorry driven by one Fred Hillier so that we should have at least some sort of home but we were both anxious to be put on a tank; although those professing to know said that the squadron was over strength in gunners and operators and we were correspondingly depressed.

The squadron had just returned from the rest camp at St. Aubin-sur-Mer and all the tanks were in workshops save for three replacements. We thought we had struck lucky one evening when Sergeant Ellis ordered us to get one ready to move. This sergeant was not particularly popular, we learned, but any commander was better than none. However, it transpired that he was our commander only for the evening, to demonstrate flame to an infantry battalion. I acted as driver on this occasion and was quite pleased with myself as it was the longest period for which I had driven a Churchill. I stalled the engine once but we were stationary at the time so the lapse was not noticed. Shag, as gunner, had nothing to do, so we hoped that a favourable opinion might get to the major.

The tanks being away it was feared that time would hang heavily on our hands and discontent be engendered thereby. I never felt discontented at having nothing to do but all commanding officers know that idleness must be prevented at any cost so we had PT and drill parades. With miserable memories of the Training Regiment I was pleasantly surprised to find that field unit standards were far more reasonable.

PT was tried first. First parade was at ten o'clock to count heads. Paddy Scallan, the Squadron Sergeant-Major, took on the job of PT instructor and he was about as keen as the rest of us. So we jumped about for a bit, without much exertion and then started to run round in a circle. Then someone disturbed a wasp's nest and it was every man for himself. My hair was very long and wasps got tangled in it and stung me so I had a headache for the rest of the day. About half the squadron got stung and that finished the PT.

The next morning they tried drill. The field was very bumpy and the wasps were still on patrol so Paddy just marched us out to the road, fell us out for a smoke, then marched us back again. The following morning there was no parade at all.

Our dirty washing had piled up in B Squadron and this seemed a good chance to get it clean. The water from the River Odon was not very pure to begin with, especially as there was a cow rotting away just round the bend, but after we had boiled our shirts in a petrol tin we saw just how dirty we had been. I scraped away the scum by the handful and then we rinsed the clothes in the river on the end of a rope.

Then there was sewing. The regiment, hitherto independent, had just been assigned to the 79th Armoured Division and we had to fix the triangular bull's head flashes to our tunics. This was a most wearisome task and took all of one day. We had just finished when an acquaintance told us that George Ive was looking for us. George was the MT[32] Sergeant and the only reason he should want us that we could think of was that we were due for some fatigue.

George was very fair about fatigues. I had been mess orderly in D Squadron on one day when he was Orderly Sergeant and had neglected to turn up for the washing up after tea as I wanted to go into Creully. I had just got into my best serge and in a moment would have been clear of the field when George came rushing along and caught me. I thought I was for the high jump but he suggested that as I had never been mess orderly before I did not know that I had to wash up after tea. I was only too pleased to agree with him.

But it was a tank. George saw us that evening with the good news. He had been the MT Sergeant, with occasional jobs as Q-bloke[33] and this latter was his real métier. However, after several courses he had been pronounced competent to command a tank and had been given the fourth, or 'Charlie', tank in 13 Troop.

The four-tank troop had just been instituted in the regiment. Originally, in each squadron, HQ Troop had four gun tanks, two having Ninety-fives and two Seventy-fives and the five flame troops had three tanks each. Now three flame troops would have four tanks and one three so that, on detachment, each flame troop could have the support of a gun tank.

George had a lot to tell us. Shag was gunner, I was wireless operator. Dusty Miller, our flame gunner, was formerly in the AA Troop. Jack Rodaway, driver, had been a co-driver in HQ Troop and

32 MT. Motor Transport.

33 'Q' Bloke, or 'Q'. Traditional title for the Quartermaster sergeant, the man responsible for issuing everything that had to be signed for except pay.

was the only member of the crew to have been in action. Our tank was 252033 and George advised us to get our kit stowed as we should be moving in the morning.

This was good news but incorrect and Shag and I spent the afternoon, as usual, exploring the surrounding countryside. Whatever happened in the morning, no one bothered us after dinner. We could bathe in the Odon, taking care to be upstream of the dead cow. It was an attempt at cleanliness but neither of us was very fond of water. Or we could go blackberrying. Otherwise there was a German Seventy-five in the field beyond the old D Squadron harbour and in a corner a score of neatly marked graves that had to be inspected. Or we might go down to the little cluster of houses lying just over the road. We were cautious in this, having vague notions of the penalties for looting.

We rummaged these abandoned houses several times but they contained nothing of value. Plaster fell from the ceilings and walls where peeling wallpaper revealed rotting lathes. The air was heavy with the sour smell of decaying food. A wardrobe with the doors wrenched off, contents scattered over the floor - underclothes and old stockings, a summer dress, an odd shoe and bedroom slippers - mixed with bricks and buttons, religious books and broken glass. The bed broken and filled with plaster, the round table standing in a corner jumbled with cardboard boxes, identity cards and ration books, spoons, buttons, odd trinkets and coins, letters and picture postcards. Lopsided on a wall was a cracked mirror and a crucifix above a framed text. Shag and I would turn it all over and then creep back to tea feeling guilty. On this occasion we met 'Dan' Duffy, the squadron commander, as we entered our field. He was a small but thickset man with bloodshot eyes, a red moustache and an abrupt manner. We saluted him reluctantly and submitted to a cross-examination as to our movements. He accepted our explanation that we had been fishing, without luck.

In the opposite direction we could explore the tracks leading out to the Bretteville-Caumont road. Here there was a wrecked Italian truck and a burnt-out Daimler of the 15th Scottish Division, with two graves. There were also lots of bits of German infantry weapons, which interested us greatly.

Dead cattle lay about in the fields, bloated and rotting. The smell of decaying flesh was everywhere. There were no birds. The only living animals we saw were some horses, well groomed and fed, in the stables adjoining a large mansion. There was no one about and it was all rather strange and spooky. The funny thing was that the house and furniture were untouched save for the library. Lots of the books had been torn up and the pages strewn about the room and outside. I could not explain that - there was a lot worth having in the house without doing wanton damage.

One evening a truck ran into Caen for such people who wished to see the film of J. B. Priestley's 'They Came To A City'. I believe this film was shown in Caen before its premiere in London, as a compliment. In my case it was wasted for it was so boring that I walked out after ten minutes with Shag and Taffy Wakelyn, who was wireless op. for the Fitters. I was feeling fed up, anyway, as I had neglected to polish my boots before going to the office for my pass and Paddy had told me off.

The darkening streets of Caen held little of interest to the soldier and the few French girls that were about failed to respond to Taffy's "Bon soir, mademoiselle. Ça va?" So we went to the NAAFI and queued for tea and biscuits. By the time we got to the counter, there was only tea. It was a relief to get back to Bretteville and bed.

Now the rumours began again and the Fitters were working overtime getting 'Dan's Circus' in running order. All the squadrons had done well on the Falaise Gap but C was reckoned to have secured the best collection of German vehicles. At this time it comprised a motor coach (long used as an ideal squadron office), two powerful motorcycles, a half-track motorcycle, two cars in working order and several that were not, numerous trailers and a Bren Gun Carrier that had been captured by the Germans in 1940 and incorporated into their army.

At last there was definite news. In the morning we were to break trailers, load on transporters and proceed to the area of Le Havre. The only disappointment was when we tossed up and I had to go with Dusty and the trailer when I wanted to ride with the tank. But that did not really detract from the pleasure of being somebody and doing something at last.

* * *

The dew was still on the grass when Shag and I took our kit over to the tank. It meant several journeys but it was all jumbled on the floor of the turret by the time the rest of the crew arrived. It was the first time I had seen them all together but there was no time to get to know each other this morning. Jack started the engine and opened his pannier door[34] so that he could hear our shouted orders. I removed the sledgehammer from the gearbox decking. Dusty found a pair of pliers and fumbled at the split pin that ultimately secured the trailer to the tank. Shag and George fixed the legs one at each end to support the trailer after the link had been broken.

All went smoothly. The pin came out, Dusty shouted, the tank jerked forward, I clouted the revolving part of the link and the trailer was broken. Surplus fuel dripped from the hanging nozzle at the back of the tank. George told us to burn this, which was a standing order on security grounds. Dusty plugged both apertures with cotton waste and put an old kit bag over that part of the link attached to the tank before it was swung up and over to the right to be secured in its bracket. All that was left to do was to pin the towing link into position on the trailer and then we could warm our hands at the blazing fuel in the ditch and I could get a good look at my new comrades.

Jack was a typical driver - thickset and untidy - and although his hair was thinning he wore his beret only rarely and when he did it was perched on the top of his head like a saucepan lid. He was one of the

---

34 Pannier Door. The Churchill had a door on each side of the hull to enable driver and co-driver to escape if necessary. On the Mark VII the doors were round, on earlier Marks rectangular. The doors were, of course, of great assistance when it came to internal stowage.

original members of the regiment, his 'first three' being 629 - most of the ex-infantrymen were now drivers and co-drivers while the turret crews, in general, were younger soldiers from the Training Regiments. Dusty was one of these, a tall, thin, quiet Londoner with a poker face. He looked reliable and we soon found out that he was. George had been a solicitor's clerk and retained a somewhat clerical manner. Shag I had now known for some time and liked, although he had his mad moments.

The big artillery wagons known as Matadors were late in arriving but this was expected and once they did come the hitching up operation was performed without mishap. Dusty and I took our places in the truck as the tanks were lining up to rendezvous with the transporters.

Bumping over the ruts, we passed the wrecked Daimler that marked the entrance to the squadron area and drew out on to the Caen road. A French farm worker, waving frantically and pointing into the ditch, drew our attention to a trailer handling bar lying there and in the first flush of our enthusiasm we stopped the Matador[35] and retrieved it. This halt left us well behind the column and when we entered Caen without catching up we began to wonder if it had turned off somewhere along the road. We turned round - a complicated business in the narrow street - and sped back to the commencement of the Caen Bypass. This was just being completed - Caen was a hopeless bottleneck - a bumpy, rust-coloured track full of puddles and smeared with a film of mud, crossing the canal by Bailey Bridge and bordered below the embankment on either side by rows of white crosses.

Luckily - for we had no idea of our destination - we found our convoy drawn up on the verge of the Falaise road. The leading Matador had hit another truck and made a wheel change necessary. On this first stage of the journey the convoy was trying to keep together.

---

35 Matador. Towing vehicle for the heavy artillery, 5.5s and above and consequently capable of handling our trailers.

A misty drizzle and grey skies lowering over the devastated countryside made the prospect far from attractive. The Germans had suffered severely - witness the large number of half-track and horse-drawn vehicles abandoned, burnt out or overturned into the ditches. A Tank Delivery Unit emphasised our armoured might but the possible fate of those glistening Shermans was only too obvious. Their sisters lay wrecked, brewed up, blown up and rusting, all along the long road.

It was said the Germans had nicknamed the Sherman 'The Ronson Lighter' owing to its tendency to catch fire. It was believed that only weight of numbers got the tanks through. There was something pathetic about the knocked-out Sherman and quite aside from one's feelings for the crew one felt pity for the tank. On German wrecks the long gun with its tremendous muzzle brake always drooped and looked defeated but still vicious. With the Sherman the naked muzzle cocked skywards and surprise, pain and bewilderment were depicted in every line.

We left the Falaise road at St. Julien-le-Faucon, passed through St. Pierre-sur-Dives and on to the road I had travelled with B Squadron. The body had been moved from the ditch at La Bosquetterie but little else was changed. The road curved down into Lisieux between thick woods and along the river valley the meadows stretched damp and green, beautiful after the dusty plain of Caen. The bridge, surrounded by bomb craters, had collapsed into the stream and the gap had been filled with rubble around large pipes to provide a crossing. The railway line running parallel to the river was twisted grotesquely, the embankment crumbling into the water. For the first hundred yards beyond the bridge, the road was flanked with walls of debris and then the battered houses were habitable again. The white cathedral, or whatever it was, towered on the skyline over all the devastation below, apparently unscathed.

German tanks must have been concentrated in this area for there were the wrecks of several self-propelled guns in the town and tanks proper in the fields beyond. At the top of the hill, where two roads joined, a Mark IV[36] had been run into the ditch. Turret and sides were systematically guarded by spaced armour - how different from our own makeshift welding of track-plates.

It was late in the afternoon when we came to the Seine near Pont de l'Arche and the rays of the dying sun glinted on the swift current rippling under the pontoon bridge that had quickly replaced the permanent structure. Into Rouen the road ran by the river, on one side towering chalk cliffs, on the other the sparkling Seine with its islands drooping weeping willows in the water. Here and there a half-submerged barge rusting under the bank struck a discordant note. On the road chalky dust swirled in our faces. In the riverside villages people stood on their doorsteps and actually smiled and waved.

Although the mere fact of being in the army was enough to destroy one's interest in the artistic and historical associations of the countryside in which we happened to be, I did want to see something of Rouen but was afraid the fast-gathering dusk would prevent this. It was still light, however, as we entered the town. Along the river bank twisted railway lines, shattered warehouses, wrecked cranes and listing barges loomed out of the mist of an early September evening. The fallen bridges were black against a golden sky and by one a queue waited patiently for the ferry.

In the centre of the town there seemed to be some confusion on the part of the Matador drivers. Little groups of lorries and trailers passed and re-passed, the crews jeering at each other, vanishing round a corner only to re-appear the next moment on another road, going in the opposite direction. But at last we found the road out of the city and then, as is quite common with army transport after nightfall, got properly lost.

It was drizzling again. Dusty and I were cold. The Matadors were heavily sprung and thus unpleasant to ride in when lightly loaded

[36] Mark IV. The Panzerkampfwagen IV was the heaviest German tank until the advent of the Panther and the Tiger and, at this stage of the war, mounting a high-velocity 75 mm. gun. Apart from being a standard gun-tank, it was the basis for a whole family of specialised vehicles (see SP etc.).

and there was no chance of sleep. My canvas window would not shut, the draught was biting and the sleet swept in upon us.

At length we stopped, the drivers conferred and then walked away. Dusty and I climbed down to warm our hands on the radiator. There were two red lanterns and an MP[37] sign pointing to a tent in a field. Then our drivers returned with the information that we were "halfway to bleeding Dieppe."

We turned and jolted back the way we had come for what seemed ages. Then, leaving the main road, a village shone in the glare of the headlights. We halted in a sunken field. The engine stopped. The drivers made no movement and it was too dark to see anything. Too tired to care, we made our beds in the back of the Matador and got into them.

37 MP. Military Police, the unpopular 'red-caps'.

CHAPTER 4

LE HAVRE

When I awoke it was a bright sunny morning and I could hear the clatter of Churchill tracks in the distance. The Matadors started to charge about the field sorting the trailers into Troops and Dusty and I stumbled around in the wet grass without any clear perception as to what had to be done. We were both unfamiliar with the use of the trailer legs and there was a shortage of petrol cans with which to block the wheels. Our tank was third in the column and fortunately the trailer link was on its good behaviour. This was not always the case - in soft ground the tank was not delicately manoeuvrable and to fit the nozzle attached to the tank into its aperture on the trailer was then no easy task.

Breakfast was ready by the time we had drawn up behind the rest of the Troop. The cooks had been operating in a cart shed at the corner of the field and sausage and beans went down very well. This was to be our last cookhouse meal for a long time - henceforward we were to fend for ourselves.

After breakfast came a long wait for an opportunity to get out of the field. I spent the first hour in stowing our kit properly as Shag had been too lazy to do anything about it and it was still lying on the floor of the turret where we had left it at Bretteville. The road was packed with traffic moving towards Le Havre. Churchills of the King's Own and 9th RTR[38] passed, many showing signs of recent action such as rent mud shields and missing bogies. Then a long line

---

38 RTR. Royal Tank Regiment. This was the 9th. Battalion, a battalion of the RTR being the equivalent to a regiment of the Royal Armoured Corps.

of Carriers and trucks. Following, a squadron of Flails[39] swung round the corner, their chains scrabbling in the dust. A bus-load of reinforcements from 269, our Delivery Squadron - at this there was a rush to the gate to renew old acquaintance. A long line of Recce Honeys, bearing such names as 'Jeanne d'Arc' and 'Jerrican', ungraciously accommodated themselves to the slow pace of the rest of the traffic.

Towards midday it began to rain and simultaneously there was a break on the road. A few minutes of feverish activity and we were strung out in the gap. The skies were grey again, the steady drizzle blanketed the landscape, the hammering tracks steamed on the wet tarmac. The turret crews were wrapped in waterproofs, gloved and scarved, smoking damp cigarettes and trying to prevent the moisture from seeping into the turret. On the radio the Andrews Sisters were singing - the operator on the tank in front was beating out the same time as me on the hatch padding.

The countryside was sparsely inhabited and there were only scattered farmhouses near the road but despite the rain people were standing in the gardens to wave. We had a German tin hat which I had picked up at La Bosquetterie strapped to the gun muzzle and the French pointed and shook their fists at it.

Then came a little town with narrow streets and sharp corners. It was congested with farm carts and evidently market day. The tracks screeched and ground, beating madly as we wormed through, commander and operator leaning anxiously out of the turret[40] with their microphones to their mouths. A horse was restive and several carters were struggling to restrain it. We threw cigarettes to people

---

[39] Flail. The Sherman Crab, described in the text. The 79th. Armoured Division had three regiments of Flails: Lothian & Border Yeomanry, 22nd. Dragoons and Westminster Dragoons.

[40] 'leaning anxiously out of the turret'. The driver of a Churchill sat below the level of the top of the tracks which projected forward on either side of him. He had a round vision aperture (and two periscopes for use when closed down in action) but his view was very restricted. Thus in tight traffic situations he relied heavily on commander and operator to keep clear of obstacles, especially as an air louvre stuck out on either side. When 'closed down' the commander had his cupola with 8 periscopes and the operator had a single periscope but guiding the tank then became even more tricky.

crowding the pavements. There was a heap of men, women and children in the road and then they were all jumping for the comparative safety of the pavement as the rear of the tank swung over. Amusement in the turret and chatter over the I/c[41] about the girls. I flung some cigarettes to one and there was another scramble which the tank behind had to swerve to miss.

Then out of the town and pounding down the road once more. For the first time we had been greeted with flowers and I had a bouquet stuck in the B-set[41] aerial base and a large red rose behind my cap badge. In return we hoisted the Rear Rally flag[42] on the aerial in such a way as to be the tricolour. Flown properly it was the Dutch flag so we would find it useful.

Then the column slowed suddenly and stopped. Our engine panted softly and steam rose from the tracks and exhaust covers. Jack stood up in his seat and grinned up at us, his face all muddy, but dropped down almost immediately as the leading tank turned off the road along a muddy track and stopped at the far end of a line of beech trees. The rest of the squadron followed.

The engine died, coughed twice and was silent. The wireless whined and faded out. I put off the master switch and descended stiffly to the ground and already Shag was in the ditch and filling some old margarine tins with petrol. I put water into the dixie. Tea. Several French children watched us drink it, appearing suddenly from nowhere in the way children always do and very interested in every move we made. They went barefooted in the wet grass and it made us cold to look at them. The rain dripped steadily through the branches and we huddled round the fire, the petrol soot blacking our hair, eyebrows and stubble. It looked very odd on Shag, who was fair both in hair and complexion.

---

41 I/c, B-Set. See description of the 19 Set in the text.

42 Rear Rally Flag. A hangover from pre-war exercises. I did not know what it was for and never saw it used properly.

When we had thawed Shag and I dragged the bivvy[43] over the bank into an orchard next door and erected it. George wandered away on some business of his own. Jack lost his spoon and blew up about it - the first of many unpleasantnesses over his cutlery, which he was always losing. Dusty was fiddling about on the trailer. No one ever asked Dusty what he was doing. It was always something necessary, done quietly and well.

Shag and I, who usually shared a guard, were on in the early hours of the morning and prowled through the orchard in our greatcoats. I had my pistol in my pocket but Shag could not find his and had armed himself with a pick haft. We skirted a pond on the far side and attempted to enter a barn for shelter but the rusty hinges squeaked and we desisted for fear of officers.

Soon after, the rain stopped but water was still trickling down the bank into the bivvy when we returned to it. It had been a mistake to pitch it there for George, who was sleeping at one end, got very wet. In the morning there were a lot of blankets hanging out to dry.

* * *

Le Havre, strongly fortified, was supposed to have a garrison of about 12,000. In theory and in the newspapers, it was the Canadian First Army that had to attack the town but in fact it was the British 49th and 51st (Highland) Divisions.

C Squadron of the 141 was attached to 152 Brigade of the 51st. With us were the Flails of the 1st Lothian & Border Yeomanry to deal with any minefields and the AVREs[44] of 16 Assault Squadron of

---

43 Bivvy. Short for 'bivouac'. The tank carried a number of tarpaulins, or tank s heets, which we used to construct extremely primitive shelters.

44 AVRE. Armoured Vehicle, Royal Engineers, described in the text. The 79th Armoured Division had three RE Assault Regiments but, like the Crocodiles, these operated as separate squadrons or half-squadrons. The REs were a very versatile organisation. The main accessories which I saw in action were fascines and the SBG (small box girder) bridge.

Royal Engineers who would lay Bailey Bridges[45] over anti-tank ditches, or fill them with fascines, and who would then be at liberty to beat holes in any bunkers with their petards.

The Flail or, to give it the official name hardly ever used, the Sherman Crab, was a standard tank with a rotating cylinder on arms which fitted across the front and on which were mounted a large number of weighted chains. When operating these flailed the ground and exploded mines[46] so as to clear a track through a minefield. The Sherman retained its armament so it could also act as a normal gun tank. Successful as the device was it seemed a thoughtless act on the part of some military genius to attach it to the relatively thin-skinned Sherman whose crews had to operate in close and slow-moving order often at point-blank range.

The AVREs, Armoured Vehicle Royal Engineers, were Churchill Marks III and IV, again thinner-skinned than our tanks. The turret weapon was a Petard, a 290 mm. spigot mortar firing a 'Flying Dustbin' containing 26 lbs of explosive up to about 80 yards. The 'Dustbin' was muzzle loaded by the co-driver reaching up through his hatch which, again, seemed a dodgy occupation. As a demolition device it was also successful but, in addition, the AVREs performed a whole range of engineering tasks. The most spectacular piece of equipment was the SBG bridge mentioned above. This was a 30-foot girder bridge attached to the front of the tank and sticking up at an angle of 45° ready to be dropped across obstacles. As the campaign progressed the AVREs were continually adding to their repertoire and we had a great respect for them as, indeed, we had for the Flails.

So far as Le Havre was concerned, on September 4th a demand to surrender had been rejected by the German commandant so preparations were made for our assault. In addition to the land forces, it was said that the battleship 'Warspite' and a monitor were to bombard the fortifications and there was to be heavy bombing.

---

45 Bailey Bridge. A prefabricated steel bridge, one of the most useful British inventions of the war. The smaller sizes could be transported ready for use (see AVRE). Larger ones were put together like Meccano.

46 Mines. The main German anti-tank mine was the Teller plate mine, about the size of a dinner plate. Their anti-personnel mines included Schu mines and wooden box mines; these latter were, of course, designed to be difficult to clear.

* * *

It rained intermittently all the time we were harboured under the beech trees, coming down with especial force when the moment came to move nearer to Le Havre. So we were thankful for our gas capes, which were now getting a bit the worse for wear. In fact, we had no suitable clothing for wet weather as yet and the lack was especially hard on Jack. Water would accumulate in the engine compartment and every so often would surge under the turret into the front. His seat was raised a few inches from the floor but every time it happened the legs of his trousers would be soaked. Dusty could avoid this by sitting up on the track guards.

Major Duffy stood by his staff car to watch his 'boys' pass. We always kept a good lookout for that staff car, waving it by as soon as it hove in sight. Once it was ahead everybody could face the front to watch for low branches, make themselves comfortable and light up cigarettes and pipes. I still cannot understand why the rule forbidding smoking in WD[47] vehicles is retained for everyone does smoke and attempts to enforce the regulation are only spasmodic. The Americans seem to get on very well without it for I do not believe there are any more fires in their forces caused by cigarette ends than there are in ours. Perhaps the rule is retained as a peg to hang a charge on if necessary, like the notorious Section 40 of the Army Act 'conduct prejudicial to good order and military discipline'.

Anyway, we kept the cigarettes out of sight as we lurched out on to the road. All down the column Rear Rally flags fluttered from the wireless aerials, a cheering touch of colour in the drab light. The rain beat down and yellow mud spurted in our faces as we wallowed over the potholes. I began to think favourably of the snug cab of the petrol lorry but was soon cheered by the honour and glory attached to our tin hat, which attracted the attention of several civilians at a halt when we had to get off the road to let a squadron of Flails go by. The French wanted to know when and where we had killed the German and I spun

---

47 WD. War Department.

them a long yarn about the "lance-flamme" being "pas bon pour les Boches." It was some compensation for a wet backside.

The echelon was harboured in an orchard around the outside of which we parked the tanks. I found time amid the hubbub of arrival to pick some blackberries but the rain had spoilt their taste. Jack and Dusty went off to draw the compo[48] pack and returned much put out as they had been issued with an E-pack, Haricot Oxtail; which was the least appetising of all the compo packs. Nevertheless, it was convertible currency and we exchanged three tins of Haricot Oxtail for five eggs and a pat of butter at a nearby farmhouse.

When we returned to the tank an officer was talking to George. Jack, who had naturally been busy within earshot, whispered that George was leaving us, being replaced by Mr. Grundy. This officer normally commanded the fourth Mark V in HQ Troop, 'Sultan', but this tank had been longer in the workshops than the others and had not yet caught up. Until it did we were to do duty as a support tank.

It was strange having an officer on the tank but Mr. Grundy was a very decent chap and no trouble at all. He was liked in the squadron and Jack spoke highly of him, which was a recommendation indeed. At present all we could do was feed him and whatever he got, poor fellow, he praised as being very nice. It must have cost him an effort to say that sometimes for our training had been concerned with fighting the tank and the much more difficult task of living on it had been ignored.

We discussed the advisability of dropping the trailer and replacing the Flame Gun with the spare Besa. Jack, whose word was now generally accepted as law, said it would be best to wait until the last moment, as 'Sultan' might turn up and all our work be for nothing. We asked him if it was best to be a flame tank or in HQ Troop and his

48 Compo Pack. Each compo pack provided enough rations for 14 men for one day. We were issued with one pack every three days (see text). Each pack contained a main meal - A being Steak and Kidney, E Haricot Oxtail, F Corned Beef, plus all the accessories, such as tinned pudding or fruit, cigarettes, tea-sugar-milk powder, even a rather slippery toilet paper. The empty box, with a hole carved in the bottom, was just the right size to provide a comfortable 'thunder box' which was carried on our trailer.

verdict was that HQ had all the advantages. Not only was their business to stand back and give covering fire while the flame tanks were getting within range but they had more speed if less armour, knew what was going on, and stood a chance of better rations.

In the afternoon I was detailed to take over the 'Administration Net' in the absence of the scout car[49] 'Twenty dog' that usually performed this duty. It was the first time I had actually worked the radio in earnest and I found the vigil a strain. I never did learn to whom I had been talking and never heard the Administration Net mentioned again.

This task prevented our tank from accompanying the rest of the squadron to give a flame demonstration to troops of the 51st Highland Division. It was the first time this particular battalion had worked with a flame regiment and they were alleged to be more afraid of us than of the Germans. In any case, the 51st had a reputation for not liking tanks. To dispel these feelings they were to be given a preview of the show.

Le Havre looked dodgy. 152 Infantry Brigade were on the right flank. There was an anti-tank ditch to be crossed at point 'Rum', strong points marked as numbers 8 and 11, the village of Fontaine-le-Malet, the Forêt de Montgéon and strong points to the right on Mont Trotins. For our part, 13 Troop were to emerge from the Forêt and attack on the right flank of some 88 mm. guns[50] situated on the southern part of Mont Trotins, flaming two 20 mm. and a barracks on the way. 14 Troop had the left flank while Shermans of the East Riding Yeomanry made a frontal assault. We consulted the oracle and Jack was of the opinion that if we did, after all, go in with 13 Troop then we were in for something definitely dodgy.

---

49 Scout Car. Known as the 'Dingo'. A four-wheeled armoured car without fixed armament, used for recce and communication purposes. A very pleasant little vehicle.

50 88 mm. Anti-tank Gun. This gun, originally an anti-aircraft weapon, obtained a legendary reputation in the Western Desert in the anti-tank role. It had a very high muzzle velocity and could knock out any allied tank. German anti-tank guns commonly in use were the 75 mm. and the 50 mm., the latter being the most numerous. The only really effective allied anti-tank gun was the 17-pounder (76 mm.).

Everything was very thoroughly prepared. Not only was the briefing exhaustive but to exclude the possibility of mistakes a practice attack was held over ground supposed to resemble the real objective.

We started early and badly, for as soon as we were on the road my air louvre, which stuck out from the side of the tank, hit a telegraph pole and Jack blamed me. We stopped in a clover field for breakfast and Shag and I cooked. The food went well but I had some trouble with the tea and at length managed to get a dirty grey liquid into five mugs. The others would have passed it for the rain was coming down in torrents and all that was needed was something hot and sweet but Jack, never tolerant at the best of times, had already been sorely tried and complained bitterly. When we had finished I found the wireless set had drifted off frequency and I had to get Charlie Clark, Major Duffy's operator, to give me a netting call all to myself.

The 19 Set, which was my particular responsibility, took up most of the back wall of the turret. It was really three sets in one: the A-Set, which was the main channel of communication; the B-Set, which we were supposed to use between tanks in a Troop but which was tricky and unreliable; and the intercom (I/c) system. We also had a separate 38 Set which was supposed to let us talk to the infantry but this was never used.

Getting the set on net meant, for the A-Set, so tuning the set that all the tanks could hear and speak to all the others. It was a matter of nice adjustment, with an at first sight complicated procedure involving a tuning call in which the CO's operator repeated the squadron's call-sign[51] for the day to enable a rough setting, followed by a netting transmission to produce the fine setting by the elimination of a whistle. Here I was finding the difficulty. By the time I was sorted out and pronounced to be on net we were moving again, to the scene of the mock attack.

[51] Call-signs. The squadron call-sign was changed every 24 hours, at midnight. As an example, if the call sign was Tare Baker Fox, the Troop tank of 13 Troop would be Tare 3, the troop tanks Tare 3 Able, Baker and Charlie. If I wished to call the Troop tank I would use only my call sign, as he would know I was calling him, but if calling the Able tank I would have to use both call signs. Examples of these procedures occur in the text.

I was disappointed. Even in practice I had expected some excitement but everything was most casual. The Flails pounded a patch of earth into a slightly more sticky consistency, the Shermans chugged across the valley with the infantry wading behind, knee-deep in the wet grass. We stood about in the rain and got soaked. I could not see that anyone was the better for the exertion but all the officers seemed pleased.

We always got a lot of maps but little time to study them. There was a Defence Overprint which showed everything down to a single foxhole. Sometimes there was a Minefield Overprint as well. The information was gleaned mainly from air photos, augmented by ground reconnaissance. It was usually only a few days old and gave a fair idea of the opposition we might encounter. Air photos added to the realism of the maps but they were harder to interpret and we did not get them so often. What the maps could not show, of course, was whether or not there actually were guns in the positions marked.

We moved up to the Forward Harbour[52] on the afternoon following the practice attack. 'Sultan' had caught up and there was another change of commanders. We now had Steve O'Neill, who was reputed to be steady and whom I had known in D Squadron when he was transferred from the Recce Troop. We were back with 13 Troop. Although Steve was only a corporal he was senior in the Troop to George, who was left with the echelon. I forget what had happened to Steve's own tank. It was either getting a new engine or a new turret ring.

The move was made in sunlight, welcome after the leaden skies and continuous downpour to which we had become accustomed. Our new harbour, a ploughed field, was considerately placed amid several batteries of 25-pounders,[53] all heavily in action.

---

[52] Forward Harbour. A number of tanks gathered together overnight or for an appreciable period of time are said to be 'in harbour'. Sometimes a Forward Harbour was nominated to be the forming up point immediately before the start of an attack.

[53] 25-pounder. A highly mobile and versatile artillery piece, firing HE and smoke and, sometimes, AP shot. The most common RA gun.

There is a vicious crack to the 25-pounder that places it in a category by itself in a list of explosions. Deep in their pits surrounded by empty ammunition boxes, old compo packs, sheets of galvanised iron and swathes of netting, the little guns leaped and bounced like infuriated terriers at a gate. The shells wailed incessantly and I felt that at last I was getting near to the real thing.

Overhead an observation Flying Jeep circled wearily. The artillery men told of one, earlier in the day, which had flown so low as to enter the trajectory of the shells and had been blown to smithereens. These little aircraft were certainly worked hard. One afternoon in B Squadron we had been harboured in a field next to one from which the Jeeps were operating. There were about half-a-dozen of them and the field was very small and pocked by cows - indeed, the cattle still occupied one end. The punishment the planes took on take-off and landing must have been terrific for they jolted and bounced all over the place. They never seemed to get any maintenance - just down, refuel and take-off again.

I sat in the sun and watched our echelon jolting across the field to bring us petrol. A little to the east a group of Engineers argued around a bundle of fascines they were trying to hoist on to their AVRE. Over Le Havre great clouds of smoke rose in the still air and we climbed on to the tank to watch through binoculars as the Halifaxes and Lancasters, bomb doors open, flew steadily in, undeterred by furious flak, until the bombs tumbled down out of our field of vision.

For Operation Astoria, the liberation of Le Havre, the RAF had laid on a most comprehensive softening-up programme and the highlight was to be a thousand-bomber raid on the dock area. We were watching the attack on the outer defences prior to the assault by 56 Brigade. 152 Brigade was not to move until midnight.

After I had more experience I was still unable to decide whether or not, from the point of view of the army, the advantages of a bombing raid outweighed the disadvantages. At Le Havre, admittedly, all went well, but other operations were not so fortunate. I have already described the mess made of our A Squadron echelon by the USAAF. Later, at Sangatte, we found it impossible to reach our objectives because of craters made by the RAF which also provided cover for the opposition.

The small fry - Typhoons and Thunderbolts[54] - were even more impartial than the bombers and when Tiffies were operating anywhere within five miles we had to be ready to duck. There were many stories of our tanks being shot up although I never met anyone who had been, not by the Tiffies. My own experience leaves open the question of the standard of tank recognition attained by the ground attack aircraft. During the River Roer operation we were parked near a German Panther tank used by the Coldstream Guards Tank Battalion as a Forward Observation Post. A Thunderbolt saw this Panther and recognised it as German despite recognition sheets and white stars. Fortunately there was only one bomb, which missed, and the pilot then machine-gunned all the tanks in the area. With similar success.

* * *

Three o'clock in the morning. My brain is not functioning properly. Someone bangs on the top of the turret and tells me to get on the air. The master-switch is in an awkward position, under my seat in a recess of the hull with the batteries and it is a struggle to reach it. Reach up, the set whines and the hiss of the headphones is loud in the silence of the turret. I can hear Shag and Steve messing about on the engine-deck for the guns have ceased firing and there is only the roar of the cooker and the odd clang of a tool. I rub the sleep out of my eyes, disentangle my hair, light a cigarette and cough painfully. My mouth is dry and my feet ache as they always do when I have slept with my boots on.

The call comes faintly, then louder as I move the dial. "Able Baker Charlie Dog... Able Baker Charlie Fox... Able Baker Charlie Love..." My fingers are all thumbs. The set whistles, it dies to a groan and then I have silenced it and locked up on the frequency with a penny brought from England specially for that purpose.

---

54 Thunderbolt. Although the Republic Thunderbolt was designed, and mainly used, as a long-range escort fighter, by this time the USAAF was also using it for ground attack although, as it was not fitted with rockets, it was not so effective in this role as the Typhoon.

"Hullo. All Stations Tare Tare Baker, report my signals. All Stations Tare Tare Baker, over."

The Check Call. We answer in rotation - HQ, 11,12, 13 and 14.

"Hullo, Tare Three Baker. Hullo, Tare Three Baker, OK, over."

Then a long wait for me while other sets follow the commands of the CO's operator and are adjusted to his satisfaction. At last, "All Stations Tare Tare Baker. OK, out."

By this time Dusty and Jack have made the tea. I go out to the engine-deck and shiver, stooping to warm my hands in the exhaust jets. I am pleased to be able to report that we are on net. The tea is sweet and hot and goes down well and I have nothing more to do so I can sit on the engine deck and drink it quietly and get warm.

The other tanks are a blur in the darkness. Someone stands by the air louvre and shouts at me. Jack has revved the engine to warm it more quickly. I shout, "Can't hear you!" and point and he goes away.

We start late. Jack says it is usual. I am not quite sure how near we are to the front line so I play for safety and stand on the floor of the turret, peeping out of my hatch. I wonder if I should close down and watch the outline of the operator on the tank in front. He seems undecided. At length I get tired and ashamed of opening and closing my hatches and leave them half open in the vertical position so that I can drop them with one sweep of my hand.

Artificial moonlight. Searchlights spread low over the fields. A line of men and Carriers moves down the side of a hill, silhouetted against a pale violet glow. We lurch off the road, giving way to a long convoy of trucks. Gun flashes stab the blackness - blackness doubly intense in contrast to the searchlights. Fires are burning, winking patches of red, on the hillside towards Le Havre. Beyond the hill the flicker of exploding shells.

Then there is the faint glow of dawn. Dim shapes become trucks, tanks, Carriers and Jeeps. I doze and when I wake it is almost day. We stand on the side of a hill behind a squadron of Flails. The Lothians are moving about their tanks and we are emboldened to sit on the engine-deck and warm hands and feet on the exhaust.

There is a line of ragged, dirty figures, coming over the brow of the hill and down the slope towards us. Prisoners. They are unshaven and bleary-eyed, bewildered and miserable old men for the most part, but one tall blonde fellow is bomb happy, laughing and singing and falling over the ruts. Or he is drunk. There is only one Tommy as escort and he looks ill. His face is grey and strained and he holds his Sten as if it were trying to get away from him.

Jack has left the driving seat and is demanding a brew. His face is stung red, ginger stubble blotched with mud. He is very cheerful and wide awake, which is more than I am. Dusty gets the cooker and dixie. Shag scalds his fingers opening the water can. It has been lying on the gearbox decking right behind the exhaust and the water is almost boiling. I bring the tea from my store in the turret and we manage to get the brew into mugs before the order comes to move on. The tank behind is not so fortunate and follows with cooker and dixie balanced precariously on the back bin.

Over the hill and it looks like time to close down. There is a long grass slope down to a wood, with thick poles at intervals, and the tanks spread out, each Troop making its own road. About a mile ahead a water tower is being shelled. Rising above the greenery of the woodland, the white stonework gleams in the sunlight and the shell bursts are black patches on the clear blue sky. We do not know if they are British or German. I ask if the wood is the Forêt de Montgéon.

Steve looks at his map and cannot decide but thinks it might be. The B-Set - another attempt to use it for inter-troop communication - suddenly emits a piercing whistle and I twist round to deal with it. I am not successful and Jack shouts, "Shut that bloody thing off, Smudger!" All members of the crew can hear what comes in over the air because of the 'filterthrough' from A or B-Set to the I/c system.

So whistles irritate everyone. The B-Set is supposed to be on net to the Troop Leader but I bow to experience and it is silenced.

Some tanks are moving along a valley to our left, through the remains of a wood. The charred ground smokes and bursts spasmodically into flame as the tracks churn it up. The turrets swing methodically to left and right. Steve thinks this is 'Rum' but Jack chooses this moment to say that the throttle needs bleeding and we ought to do it before we go any further. Steve tells me to call the Squadron and detail our problem.

After I have reported I try to get the Fitters to our assistance but they are deaf to my calls - Jack has the answer, they are netted to the BBC.

'Rum' is a track junction near a large country mansion. A Bailey Bridge spans the anti-tank ditch and the AVRE that laid it is sticking up in the air with its nose in a crater. Two more are lying in a minefield and have been abandoned. A number of Half-tracks are standing about. A Bulldozer is filling in a bomb crater in a desultory fashion.

A few hundred yards ahead mortars are bursting in a cornfield, great gouts of black and red against the golden wheat. They disturb the columns of prisoners that trudge along the track to a field behind the house - at every explosion a ripple of alarm runs along the line as those nearest start to run and are gradually stopped by those in front.

Behind the house they are searched by a few MPs and a large number of assistants. We are among these last and I get my first close view of the Germans. The prisoners look so miserable that my feeling that I ought to get my hands on something worth having is subdued and I am angry with myself but cannot overcome my scruples. So my acquisitions are limited to a camouflage jacket and a compass, which will not be needed any more, anyway.

During the afternoon I return to the tank and listen to the battle. All seems well. The Shermans are chattering away most of the time about haystacks, white flags and prisoners coming out. Presently the

Fitters turn up and we show them our trouble and ask them where they have been - at which they laugh.

It takes half-an-hour to fix the fault - a leaking joint - and we move forward over the battlefield. A single track winds between two white tapes keeping us clear of the minefields. A Flail lies heeled over in the crater made by the mine which disabled it, the crew leisurely repairing the track. Steve says he saw British soldiers, dead, in a ditch. I look back filled with morbid curiosity but cannot see them.

The mortaring has ceased. We dip into another valley. The slopes are pocked with craters, scored with ruts, the trees shattered. A church tops the far slope. As we climb I see a board, studded with bullet holes but still legible, reading 'Fontaine-la-Malet'. The village is in ruins and vehicles are parked among the rubble while lines of troops are moving down the cratered street.

A puppy runs out of a crumbling house and is caught by an infantryman. He holds it up to us and I scramble across the engine-deck to take it. One of the HQ tanks, Captain Barber's, has a duck, Henry. Now we have a better mascot. We christen her Peggy.

On the corner below the village is a barn. The big door is down and we see the rafters festooned with onions. Jack stops; I jump down. Shag gathers them up from the track guards and visions of chips and fried onions fill our minds as we enter the Forêt de Montgéon. The path is littered with brand new bicycles. The Carriers pick them up but we cannot stop as to do so would block the road. German prisoners are filling in craters. They draw back to let us by, then leap as the tank lurches towards them. I think Jack did that deliberately and shout a warning, but he only laughs.

Another little village on the edge of the forest. The street has been blocked by rubble and the alternative route is through the back gardens. The black earth is soft and our tanks have left great ruts which hamper the smaller vehicles. A Wasp[55] - a Carrier with a Flame Gun - bogs as we come up. Jack swerves to pass but Steve

[55] Wasp. A Bren Gun Carrier fitted with a Flame Gun. This was the only example I saw.

stops him. In no time the infantry have a tow line from the Wasp to the rear of our tank. We jerk forward, the hawser cracks, the Wasp stands on its nose and lurches out of the rut. Shag runs down the track guard and casts off, and a moment later we are drawn in behind the rest of C Squadron.

The harbour is just beyond the village, in the ploughed field forming the side of a valley. Below the field are summer houses and bungalows with gardens. Then a narrow chalk road and on the bare slope opposite the German gun positions we have come to take. Little parties of Germans, white flags prominent, emerge from straggling copses in the distance and they are eagerly gathered in. As we halt the Second-in-Command, Captain Barber, moves off to collect a party, hoping to beat the infantry who are running to loot them first.

Beyond the gun positions two farmhouses are burning, one peacefully, the other with spasmodic eruptions during which great chunks of masonry are flung into the air. The whole rolling countryside is dim under a haze of blue smoke.

Aeroplanes appear out of the sunset and drop leaflets promising safe conduct to the German soldier who produces one when he surrenders. These flutter down, pink in the dying sunlight, and we collect them as souvenirs as the majority fall in the field next to us, far from the area where sporadic machine gun fire indicates continued German activity.

Dusty and I raid the gardens and a sack of cucumbers, tomatoes and potatoes is handed to Shag with instructions for supper - it is his turn to cook.

He and Jack have stopped some prisoners who have been at work on the road. One of these carries a camouflage ground sheet which Shag covets, as four of them can be buttoned together to form a snug little bivvy. After an argument he gets it.

Our infantry now in the gun sites are reluctant to show us the store bunkers when Dusty and I go there after tea. We find the door after some trouble but are hampered by the darkness and I make a note to supply myself with a candle at the earliest opportunity. There are cigarettes, 'Jan Mart' brand, and cigars. Bottles of Vichy water in straw packing, rack on rack of them. Intrigued by the labels, we take several.

Shag and I are on guard. It is our first near the front and we do not know what to expect, so we stand with our backs to the tank, thinking of German patrols creeping along the hedges with long knives. Taffy Wakelyn had told us that he was on guard once near Caen and had sat down in the shelter of a hedge and, of course, gone to sleep. He woke up hearing voices and, in the moonlight, made out the shape of German tin hats on the other side of the hedge. So he just sat tight and they passed and he thanked his lucky stars he had been asleep and so escaped their notice. It seemed a bit far-fetched when he told the story - in the NAAFI at Caen - but now I can believe every word of it. The searchlights waver. All else is still. Half an hour passes slowly.

* * *

I was only half awake when we entered 'Looahve' as the local dialect has it. In fact, I did not know it was Le Havre for, preoccupied with the events of the previous day, I had forgotten we were anywhere near the town.

No one in Le Havre could have slept much that night. Crowds of waving, cheering people jammed the streets, for the town was out to welcome us and the tricolore drooped from every window while the children waved French, British and American flags. We had replaced our tin hat on the gun muzzle with these three ensigns, presented to me by an enthusiastic old lady. They made a brave show and attracted more attention than had the tin hat, which was our object.

We breakfasted in a narrow street which was crowded with people only too anxious to talk to us, to give us cognac, and to smoke our cigarettes. An old lady took Jack and I into her house, gave us French beer and lemonade and stuffed our pockets with pears. This set the fashion. We produced our canvas bucket and soon had it filled with fruit.

One girl could speak English and said her mother lived in Rochdale. Jack promised to write the news that the daughter was safe but I do not think he ever did. Jack had had a girl in Bretteville whose home was in Le Havre and he wanted to see if the house was still intact. I found a postman, who might reasonably be expected to know the locality and found it was quite near, only a few streets away. However, Jack was busy with the Rochdale girl and when I gave him my information only told me not to bother him.

One man was at great pains to explain how they had prayed for our bombing raids even though so many townspeople had been killed. He was drunk and very eloquent, gesticulating and pestering me to come and look at a bombed house. I did not want to look at ruins. I had been washing and when I got my attention back to the bowl the soap was gone. I thought they might have tried asking for it, first.

In order to light the after-breakfast cigarette it was necessary to get inside the tank. We had to stop distributing cigarettes, anyway, as the fighting to get near us became serious. One large woman with gold teeth flung a whole basket full of pears on to the engine-deck and I was almost crushed in trying to reward her.

Peggy chose this moment to make her appearance. She had been sick twice and dozing against the exhaust stacks and now marched down the track guards, where she was an immediate hit. There was a chorus of "Oh! Le petit chien!" and all the children were lifted up to see. They all had to know if she was French or German and were very relieved when I told them French.

All the time we could hear the Shermans banging away and now moved up to join them. The streets, as we neared the sounds of conflict, were still jammed with people and all the men, and many women, carried bottles. The girls paraded in couples as they always do and the tank behind us was short two members of its crew.

Jerry was just around the corner in some houses the Shermans were shelling. The FFI (Force Francaise de l'Interieure), too, were very active, collecting arms and imprisoning collaborators. They drove wheezy little cars at speed on the pavements - we took up all the road - with complete disregard for the pedestrians but no one seemed to mind. I took a long time to convince one man he was not going to borrow our Bren. I regretted that such a thing was absolutely impossible as the regulations of the army strictly forbade it but gave him a spare hand-grenade and made him happy.

When I saw him again he was part of an escort surrounding a very old, grey-haired civilian. The old man was shaking all over and had to be half carried. The crowd cheered lustily and called him names that I wished I could translate. Someone said they were going to shoot him and all the civilians laughed and cheered again, and I felt sorry for him for he was so old and the crowd seemed so brutal about it. Maybe it was justice but not English justice. There was more shouting and cheering and a lorry passed across the top of our street with more civilians, women among them, all heavily guarded by the FFI. These latter, I noticed, were all extremely dashing young men with German rifles slung across their backs. I thought they were acting like bullies and would be better employed, and could use their rifles, with the Shermans round the corner. I suppose it was natural for the French to hate the collaborators more than the Germans but it would have been in better taste, I thought, to have helped us beat the Germans before dealing with their private affairs.

Then Reggie Webb, commander of our Able tank, forced his way back along the column and told Steve to pressure up as we were going to flame just round the corner. Steve got down and unscrewed the gas bottles while Dusty did his drill at the front of the trailer. I loaded the guns. Shag woke up, put on his headset, and went to sleep again.

The tank ready, we searched for a private wall against which to relieve ourselves but there was none and modesty had to go by the board. For in this our first action we did not want more physical discomfort than was absolutely necessary. Steve stood at the end of the street and right-dressed us[56] and made as much noise as he could but none of the women took any notice.

[56] "and right-dressed us". 'Right Dress!' is the bellowed parade order for troops to align themselves, equidistant, with the man at the right end of the line. Steve, of course, was concerned only to embarrass us.

All was ready to move then, tank and crew. Nothing happened. Steve went away to sort out the trouble and returned at the saunter. The flap was off. Jerry had given in and our opportunity to fight was lost.

This made us very wild but the French were overjoyed and their efforts to make us drunk were redoubled. Bottles of rum, champagne and cognac came from every side. On the tank behind the driver had returned from his wenching and was now upside down in the co-drivers seat, dead drunk. We could see his feet sticking up.

So we drove in stately procession round the town, taking the salute, halting for long periods to let stragglers catch up. Jack narrowly missed a Jeep on one move, our air louvre passing over its bonnet. Jack said he never saw the Jeep but swerved by instinct. For me there was only a blur of green and a pale patch of face and an open mouth that I presume was swearing.

We cooked dinner but no one could eat it and the tins of Haricot Oxtail were kicked into the gutter. At one period I was sitting in a garden drinking coffee and rum with a family I had known all my life but have no recollection of leaving them. In fact, everything was becoming a bit of a dream. I went to sleep on the track guard and woke up in another street, so I must have been pretty far gone, as were those who let me stay there while the tank moved. But my French improved with drunkenness and I had several children into the turret to explain "le canon soixante-quinze, la mitrailleuse Besa, la lance-flamme et le TSF". They were particularly interested in the I/c, over which they chattered like jays.

The infantry were in an even worse state than the tank crews, having found a bunker full to the brim with cognac and champagne. Jack had brought back six bottles of Bollinger. I said I thought it was supposed to be good champagne and we drank it from tin mugs, sitting solemnly on the track guard in a row. I cannot say that it was appreciated.

The infantry had got hold of some German cavalry horses and held races in the streets and drinking bouts in the gardens. Carriers picked up those who were too drunk to go further. One tiny little Scotsman distributed packets of Woodbines among the Squadron in token of his appreciation of our great assistance. One of our men collected the packets behind his back and put them back in his pack.

The FFI were bringing back more prisoners from positions just along the road and among them were some French girls who had been living with German soldiers. These were laughing and joking and giving us the eye and very nice some of them were. The FFI were looking very severe and righteous, of course.

Jack and Dusty had been off together and Jack had got a bottle of cognac. His beret was perched like a plate on the top of his head, back to front, so we knew he was drunk. However, drink never went to his legs and he capered around offering his bottle to all and sundry until it was empty. Which was not long.

Then we went into a café. The tiny bar was full and the only drink was crème-de-menthe but most of us were past caring about the quality of our liquor. We sang the Marseillaise, Madelon, Tipperary, Roll Out The Barrel, Après La Guerre Finit and a lot more, separately and all together and in all sorts of languages. There was a lot of dancing round the tables and hugging and kissing and all very jolly and how the inhabitants of a liberated town ought to act. When we got back to the tank someone had pinched our only tin of jam with margarine and biscuits to go with it.

At last it was over and we were moving on. The effects of the drink were being felt and the heavily bombed dock area was grey and cheerless in the twilight. The roads were choked with wire that continually tangled in our tracks. The night air was heavy and laden with grey brick dust that caked our smarting faces.

Signposts indicating Fécamp and Dieppe proved false alarms. We turned down the sunken road past the positions taken the previous day. Our air louvre scraped a field gun and limber lying tilted over in the ditch.

I should have been helping Steve to command the tank but dozed off, partly through excitement but mostly through the drink. I have a vague remembrance of a halt where I fixed the Hellesen lamp[57] on the back of the trailer but I did not know where we were, or where we were going, and did not care. I remember trying to wake Shag, who was asleep across the tool box behind the driving seats, in order that he might switch over to the other petrol tanks. A bitter struggle. For a long time he made no reply and when he was awake he would not understand what I wanted. I tapped it in morse on his wrist but he would not understand that, either. Jack had to wait for a halt and make the change himself.

Jack said then that Shag had got hold of the gear lever several times and tried to change gear - which was peculiar as Shag could not drive. Steve told us in the morning that we were halted by an impassable bridge and word came over the air to get what sleep we could. I never heard it. I awoke shivering with the dew dripping on my knees from the branches above my open hatch.

---

[57] Hellesen lamp. The standard signal lamp, used mainly as a torch.

CHAPTER 5

BOULOGNE

We were two days in harbour near Bolbec, in a field with long soft grass that made a good mattress. HQ Squadron was in an orchard nearby and in trouble. Conflicting reports reached us but it appeared that Captain Douglas-Home, who commanded D Squadron when I was there, had refused to go into action against Le Havre. It was something to do with insufficient time given to the German garrison to make up their minds whether to surrender or not. Our colonel had hushed up the matter but the captain had written to the newspapers explaining his point of view and now they were both on the mat. In the event, the captain went to prison and the colonel got a kick upstairs, going to the War Office as a brigadier.

HQ had not been in on the liberation of Le Havre so they could not see the funny side of it. They were angry with Duggie for letting down the regiment and dropping the colonel right in it and complaining that the matter would not have been hushed up had the offender been a trooper. But then HQ had very little to do except bind. We were far too busy to bother much about it although I did think, when I was told about it, that it was a bit late in the war to get squeamish over Germans being killed. Perhaps his argument would have looked better if we had actually had to fight our way into the town.

Steve had gone back to his own tank, the Baker, and we were Charlie again, under George. The change involved a complicated share-out of rations. We had dropped our trailer, some of the necessary Matadors had turned up already and George and Dusty had gone with the first trailer party to the Boulogne area. I spent that afternoon fastening my 2-inch Smoke box to the side of the back bin as Jack had refused to see it lying about loose any longer.

In the evening we stuffed the link with cotton waste and moved across the road ready to load on transporters in the morning. I was guiding Jack by waving a glowing cigarette and, cutting a trailer fine, I forgot the air louvre again until too late. 11 Troop officer, Mr. Waring, did his nut with me but there was no damage done and we reached the desired spot without further incident.

Jack produced his last bottle of champagne and we toasted ourselves. Then to bed beside the tank. It was a lovely night and we slept just between two folds of the engine sheet. After about five minutes, it seemed, I was shaken awake by the guard with the news that it was three o'clock in the morning and we had to go up to A Squadron who had a tank and no crew for it. The guard moved away and we sat up and swore a good deal before trying to find our boots and fold our blankets in the darkness.

Then an engine droned and the sidelights of a truck showed, jolting towards us. A Matador and trailer. We flung such kit as we could find into the back and left the rest with the tank to take care of itself.

Although we tried to make ourselves comfortable with sheets and bedding rolls the truck jolted and lurched and banished all chance of sleep. Still, dark trees lined the road. The villages were sombre and uninteresting. I wondered where A Squadron was supposed to be and how they came to be short of men - that was a depressing thought.

With the sun, as always, came renewed life. We sat up and could see to make ourselves comfortable. The farm labourers going to work waved to us. A girl passed on a bike and we were cheerful enough to whistle. The Matador seemed to run more smoothly and when we halted the drivers produced five eggs for breakfast.

Somewhere between Le Havre and Abbeville there is a very beautiful forest. In the early morning the sun was glinting through the tall trees and just beginning to disperse the pale blue mist that clung to the ferns. I imagined wolves, bears, Snow White and the Seven Dwarfs and was quite sorry when our driver managed to find his way out. For of course it was off his road.

A nice old Frenchman opposite whose house we stopped for dinner (Meat and Vegetables - as a change from Haricot Oxtail), stood us all a glass of 'ginevre'. I could not understand all of what he was saying but we got on very well as I was becoming expert at commenting "Oui" or "Non" according to expression. Our new friend was very proud of the fact that his son, evidently a leading light of the local Resistance, had killed two Germans. In 1940, also, he had hidden two British airmen in his hayloft for a month before they were passed on to the coast. So he had claim to our attention. He also spoke of 'les torpilles', as the French called the Flying Bombs.[58] There was a site nearby and apparently the Germans had had a lot of trouble with it, for he laughed so much in telling us about it that I could not understand a lot of what he said.

We passed through Hesdin, Fruges and Fauquembergues and spent an hour riding round Les Desvres, looking for unit signs. Our strategic number was '993' in white on a green background and we were looking for this in conjunction with the blue triangle of A Squadron or the blue circle[59] of C. All the corners, as usual, were plastered thick with signs but we could not spot ours for a long time.

Eventually we found it under an MP notice:

"THIS TOWN IS OUT OF BOUNDS TO ALL RANKS EXCEPT ON DUTY."

A Squadron was some way out of the town, reached by several miles of rutted track and harboured in a ploughed field, as usual. The squadron had no tank for us and had not asked for us to be sent up.

Being without our tank was unsettling just as we were getting used to having one but our homelessness was short. A spare crew brought

58 Flying Bomb. The V1, or 'Doodlebug', a pilotless aircraft which was the first of Hitler's 'Revenge Weapons' and which had been bombarding London from sites in Northern France.

59 Blue circle. Our strategic number for direction signs, etc., was 993 in white on a green background. Conventional squadron insignia in the tank corps was a diamond for HQ Squadron, a triangle for A, a square for B and a circle for C. Our regimental colour for these signs was light blue.

our tank up. It was waiting for us in the morning and we had to link up the trailer before breakfast.

* * *

Boulogne, like Le Havre, was strongly fortified and we were told that every advantage had been taken of the ring of hills surrounding the town. In particular Mont Lambert, to the east, was defended by concrete forts, wire and minefields and was supposed to be the hinge of the outer defences. Those of the town proper were apparently not so formidable. The garrison was estimated at 10,000.

A plan of attack had been worked out, of course. Heavy bombing was to make a gap in the outer ring of pillboxes. The infantry - 8 and 9 Brigades of the 3rd Canadian Division - were to be brought up in Kangaroos[60] (Grants and Lees, later Rams, from which the turrets had been removed to enable them to carry assault infantry). The sides of the gaps being held by the infantry, lanes would be bulldozed and the way thus made clear for the armour.

8 Brigade was to attack in the north, towards La Tresorerie. 9 Brigade was to take Mont Lambert and La Cocherie and then three columns of 79th Armoured Division units would pass through this area with three bridges over the River Liane as their objective.

* * *

During the day more of our tanks arrived and in the afternoon C Squadron was able to move as a unit to the more comfortable, unploughed part of the field. HQ Squadron was just over the hedge and beyond them was a battery of 155 mm. guns, all nicely camouflaged.

---

[60] Kangaroos. These were Canadian Ram tanks which were very similar to the Sherman but were never used in action as gun tanks. The turret was removed and 8 to 10 infantry could be carried in the space within the turret ring. 79th. Armoured Division had two regiments; 1st. Canadian Armoured Carrier Regiment and 49th. Armoured Personnel Carrier Regiment.

Shag and I erected the bivvies in a piece of long grass and got our sleeping arrangements organised. Paddy Scallan, the SSM,[61] came round trying to get rid of some of his ammo and gave me some 2-inch Smoke bombs he wanted out of the way. As I already had more than my complement it was a puzzle to know where to stow them but it seemed a good idea to increase our defensive potential as much as possible.

Then we did our washing. The opportunity was now coming but rarely, as the needs of the tank took precedence. In fact it was becoming difficult enough to wash ourselves but at least we could dry our bodies quickly but there was nowhere on the tank to store wet underclothes.

With every job done there was just time before dark to go up to A Squadron to ask Jock Fraser's opinion on the contents of a bottle Jack had unearthed. I had known Jock in D Squadron and he was something in the liquor trade and so the obvious person to go to. It was pronounced to be Benedictine but I preferred the taste of a bottle of fruit juice also brought from Le Havre although that, equally, had no label.

Overnight, gun tanks and Flails of the 1st Lothian and Border Yeomanry and AVREs of 87 Assault Squadron arrived on the other side of our field. The morning brought great exertion for the officers who were fooling about in scout cars all over the place. Exhaustive briefings and rehearsals were a feature of our part of the clearing of the Channel Ports. There was plenty of time for them. In this case I went to the wrong briefing, that held by the Flails, but it did not matter. The men never expected the plans to work and maybe the officers did not either.

Jack and I, having had breakfast while we were on guard, took the tank over to take part in the formation of our column, the rest of the crew joining us later. There was a jumble of AVREs, Shermans, Flails, Crocodiles and Churchill gun tanks, supposed to be divided

---

61 SSM. Squadron Sergeant-Major, the senior Non-commissioned Officer (NCO) in the Squadron. The way we were organised, Paddy Scallan was effectively in charge of the echelon.

into a 'Vanguard' and a 'Mainguard'. At the head marched an armoured bulldozer appropriately named 'The Sniper's Nightmare'.

We were in Column C, commanded by our colonel. On the morrow, 17th September, we should follow, and assist if necessary, the infantry attacking Mont Lambert. This objective taken, we should pass through, take the southern bridge and then act according to circumstances. A sugar factory was mentioned as an interesting and convenient second objective.

The order of the column was complicated, of course, and had been tricky to form in broad daylight. In the half light before dawn on the 17th everything went wrong for none of the commanders could remember where he was supposed to go. George did the sensible thing and stood off to one side and watched tanks shunting, officers scurrying to and fro, scout cars flying over the ruts. When things seemed to have settled down he picked a place that looked about right - fortunately neither Jack nor I had taken any notice of where we had been put the previous day so there was no argument. In any case, I was having trouble netting my wireless owing to harmonics. The CO's operator was a patient chap and kept giving me netting calls all to myself until I was satisfactory. By then the column was moving.

A winding country lane led down through the village of Le Wast to join the main road into Boulogne. The morning was grey and cold and again a thin drizzle kept commanders and operators huddled in their gas capes. More capes were spread over the driving compartment hatches but mud and dirty water spurted into Jack's face. Despite the weather the dim shapes of people at their garden gates showed that the French were wishing us luck.

We reached the main road. The tram-line at the side was choked with burnt-out wrecks of goods wagons, gaunt skeletons of rusting ironwork on ridiculously tiny wheels. By now the rain had stopped and there were gleams of sunshine as the clouds began to lift. The woods we entered at the foot of a hill were shining and our spirits rose. Shag struggled up through my hatch and sat beside me. George and I rolled up our gas capes and stuffed them into the turret and the rain and mud dried on our faces. I could smoke. My consumption of cigarettes was going up by leaps and bounds. It was a far cry from the days when I had first joined the army, when I had given up half my NAAFI ration of smokes for someone's sweets.

Our first casualty, a Crocodile of A Squadron, stood in the open space in front of a café. The crew were gathered on the rear decking peering at the engine. When I thought about the matter at all I was amazed at the chagrin displayed by crews broken down on the way into action. Since you knew then that you would live to fight another day, to be disappointed at the loss of a chance of risking your life seemed silly.

At the summit of the hill a torpedo, of all things, had been rolled off the road into the ditch and at this point we turned on to a track through the woods and halted. It seemed a convenient moment so we breakfasted and then there was nothing to do but wait. The infantry were held up somewhere, it was said.

I had a wireless watch for half an hour and then Shag and I walked up the line to look at a Flail. Of course, we were familiar with the Sherman, but it was interesting to get the point of view of their crews, who were surprisingly optimistic. In spite of what the Lothians said I was glad not to be among them. After all, they were only mine bashers but we at least got a little variety.

Back at the tank, I settled down to write home. The advantage of choosing such a moment was that if I got stuck I could, without great pangs of conscience, say, 'Well, I'll have to stop now as we're just going in. I'll finish this when we come out,' and then pack it up for that day. It was not quite so melodramatic as it sounds. Most of our letters were censored in the squadron but we were issued with 'green envelopes' which could enclose up to three letters to go back to the base post office. We had to sign declarations that they did not break security regulations and it was said that only a very small percentage of letters so sent got opened in sample checks. We believed that we could not mention place names until a fortnight after leaving a location and I used to write that I was going in, or coming out, in the hope that this would not be censored and that my relations would be able to guess from the newspapers where I was. When we checked up afterwards it had worked quite often.

The Padre was making his rounds and collecting letters and offered to look after Peggy for us while we were in action but we refused on the grounds that she brought us luck. This sounded good, even if we had had no chance of putting her to the test yet. Our colonel, in grey flannel trousers à la Montgomery, advised us to get her on the regimental strength if we wanted to keep her. It appeared that the regiment could have four dogs.

The day dragged on and the sun blazed down. I finished my letters and lay down on the engine-deck, lulled to sleep by the hiss of the wireless set and the purr of a cooker. I awoke shivering, for the sun had dropped behind the trees. I heard George yawning in the turret and asked him the time - he was the only member of the crew with a watch. He came out, glad to have someone to talk to and said that we were soon going to move as the Canadians were on top of Mont Lambert but the Germans were literally inside and this was obviously a task for AVREs and Crocodiles. I did not care what we did so long as we did something. The only emotion I could feel was boredom.

The black, bare mass of the strongpoint loomed stark against the yellow autumn sky as we wound along a narrow lane towards it. On either side, between the woods and the foot of the scarp, was a shallow trough of meadow and heathland which seemed to be mined, for a couple of Flails lay tilted over in the ditch, their crews standing about outside. We squeezed by and headed for the foot of the hill at the best pace we could make. Jack, of course, was closed right up to the tank in front to get all the protection we could.

It was getting dark quickly. Our CO kept assuring us that he was trying to get our release, rabbitting over the air to the exclusion of all other traffic. None of us fancied flaming in the dark. Then the first mortar crashed down upon us. There was a gout of orange flame and rolling black smoke and the whole tank shook to the explosion. I had had one of my flaps open for the sake of air and it was down and locked before I had time to think. The turret filled with bitter fumes, the fan hummed, and we passed by unscathed. There was another crash that also seemed too close. Then I acknowledged the order to retire. Mont Lambert would have to keep.

To turn round was easier said than done. The mortars were coming down thick and fast and George was not much good at guidance even when he could get his head outside. Although he had several periscopes in his cupola and I had one on my side of the turret we could not see close to the side of the tank. We managed in the end by taking a small tree with us. The Flail in front of us got a five-barred gate - the narrow road was very awkward for the Flails owing to the width of their cylinders. One of A Squadron's Crocodiles was saying that he had lost a track in a ditch and wanted help but with mortars dropping all over the place his chance of getting it seemed small. For what seemed ages all was confusion and then, feeling rather humiliated, we were out of mortar range and on the main road headed for La Capelle.

I opened my hatches and stretched thankfully, for I was too tall to stand upright when we were closed down. It was now pitch dark and all I could see of the tank in front were jets of flame belching from its exhaust. This appeared to be no hindrance to Jack, who had his foot hard down.

Then there was a village, a huddle of houses dimly glimpsed, and we drew off on the grass verge. I stooped down in the turret to turn off the master switch and there was a clank and a thud and by the time I had extricated myself and rubbed the bumps, the AVRE which had run into our trailer had backed off and Jack and Dusty were lashing up the door with rope. I tiptoed back to the turret and went to sleep.

* * *

During the night the Germans must have decided that the game was not worth the candle, for in the morning we reached the top without opposition. The road up the side of Mont Lambert was steep and winding, a cart track reinforced with rubble, flanked on either side by high banks clothed in gorse and brambles. Under the bank at the top was an AVRE, still smoking, and from the wreck rose the stench of charred flesh.

There was a straggling village on the top of the hill and little knots of prisoners were being driven down the street. There were several large bunkers with AVREs standing about amongst them but no sign of German guns. With another tank we drew up beside one of the green mounds and waited. I started spreading jam on biscuits for breakfast.

Then a Churchill gun tank drew level with us. With a rending of metal its air louvre wrenched away our near side rear wing. The offender stopped. From the cupola a pink face peered back at us. Jack stood up in his seat and shouted and waved his fists. The officer, Lieutenant Macksey of A Squadron, with whom I had been on the flame course, got down and came over to us. Jack, who had no respect for rank when his blood was up, swore at him. Shag and I were giggling in the turret and George was scandalised. The officer was apologetic - with Jack in a flaming temper he had not the chance to be anything else. Then his tank moved on and a little later we heard him babbling about the number of Germans who were surrendering to him. Jack, only slightly mollified by the apology, was still muttering about his wing.

There was nothing to do on the tank and we could not sit there for long. We had had enough of that the day before. The nearest bunker was evidently a store and Shag and I took a brand new rifle each, filled our pockets with ammo and a sack with tinned fruit and vegetables, boxes of sweets and brown bread. Some of the tinned food was Italian, a watery mixture of carrots, runner beans and celery. The green labels looked impressive, however, and we packed it on the trailer to flog to civilians. There were a lot of German uniforms lying about and I decided to make a collection of epaulettes and although there were only infantry with white piping, they would do for a start.

Then we found a German lorry in a cutting. It had been most carefully camouflaged but then the Germans did not rely on motor transport to the extent that we did and I suppose a lorry was more valuable in their eyes than it would be in ours. In fine style, I blew the lock off the toolbox with my pistol but there was only a Red Cross box and a few tools worth having.

We could never keep cutlery on that tank. As fast as we got a knife and fork each they got lost. I decided to end this state of affairs and the source of many rows with Jack and collected a headset satchel full. Many were forks and spoons combined, most useful articles. This was the only looting that ever received George's approval - at all other times his legal training got the upper hand and was revealed in varying expressions of disgust according to the value of the article acquired.

It was getting dark when our column was re-formed, all mixed up, and we took the road towards Ostrohove and Boulogne. We passed a Kangaroo lying on its side in a bomb crater. The fields were scattered with portable flame-throwers abandoned by the infantry - named life buoys on account of the shape of the fuel tank. Little groups of prisoners stood on the verges, white flags prominent. There were dead cattle everywhere. At one spot a number of large naval shells had been unearthed by the Engineers and were fenced from the road by white tape.

On the outskirts of Boulogne a house was on fire and we took the opportunity of warming up our Besa, sending the tracer ricocheting from the roof as we sped by. Soon we had worked our way into the town, the streets became narrow, there were craters everywhere and then our speed slowed to a crawl.

Action was imminent now, for the leading tank, commanded by that officer who had incurred our displeasure earlier in the day, came up on the air about a flame-thrower that had taken a crack at him. He said it shook him. The news shook us. We could see nothing as Jack had prudently closed right up to the tank in front as was his normal habit. Then the second tank in line came up.

"Two-two[62] has had it," cried the commander.

"What's that?"

62 'Two-two'. Strictly speaking, this was the call sign for the Recce Troop of a regiment. In this case it seems to have been allocated to the leading HQ tank in the column which was, perhaps, reckoned to be acting in a Recce capacity.

"Two-two has been knocked out."
"Did you say knocked out?"
"I said knocked out. The poor bugger's brewed up. There is an ant[63] on the cross road."
"An ant? Is there? Did you see what happened?"
"Yes. He brewed up straight away. But I think they all got out."
"Is it blocking the road?"
"Yes."
"Can you see a way round?"
"No."

Silence. They were digesting that one. In my tank there was a babble over the I/c:
"Listen! Did you hear that?"
"Yes. Two-two's had it."
"Who's Two-two, Smudge?"
"Whatsisname. Macksey, bloke who hit our wing."
"They said they all got out. Who's his crew?"
"Dunno. A Squadron. Do you know, George?"
"No. Did they say an anti-tank gun?"
"They did indeed."

Silence again. We supposed they were trying to think of a way round the burning tank. Shag set to changing the barrel of the Besa. There had been a 'premature', a bullet was jammed in the barrel and it was quicker to put in the spare than to clear the jam with a cleaning rod. We carried a spare Besa to fit if the Flame Gun was dismounted.

It was very dark in the narrow street, despite the flickering light from the front of the column which I imagined was the burning tank. The houses towered up on both sides and I did wonders with my periscope trying to see in every possible window. Everyone was getting on edge. Up front they were beginning to doubt the presence

63 'Ant'. The code word for artillery, as laid down in training. There, we were given a list of code words for use in the interests of security, such as 'Bandits' (enemy), 'Hornets' (tanks) and 'Eagles' (aircraft). These were never used and this was the only time I heard 'Ant'.

of an anti-tank gun and were talking of bazookas.[64] This brought everyone's eyes to the periscopes.

A Sherman, better able to manoeuvre than the Crocodiles, had been searching for a way round the wreck and now reported failure. The officers chatted over the air about the advisability of staying put for the night and then came the order to close up, to squeeze round the corner nose to tail, and to get every man outside armed to the teeth. Our CO advised that one man, armed with a Sten, walk beside each tank during the closing up operation. We offered this job to Dusty but he said the responsibility was too great for him and he felt it should be that of the tank commander.

However, we closed up without incident and all the crew descended save for me, for the wireless had been playing tricks all day and this seemed to be the time to find the trouble. Shag and Dusty took the Bren Gun and I traversed the turret towards where the Germans were thought to be. Then I put my captured rifle on the roof, my pistol handy on a ledge and, having thus done all I could in deference to the situation around me, found a fresh packet of cigarettes and got to work. That would be about eight o'clock.

By about midnight I had changed all the valves and checked and cleaned all the connections and decided I needed a blow. I climbed down to find Jack standing by the wing. It was a brilliant autumn night, moonlight, but faintly misty towards the river. Dusty and Shag, Jack said, were on the corner with the Bren. Shag had been into a cellar and come out at the double with a story of its being full of Germans. No one, so far, had investigated. George had not been seen for the last hour.

For the most part everything was very still and our whispers seemed to carry a long way. But every so often a shot would echo down the street, then a flurry of shots, a yell, and silence. Jack said that had happened several times so quite a few people must have

---

[64] Bazooka. The Germans had two types of rocket-propelled anti-tank hand-held weapons. They were extremely effective although only short range. The most common was the 'Panzerfaust', a stubby weapon rather resembling a toffee apple in appearance.

copped their lot. I said I would go and see if Shag and Dusty were all right but I did not go. My feet made such a noise on the road that I returned to Jack after a few paces.

There was an explosion, then another burst of firing. Two figures detached themselves from the shadow of the next tank for a moment and then fell back into the gloom. Nothing else moved.

I got back into the turret but was now conscious of what was going on outside. Every so often someone would think he saw something and shoot at it and half a dozen others would join in. We only knew that Jerry was somewhere near but just where was a different matter. Jack had said he had heard we were completely surrounded, which was not a very cheerful thought.

I stuck to my work in the faint light of the festoons.[65] Shag came in about two o'clock with the news that Canadian infantry had taken over and he was going to get some sleep. I worked on for a bit. Got out some more cigarettes and smoked them. Jack snored and Shag kept twitching in his sleep and distracting my attention. Around four o'clock, as near as I could judge, I tried the set and it worked and woke Shag. He stretched and knocked down a tin, which fell with a clatter and woke Jack. They snarled at each other for a bit and then dozed off again. Having carried out the few tests I could make without someone on the receiving end and finding everything to be in order, I switched off the lights and settled down on the Immediate Action[66] ammo bin. Shag woke up again, swore at me for making a noise, I swore back and he went to sleep.

It was getting light now so I did not try to follow his example but ate some boiled sweets and read. After a bit George peered into the turret. I had not seen him all night. He asked where was Jack. I knew that was coming. George was in perpetual fear that Jack would get fed up one day and run away and leave him. So whenever Jack was not immediately in evidence George would be running around looking for him. This trait always infuriated me but I concealed my

---

65 Festoons. The internal lights of the tank, similar to those in a car.

66 Immediate Action (IA) Bin. The turret container for a mixture of 75 mm. ammunition for immediate use.

feelings now and asked what was going on. He said he was just going up to see.

Another thing, George was always 'just going up to see'. He wandered away and I transferred my attention to chocolate and cigarettes. An engine started up and ticked over. Then there was a clatter of boots on the track covers. George swung his legs into the cupola in style, put on his headset and told Jack to start up. We were just going up the road, George said, but he did not know what for. But Jack must keep close up.

We chugged along the street - the way was evidently clear now - and turned in to a bare patch between the houses on the hillside. On our left and below the town was spread out in panorama. Ahead and behind our tanks were scattered and turrets began to creep menacingly round towards the town. I put the Seventy-five safety catch to 'Fire' and started the fan.

"Seventy-five traverse left," said George. "Steady! Hold it! Fire!"

"Eh?" Shag looked at me and burst out laughing.

"Fire!" repeated George, irritably but with less force.

"What at?"

"How should I know?"

"Well, if you don't know... What am I supposed to do about it?"

"Fire at anything."

"Stand back, then!"

The gun thundered, leaped furiously back, the empty case clanked against the guard and clattered to the floor. I thrust in another round. The breech clanged to.

"OK!"

"Stand back!"

Crash! Clank! Clang! We fired several rounds.

"I've knocked a factory chimney down" reported Shag.

"Good going!"

I hammered at a round that refused to enter the breech but the brass case was buckled and George flung it outside. Then came an order to lay smoke to help the infantry across the river. The smoke rounds were light and easily handled after the HE - also they were more robust.

Shag fired and the round was not ejected as the charge was not powerful enough to make the gun recoil fully. My brain, numbed by the explosion, did not grasp this fact and struggled to remember the misfire drill.

"Whassermatter, Smudger?"

"It ain't gone off!"

"Course it has, you bloody fool! Smoke don't eject. Open the breech!"

I extracted the case and bitter, stinging fumes filled the turret to set us coughing. But firing smoke was much more fun as we could see the results plainly. A white cloud filtered along the river valley and columns of smoke left by the falling shells drifted slowly downwind. We had fired all the rounds in the IA bin and Jack and Dusty were kept busy passing up fresh supplies from the racks in the front. We fired all our smoke and then went back to HE.

German mortars on the hills opposite had our range by this time and bombs fell thick and fast among us. Also some Eighty-eights, we judged, were firing air bursts. In fact, it began to get uncomfortable and most tanks were talking about ammunition shortage. Withdrawal was mentioned.

We were closed down, of course, but I could see enough through my periscope. There was a splintering of orange flame, billowing black smoke, and a house slowly crumbled before my eyes.

"Shag!" I called.

"Sir!"

"I can see a mortar! Traverse right a bit. See that big white building like a school?"

"Yes."

"About seven o'clock from that. See that house with the shiny red roof?"

"Yeah."

"Just above that. There it goes again. See it?"

"Yeah. Stand back!"

We watched for the shell to burst. The drifting smoke made it difficult.

"No." I said. "Go up a bit and to the left, Shag."

"What are you firing at?" asked George.

"Mortar. Stand back!"

"That's it!" I said. "Up a bit and you've got him!"

"Stand back!"

"You got him, Shag!" I shouted. "You got him! That was smack on! That'll keep the bugger quiet."

"Now get the other ninety-nine," said Dusty.

To give point to the remark a bomb crashed a yard or two from the tank and sent sparks flying from the armour. However, we were moving forward now and our fire became spasmodic.

The mortars continued to bombard the same spot after we had pulled back into the street for breakfast and then the only risk was from the occasional shift. Jack and I were caught in a garden where we were picking tomatoes and for a few uncomfortable minutes we burrowed behind a low wall. Then there was a lull and we sprinted for home.

Soon, however, the firing died away but not before one of A Squadron's tanks, 'Steed', had been hit by four bombs almost simultaneously. Back bin and exhaust stacks were ripped off, wings and track guards torn, the whole vehicle pitted with scars. Fortunately, there was only one member of the crew on board and he was safe inside. The others, like the majority of the squadron, were away after loot. Most of the houses near our tank, however, were in ruins and the only person I envied was one trooper with a beautiful fishing rod.

I was looking for the Fitters at the rear of the column when Mr. Macksey was brought up in a Jeep. He was wounded in the shoulder, very pale, and either slightly delirious or else wildly excited. The officers rushed around to shake his hand and soon there was a crowd to hear his story before he was packed off to the dressing station.

After baling out the previous evening he had crawled up a sewage pipe but had emerged when the Germans started to shoot up it. They had taken him to their HQ where all their officers were arguing as to whether or not they should surrender and he had had his say. Eventually they had decided that they would become his prisoners.

It was now reported that the bridge, our objective, had been blown up. That being so we were released and in the afternoon moved out of Boulogne to Les Desvres. It was cold and raining again but snug in our bivvy and Shag and I could fight our first real action over again without having it belittled by the voice of experience.

* * *

Boulogne town had been cleared and mopping up was all that was necessary in the dock area, but the forts around Le Portel still held out. C Squadron was now concentrated at Les Desvres and our half squadron moved back into the town the following afternoon. My wireless set, however, had now given up the ghost completely and we were left behind with orders to follow when ready. The usual procedure was simply to fit a new set, which I could have done myself, but just at that time there were none available. Fortunately, the signalman attached to the squadron was most co-operative, which was not always the case with attached troops, and he dropped everything to get us on the road.

We did not know in which part of Boulogne the rest of our tanks were harboured and as we rattled along towards the town I tried to pick up a call and get the position but without success. It appeared they had closed down for the night. George kept asking the way and eventually got us to the Citadel, an immense domed building with massive bastioned walls overlooking the town. Lots of people had seen hundreds of Crocodiles and only skilful sifting of information brought us over the river to find the tanks drawn up in a wide street along the side of a square. The square had once been green and there were little patches of grass still, on top of air raid shelters. The rest was covered with piles of railway sleepers and metals, pipes, tree trunks and other timber.

It was dark when we arrived so we pulled in at the rear without any fuss and switched off everything, hoping to remain unnoticed and thus escape a guard. But George wandered away to report our arrival despite our protests and so I walked down the line of tanks in search of news. Shag, however, got the most important news without moving from the tank. A bunker had been discovered, down by the docks, that was said to stretch for miles and to be crammed with everything that we could possibly need. Some blokes were just going down, he said, and if we hurried we could catch up with them.

So we ran down the street, stumbling among bricks, twisted tramlines and German rifles and steel helmets that were littered everywhere. Shag said for God's sake not to smoke as there were still snipers about. It did not seem very likely to me but it was best to be on the safe side.

A glimmer of light from a doorway indicated the bunker and then I went headlong over something lying in the road. Forgetting the snipers, Shag lit a match, my stomach gave a heave, and we got inside hurriedly. It was a dead man and not a pretty sight.

The first need was candles. We had a stump each, as usual, but this promised to be a long search. The Germans had laid in a good stock, however, and they were littered all over the place, so we had no difficulty.

The bunker certainly was huge and I could believe that it really did stretch for miles underground. Room after room was packed to the roof with cases and sacks. Still others had shelves loaded with tins of coffee, sugar, dried milk, butter, ham and cigarettes. There were big crates of cigars, so many that the cigarettes had been contemptuously flung aside and littered the floor in their thousands. In another room someone had overturned a forty-gallon drum of jam and the floor was deep in sticky slime. Just beyond cardboard cartons of boiled sweets had been split open and trodden into treacle. The farther we went, of course, the more intact were the stores, until we were walking along alleys between piles of crates with no idea of their contents. But we were afraid of getting lost and in any case a proper exploration would take too long.

Shag had found a sack and we took samples - milk, ham, peas, butter, meat, cherries, apricots and tobacco. With this and a packing case stencilled '1800 Zigaren' we staggered out of the bunker and tried to find our way back to the tank. We must have walked past our corner because we had gone a long way unsuccessfully before I flung down the sack, which had been heavy enough at the start, and said that was far enough. Everything was very quiet and we conferred in whispers. We knew we should have followed a set of tramlines but must have missed them so decided to turn back. Luckily, although we did not find our tramlines, we fell in with another bunch of marauders with a better bump of locality.

Undaunted, we made another trip as soon as we had stored the fruits of the first. By this time a house that had been smouldering on the other side of the square had burst into flames, giving us a landmark. The black lettering of 'Estaminet' stood out clearly on the wall in the glare of the flames leaping from the windows beneath. Presently the roof and flooring collapsed inside the house sending a column of sparks hundreds of feet into the air, and after this the fire dwindled although the ruins were still glowing when I went on guard in the small hours of the morning.

We moved forward at daylight. The German prisoners were reputed to be stinking with money and festooned with watches and our officers were as keen to get at them as we were. The few civilians left in the suburbs were ransacking any German positions left unguarded. One lady had a beautiful blue jersey but the tanks moved while I was bargaining for it. I had to leave it.

This part of Boulogne had suffered severely, both in 1940 and during our assault. The roads were one continuous line of craters, some partially filled with the wreckage of neighbouring houses. Gradually we worked our way through the tangle of debris and entered narrow lanes winding up the hillsides beyond the town.

The fields on our flanks were marked as being mined and were full of barbed wire choked with long dank grass. Anti-glider posts were in every field and from each the orange and black skull-and-crossbones mine warnings swayed in the wind. Some of these minefields were reported to be dummies but as yet no one had ascertained which. Apart from ourselves the countryside seemed deserted. I stood on the turret floor, sheltered from the wind and peering across the desolate landscape. I kept a store of German boiled sweets under the smoke bomb bin but at the rate I was now consuming them they were not likely to last long.

Some Canadian Shermans were drawn up in a field by two German bunkers. These positions had originally been sited in a wood but the trees were blasted down to stumps and tangled greenery. The concrete pillboxes were unscathed as far as I could see.

We all went looting except George. However, he was willing to accept a box of armourer's tools which Shag brought him and said he had a buyer for them. When we returned Major Duffy was running round in circles and cursing us all. The crews were getting ready to move, but slowly in order to give their brews time to come to the boil, and this was obvious to our CO.

Parties of Germans - dejected, ragged and filthy - toiled up the slope towards us. We stopped them as they came level and they stood apathetically as we went through their pockets. Then we waved them on and a few yards further along the road they were stopped again and the whole performance enacted anew.

On the distant hillside was the ruin of a structure of girders, a gigantic wreck silhouetted against the grey sky and reminding me of pictures of crashed Zeppelins. We were told that this was a Flying Bomb site. Nearby we could see two Shermans entirely surrounded by a mass of German soldiers all eager to give themselves up. The Canadian guards would not let us stop the columns of prisoners, so we ran down the hill to meet them, dived into the ranks, marched back past our tanks collecting money as we went, fell out when the supply was exhausted and then down the hill to meet the next lot. Most of the Germans were either good-humoured or indifferent about it. Jack was particularly good at this work and at the end of the day had got about thirty pounds worth of francs.

In order that the tanks should not be completely abandoned while at the same time giving us the chance to pick up something valuable, it was decided that two men from each crew should visit the Flying Bomb site. Jack and Shag won the toss. Jack brought back a camera, Shag, a wireless. Shag had started with a bicycle as well but had sold it to a civilian on the way back. He was particularly pleased about this as the Frenchman had only to walk up the hill to collect as many as he wanted. We voted that he should keep the whole proceeds of this sale.

That evening we returned to Boulogne and spent the night on call. In the morning Shag and I went down to the bunker again but the Canadians had slapped a guard on it and were removing the contents systematically. So Boulogne had nothing more to offer and that evening we moved out, mixed up with a column of Flails that had appeared from somewhere nearby.

A few minutes later we found ourselves with only one tank in front of us, on a lonely road that none of us could remember having travelled before. I called up the other tank,

"Hullo Peter Three Charlie, message for Peter Three Able. Do you know where you are going? Peter Three Charlie to Peter Three Able, over."

"Hullo Three Able. No. Do you? Over."

"Hullo Three Charlie. No. My Sunray[67] would like to talk to your Sunray. Over."

"Hullo Three Able halting now, out."

So George and Reggie Webb held a consultation in the road. Dusty and Shag were asleep and Jack and I were too cold and tired to care where we were. By the time a decision had been reached two Flails, also lost, joined us. We moved on along narrow and roundabout roads, stopping every mile or so to argue and making it a very slow business. When we did get to Les Desvres we were all too tired to do anything and Shag and I elected to sleep under the tank to save the labour of putting up a bivvy. We also did a 'bivvy guard', tossing up for who should put on his trousers ready to say "who goes there?" should the need arise. Shag lost, which meant that I could go

[67] Sunray. The code name for any commander, of whatever rank. This was one bit of the security system that was in regular use.

to sleep, and in the morning Shag could not remember whether he had called the next pair[68] or not.

68 'next pair'. Normal abbreviation for 'next pair of men on guard'.

CHAPTER 6

CALAIS

An assault on Calais and Cap Gris Nez naturally followed from the taking of Le Havre and Boulogne. The Germans had flooded large areas and while this made an attack more difficult it also made it less urgent as our lines of communication into Holland could not be menaced. So perhaps the capture of Calais was more for the sake of tidiness than anything else, although no doubt it was thought to be a good thing to get the guns which had been shelling Dover out of the way. Dunkerque, which also guarded itself with inundations, was left until the end of the war and we were told it was useful as a training ground.

7 Brigade of the 3rd Canadian Division was to attack the positions on high ground at Belle Vue and Chateau Pigache and then would move on to the town. 8 Brigade, which had with it C Squadron of the Lothians, 11 and 13 Troops of 141 RAC and a Troop of 284 Assault Squadron RE, would attack the position known as 'Noires Mottes'. This position was supposed to include four 16-inch guns among its defences and it was alleged that these had been turned to face landward. 9 Brigade was held in reserve and would go on to Cap Gris Nez. There would be heavy bombing as a prelude to the attack.

* * *

There was no particular reason why we should change our harbour, for although the new one was perhaps a little nearer to Calais it was still in the neighbourhood of Les Desvres. However, it was a change for the better. The entrance was difficult from the narrow lane but, once inside, instead of knee-deep rank grass and muddy ruts we had short springy turf. Also, there were many fallen elm trees and we built huge bonfires. I had my first bath since leaving Bretteville by the side of a bonfire in pouring rain and it was lovely.

We now had three complete German bivvies. Jack and Dusty shared one, Shag and I another, and George had the third to himself, apart from the compo box and the cooker. I do not think George ever really adapted himself to the free and easy life of a tank crew. It seemed his heart was really in the quartermasters stores where he could stand behind a counter in a neat battle dress and refuse to issue things. So there was always a certain amount of friction. Jack was a very strong character and Dusty would never allow George to assert himself in his department, so his tendency was to confine his orders to Shag and myself. To give him his due, he was a very kindly person and had one great asset - he always secured the best of anything that was going.

He called me at eight and told me off for missing the check net at seven. I said no one had told me about it, he said he had, I said he had not, Jack supported me and George went away. I went over to the Able tank and Chung, the operator, who was already up and cooking breakfast, said that he had forgotten and so had everybody else so far as he knew. So the expected storm did not materialise. In any case, the attack was postponed for twenty-four hours because of rain, everyone looked upon it as a holiday, and no one was inclined to look into the slackness of the wireless operators.

Peggy, however, was not happy, for it seemed that German ham did not agree with her and we had to forbid her to enter the tank. In any case she would never stay in her bed in the pannier at night but always kept whining outside the bivvy until we let her in to chew the blankets. Her being sick was a nuisance. The trouble was that, selfishly, none of us was inclined to take the sole responsibility for looking after her.

That evening - and it was cold enough for greatcoats and scarves to be welcome - we were herded into the back of a truck and jolted along a cart track to be briefed at the nearby village school. Some ingenious person had constructed a sand table in the largest room. All the furniture of the school had been requisitioned and we sat perched on forms round the walls while the room filled with steam from our greatcoats and with cigarette smoke and was soon at sweating point.

Of course, there was a lot of blood and thunder because the officers were always extremely enthusiastic. Perhaps the rows of stolid faces staring glumly at the sand table gave an impression of lack of interest on our part and they thought our morale was flagging. The truth was that none of us, not even novices such as myself, expected the action to work out as it was planned and so there did not seem much sense in telling us too much about it. It was extremely difficult, in any case, to recognise on the ground what you had seen on a sand table or a map, especially with the tank closed down and only a periscope to look through. Any idea of using one's initiative outside the limited arena of fighting the tank was out. All our tank could really do was follow the tank in front and hope the Troop Leader knew what he was doing.

Anyway, officers of the Canadian North Shore Regiment told us how they and we were going to take three positions on the escarpment which sheltered the big guns. They made jokes about the loot to be gathered - they seemed particularly keen about wireless sets - and promised a general share-out after the action as the tanks would be too busy to collect anything for themselves. We were sceptical about the value of this promise as they had not previously been conspicuous for generosity - witness the Boulogne bunker.

The Flails seemed confident of getting through the minefields although this did not tie up with the prospects as outlined by the AVREs. They had a Conger[69] - a hose filled with explosive - ready to be fired across the minefield and explode a path should the Flails be held up. The Artillery, deputising for the RAF, informed us that a heavy bombing raid had been laid on to soften things up. Furthermore, such a colossal number of guns had been concentrated that they could guarantee to lay a barrage anywhere within five minutes of being asked. So far as I remember we did not make any promises.

---

[69] Conger. I think this was the only time it was tried and it did not work.

Our Troop Leader, Mr. Sutherland-Sheriff (known as 'Sherry'), did however request that the platoon detailed to accompany him should look out for his tanks, named 'Sandgate', 'Sandling', 'Sandwich' and 'Sidcup', and not attach itself to the first tanks that appeared as had sometimes happened in the past. The Canadian officer concerned solemnly made a note of the names and this reference to prosaic detail led to some useful exchanges of information such as code signs and the like. So perhaps it was not all a waste of time.

Back in the harbour I aroused George's ire by eating some of the black bread I had brought from the Boulogne bunker under the impression that it was fruit pudding. It was quite good for a change but rather chaffy. I also liked the German 'knackebrot' which was rather like Ryvita but thicker and harder. I kept a packet of this in the turret as an emergency meal and every so often George would become patriotically indignant and throw it out. After the row was over I would retrieve it and with patience managed to finish the lot.

The days were getting shorter and reveille was not until five o'clock. Petrol fires blazed up all round the field as we crawled out of our bivvies and finished buttoning our clothes where there was room to move. It had been raining all the previous day and most of the night and was still spitting in the wind. We lost no time in lighting our fire and preparing the life-giving tea.

The move up to the forward harbour, along sunken, winding lanes, was slow as usual and dawn, when it came at length, was cold and dreary with grey clouds scudding low before an east wind. We were thankful to get into the shelter of a hollow where all the different tanks were assembling. Flat heathland, dotted with anti-invasion poles, stretched away to the hills with shell and bomb craters making patches of white where the chalk had been thrown up.

We hung about for an hour and then laboured on up the slope in the wake of the Flails. The ground was soggy and our tracks dug deep. A piece of rag got caught in the exhaust stack and was set blazing. We did not know anything about this until Sherry put the wind up us by calling that our tank was on fire. I scrambled down the deck and kicked it overboard.

Just over a rise in the ground we halted again. Before us grassland sloped down and then steeply upward to the top of the Noires Mottes. As always when looking across a valley, the distance looked much shorter than it really was. The Flails were beating a track diagonally across the opposite slope, which purported to be a minefield, dragging great tangles of barbed wire in their wakes. On the other side of the hill columns of smoke rose and the rumble of exploding bombs was audible above the roar of our engine. The bombers floated lazily overhead, an awe-inspiring sight when we had the leisure to look up. The infantry walked by the side of the track, hopping gingerly on to the verges as we drew level. Despite the briefing, I saw no sign of particular troops attaching themselves to us. We could see more khaki-clad, tin-hatted figures dodging about among the mounds and bushes on the summit.

Then the leading Flail heaved itself over the brow. There was a crash, a ball of black smoke, and the whole whirling contraption was flung violently upwards. The tank hesitated, seemed to shake itself like a dog coming out of the water, and then ploughed on with determination. Its mates spread out behind and the explosions came sharply and quickly.

We passed along the flailed track, up the hill, and into the hollow between two emplacements. Again the ground sloped down, first steeply, then gently away to the surf and the grey sea. At first I thought it was all ploughed land and then I realised that not one square inch had been left undisturbed by the bombers. I had never seen anything like it.

On the extreme right the village of Sangatte, with its white-washed walls, red roofs and grey stone church, was too far away to show the ravages of bombardment. To the left of Sangatte was a low line of hillocks that we presumed concealed big guns. Then, against the surf, a modern white building that was probably a coastguard station. Further to the left was another cluster of mounds. On the map the distance to the sea was 3000 yards, or thereabouts, although it looked much nearer. We argued about the range for a bit and George, after a little hesitation, said it was OK to shoot when we were ready.

"Stand back!" snapped Shag, opening fire immediately and just beating the Able tank which had crawled up alongside.

The Defence Overprint was singularly bare but Jerry had evidently worked hard since it was issued for the craters near the shore seemed packed with Spandaus[70] and as we opened fire so did they. Our infantry, who had been taking things easy, vanished into the bushes and sparks began to fly from our armour. There were so many craters that a single machine gun was not easy to spot and although Shag asserted that he could see several, George refused to let him engage them and threw his weight about a bit. However, there would have been just as much sense in firing our HE at empty craters as at the big gun positions for as far as we could see we were making no impression at all.

While Shag fired as fast as I could load, George was fitting on his gloves and complaining that his microphone was not working, two more traits that exasperated me. It was probably nervousness that caused him to smooth his gloves continually at times of stress but it annoyed me to hear him complain of his microphone and thus blame me when his gloves prevented him from pressing the 'pressel switch' properly, and to see him inspecting the tautness of the leather between his fingers when he should have been laying Shag on a target. However, we were now to be faced with something more serious than my personal annoyance.

For some time a number of infantry had been waiting to cross our front but were prevented by a gun firing from far away on our left. We watched them huddling in the lee of a large lump of concrete and Jack suggested that we draw forward to give them some help. It was the comradely thing to do but the German gunners, confronted by a perfect target silhouetted against the skyline, quickly transferred their attention to us. There was a sharp clang, the tank shuddered, and sparks showered over the front.

---

70 Spandau. This was our name for German machine guns, which always seemed to have a faster rate of fire than ours. A 'Spandau' burst of fire sounded rather like ripping paper in contrast to the steady tock-tock of our guns.

"That's AP, George," I said.
"No, it's all right. It's only mortars. Can you see it, Shag?"
"No, I can't. And it don't look like mortars to me, George."
"Yes, it is."
"Is it buggery!" came from Jack in the front. He had heard the whistle of AP before.

Then I spotted a little puff of smoke which rose from a crater near the seashore. Simultaneously there was a whistle, a crash and a clank, and sparks flew about on our near side.

"There he is, there he is!" I shouted. "Right down there! Traverse left, Shag."
The turret crept round in the required direction, very slowly I thought.
"Can you see him, George?" I asked.
"I can!" said Jack. "There he goes again."

There was another crash and more sparks. He was hitting us with every shot.

"I think I see it," said George. "Steady! You're on, Shag! Can you see it?"
"Stand back!"

The gun leapt back. I prepared to reload.

"George! There's no more HE!" I cried.
"Try the Besa, then," said George.

Shag switched over to the machine gun. The belt raced through the breech, the tracer curved well to the left. Jack and I watched anxiously, I through my periscope, Jack through his open vision block. The tracer swung still further to the left.

"Right!" I bellowed.
"Right, Shag!" yelled Jack, but above the rattle of the Besa he could not hear us.

"Oh, you silly bastard!" snarled Jack and slammed his vision block in disgust and crash! - right in the centre of the block. Then again smack in the front and down tumbled the periscope and fan on to Jack's head. He fell forward. The engine stalled. Peggy came yelping into the turret. Dusty pulled Jack up and he recovered and bellowed for Ki-gass, for me to prime the cylinders with neat petrol by means of the pump behind the turret. Shag fired the Seventy-five and then cried out that he could not traverse. I reported that our tank was hit and the traverse out of action before I saw the empty shell case jamming the turret. I kicked it out and did not send a correction. Peggy was howling and barking and dancing about all over the floor. Shag fired AP as fast as I could load but at what I was not sure. George was working away at the Ki-gass pump but neglecting to press the little button that actuated it. Jack was going mad, but the I/c was muzzy and we could not make George understand. Then Shag traversed suddenly and I found the button. Jack had his foot hard down and the engine roared into life. The German gunner was still hitting us.

I reported that we were withdrawing to get under cover and Major Duffy asked me for the position of the gun as if he was going to deal with it. I gave the map reference as nearly as I could determine and he congratulated me. Then I reflected that he probably thought it was George speaking and I was furious. However, there was no time for pettiness for Jack had started to back and the trailer, caught in a rut, had jammed round at right angles and smashed one of the rear wings. The tracks ground horribly and we guessed they were damaged.

Once we were under cover we could get back to something approaching normal. Peggy was coaxed back to her box in the pannier and I then threw out the empty cases and counted the remaining ammo. All of the HE had been fired and most of the AP. George went off to report in person, so we could tidy up without any fuss. I got out to get some biscuits from the trailer after repeated demands from the rest of the crew but when they wanted a statement of the visible damage I retorted that I hadn't hung about to look at that - not likely.

Most of our tanks were now in some difficulty. We were almost out of Seventy-five ammo and imagined that the damage outside was severe. Sherry, who had moved down the slope to encourage the infantry, was stuck in a crater and had a flat battery. Steve O'Neill, commanding our Baker tank, was behind him and could not pass. He was another sitting target for our German, who placed four shots in the back of his trailer. He was lucky it did not catch fire for, apart from anything else, he always kept his spare kit in the back of the trailer. 11 Troop had their worries also, for the big guns on Cap Gris Nez had been turned to engage us and large shells were dropping among their tanks. Mr. Waring, 11 Troop Leader, had a direct hit on the final drive and his tank was completely disabled.

The Flails, merrily exploding mines in our rear, only added to the confusion. One AVRE, also trying to get down to help the infantry, had fallen over the edge of a blockhouse and was lying on its side. The others were making a terrible fuss about it - apparently it held a captain, or someone equally important. The Germans were still very active although a tin hut on the beach, at which we had fired some of our first shots, was now blazing well.

With darkness falling, everyone tired out and completely browned off, and with no prospect of getting near enough to flame the gun emplacements, our release was obtained and the order given to retire. Sherry's tank remained in the crater and he was lucky to find a battery in a German position during the night that enabled him to get it started.

On the run back the trouble likely to occur from damaged track guards became apparent when the mud began to pile up on the air louvres and over-heat the engine. We were to experience this trouble quite often in the months to come but for the moment coped by sitting Shag on the back bin with a shovel.

The continuous racket all day long had tired our brains as well as our bodies but there was little rest for us that night. Harboured on the side of the valley where we had congregated in the morning, drenched by flurries of sleet, hungry and cold and worn out, we worked under the spotlight to drop our trailer and an air louvre to replace those damaged on Steve's tank. We boasted fifteen hits: nine bogies were out of action; a shot had pierced the track and damaged the off idler[71]; the fan and one of Jack's periscopes were gone; the Flame Gun had been hit and ruined; the near side was heavily scored about the pannier door. Since we were obviously bound for workshops we were to be pirated and would take all the Troop's damage with us.

Shag pitched the bivvies and made down the beds while the rest of us toiled on through the night. Our turn to go on guard came and went and we were still working. It was after two o'clock and still raining by the time we had finished. Even Jack was exhausted and Dusty and I could hardly stand.

However, the morning came bright and sunny and cheerful and we all went to the top of the hill to gaze at Dover cliffs, clear and white and very near across the sea that was now a rippling blue. The news went round that the garrison of the big guns was to surrender at midday but no one was very interested. I felt terribly homesick - partly because I really was affected by the sight but also, no doubt, because I felt I ought to be and that brought it on.

From the hilltop we could also see right across the broad plain of Cap Gris Nez. Bombers wheeled overhead. The whole cape was scattered with bursts of orange and red flame and rolling black smoke intermingled, here and there, with green meadows and golden corn revealed for an instant before the next bomb fell. We could hear the dull thuds as the bombs went down and more red gleams appeared in the drifting smoke. Also, in the valley near at hand, Five-fives[72] were belting away at the same target, the little black shapes of the gunners dodging about their bucking weapons in feverish activity. But it was still very peaceful, lying on damp grass in the autumn sunshine. We were not directly concerned in the action, the noise was deadened by distance, and the bursting bombs were pretty enough to make one forget their lethal content.

---

[71] Idler. The Churchill track system was, in essence, the same as on the first tanks of World War One. From the Final Drive Sprocket at the rear each track led over the hull, round the Idler Wheel at the front and returned under the 11 relatively small bogies which supported the hull. The Idler Wheel was the means of adjusting the tension of the tracks.

[72] Five-fives. The standard heavy RA gun, firing an 80 lb. shell, calibre being 5.5".

By dinner time, we were moving. The new harbour was at Firques, in a nice tidy field which had not been used by the army before. We were told that Major Duffy had been furious out of all reason with a sergeant whose tank had knocked down the gatepost on entering. Evidently he had intended the squadron sign to be erected there.

We knew our tank would have to go to workshops and were worried lest the crew be split up because of this. Other crews told us that the Major always sent a full crew if he could as - and this was one thing said in his favour - he disliked breaking up a team and would go to some length to avoid it. At last our anxiety was dispelled - and it had been a very real anxiety for me, as I had now settled nicely into the little world of tank and crew and had no interests outside it. We were all to go. Jack and I spent the evening in an estaminet where, over coffee and cognac, we could comfortably discuss the possibilities of 30 Armoured Brigade workshops at Wierre Effroy.

EXCERPT FROM BBC NEWS BULLETIN OF 15TH NOVEMBER, 1944

'Listeners who think that too little credit is given to British troops for their work on the Western Front will be interested in this news of the 141st Regiment of the Royal Armoured Corps[73].

'After taking part in fighting around Villers-Bocage, Caen, and on the main road to Falaise, the regiment took part in the drive up the channel coast, in company with Canadian infantry. It played a leading role in the capture of Boulogne and Calais, and the German commanders of both places surrendered to officers of the regiment.

'The regiment also led the assault on the German long range guns on Cap Gris Nez, which used to shell Dover and Folkestone.

'Canadian troops were mentioned at the time and Canadian troops took part in the attack but the armoured spearheads were British - the 141st Regiment, RAC.

'We would have said at the time but there was strict censorship of any mention of the British part played in the attacks - the last of which took place on September 29th - and the ban has only been lifted today.'

---

73 While mention of Divisions and Brigades was frequent, the singling out of a particular regiment - or its equivalent in other arms of the service - was very rare indeed.

CHAPTER 7

WORKSHOPS

We could not have had a better day for the run to Wierre Effroy. The sun glowed in a cloudless sky but in the depths of the winding country lanes it was shady and cool and dew still clung to the ferns. We jogged along comfortably so as not to raise the dust, meeting no army traffic but innumerable farm carts at which to wave. We could forget the army - we were on our own and out for a joy-ride.

Wierre Effroy was in the heart of the country about fifteen kilometres from the town of Marquise. It did not seem a lively spot for there were only two cafés. In one, however, the Café de l'Union, where we stopped to ask the way, we found there was good cognac and coffee and a pretty girl.

We arrived in nice time for lunch and afterwards Jack and I hitchhiked into Marquise to get some photos developed. The town was grey and dirty, most of the shops were shut, and there were only two things worthy of note. One was the constant shell warning - Gris Nez was still in German hands as far as was known. The other was the public convenience, which was very public indeed, being simply the two stalls of an urinal placed against the wall of the church. We thought it was a queer place to have put it and used it for the sake of being able to say we had done so.

The roll of films was left in a shop where the proprietress spoke English and we paid for the development in advance and left Jack's address so that they could be forwarded. However, we never received the snaps, which I consider rather a poor show.

Then we had gin and Calvados in various cafés but there was nothing else to interest us. As we had no desire to be shelled we soon started back. Some of the houses on the outskirts were shut up and swastikas had been chalked on the doors, presumably indicating ownership by collaborators. This was an excuse to talk to some French girls at a nearby window so we were held up there for some time. My schoolboy French, although improved by use in Normandy, was still less effective than Jack's sign language as far as women were concerned. He was a good companion.

It was getting dark before we finally left and there was very little traffic. A 15-hundredweight truck took us part of the way but then we had to walk for several miles until overhauled by a Jeep going to the workshops.

At that time the crew of a tank in dock did not reckon to do any work on it and we were looking forward to a week or two of complete freedom. We had erected our German bivvies in a sheltered spot by a hedge, one being placed separately to house our loot which we had removed from the tank for safety. The REME fitters pestered us for souvenirs, particularly bayonets and German belts and there was great competition in bidding for the two rifles which Shag and I had picked up in Boulogne. When they heard that Jack had a camera all the men working on our tank had to have their photos taken. Every tank coming to workshops was welcomed by the REME as a source of income as they had little opportunity to loot. But they were a decent lot and we felt we could soon replace the things we gave them, such as bayonets.

During the first day we must have told our story a dozen times and of course it lost nothing in the telling. Although even sticking to the bare bones was enough, for fifteen hits seemed to be a record, especially as the tank was still in reasonable fighting trim.

So far so good but our expectation of a holiday was rudely shattered. The workshops were short-handed and expected an order to move at any time. They were set up to handle the Flails and a Churchill was not a tank they were used to. Moreover, we were only there by courtesy as 31 Armoured Brigade had been formed and while at the moment it comprised only our regiment there would eventually be two more and all the frills including workshops. So the commandant wanted to see the back of us as soon as possible. After we had replaced the idler and nine bogies (including the coupled numbers two and three, the 'Siamese' assembly, that gave us more trouble than all the rest put together) we began to feel we should have been better employed with the squadron. Especially when we heard of the good time being had by 12 and 14 Troops on Cap Gris Nez.

However, we could relax in the evenings. Shag and I usually took Peggy for a walk to the nearby farm, 'chez Duclos', where we were well dug in. There were three girls and a boy named Jacques who spoke English quite well - especially the swear words. George was so shocked that he took him to one side in a fatherly manner and explained that he must not use them. We had so many sardines that they were able to get a good price for their eggs, so we were always welcome. Also, we made attempts to repair the farmer's car, which had been laid up for five years and was in an advanced stage of disrepair. As I still had my German rifle, despite George's efforts to lose it, we held shooting matches in one of the fields well away from the cows - it was annoying to find that Jacques was a much better shot than I was.

One evening he took Shag and I to see a crashed Typhoon pancaked into a small field and, all things considered, in very good order. The array of instruments in the cockpit fascinated Jacques and bewildered us, but we explained them all to his satisfaction. The clock and compass, of course, were gone, which was only to be expected. After seeing this and trying to fire the guns we went and called the cattle home. The fields behind the farm were littered with leaflets in which we assured the Germans that the war in the west was over, which was very interesting and nearer to the truth than we thought at the time.

Nearby was an old AVRE harbour, littered with wings, tow ropes and track plates, and Shag and I were very technical here, running about to see if any of the wings would fit our tank. However, the Engineers had left nothing of value save a tow rope to replace ours which had suffered at Sangatte.

Then back to supper, usually eggs, fried bully and beans. The German ham was finished but their tinned meat was standing the strain well. We were fortunate in having a cooker that worked well. The petrol cookers operated on the same principle as a Primus and were likewise liable to get blocked up or leaky unless carefully nursed. Needless to say, they got no such treatment, being overhauled only when they refused to work any longer. When they did function without trouble they were ideal for cooking inside bivvy or tank.

On another evening we all walked to the next village in search of a drink, the Café de l'Union having run dry. There was a rumour that a party of German SS[74] had been seen in the woods, so we were careful. It was always the SS who were credited with these superhuman feats of endurance - I suppose the ordinary German soldier was reckoned to have too much sense - but I never actually heard of anyone who had made contact with these units.

Anyway, we arrived safely and visited all the cafés, being welcomed into the bosom of the family in each as the public bar was also the family sitting room, but without getting anything stronger than coffee. In each we were forced to be amused by Hitler's will, leaving hate, grief, indignity and pain to each of his henchmen. I do not know what organisation printed these leaflets but they seemed to have been distributed throughout that village. It was, of course, difficult for us to understand how much these people hated the Germans and we found it rather embarrassing to be expected to share that hate. It was not something we thought about, much.

My visit to the wrecked echelon outside Caen had opened my eyes to the penalty of getting mixed up with the other side and the bombing of Le Havre, Noires Mottes and Cap Gris Nez had driven the lesson home. With great difficulty I secured a brush and some white paint and executed a large white star on the turret roof. Shag then suggested a mortar bomb on the gun barrel as a token of achievement

[74] SS. The infamous Schutz-Staffeln, the most fanatically Nazi of all the German armed forces. Originally formed by Himmler for internal security, the organisation was developed into regular fighting formations of Division strength and were known as the 'Waffen SS'. They had, and retain to this day, a really nasty reputation, the majority of atrocities such as the massacre at Oradour-sur-Glane having been committed by them.

at Boulogne. I did it but it looked ridiculous. Jack made a fearful fuss, saying he would be the laughing stock of the squadron. So we insisted it stayed.

The next day Jack and I took the tank down to Wierre for a test run. I commanded and a fitter rode in front with Jack. We parked outside the café where there was a convenient space. The daughter of the house, or the barmaid - we never knew which - was seated by the fire in her underclothes and made a most attractive picture. Apparently she was recovering from a chill, although in the light of later experience I now have my doubts about this. Anyway, if she had any ulterior motive she was disappointed - the fitter only made eyes at her, the thought never entered my head, and Jack talked all the time about his wife.

I drank sufficient to enable me to persuade the baker's wife to let us have several loaves without coupons, payment to be made in chocolate at a future date. It gave us some satisfaction to recall this after we had given up hope of getting our photos from Marquise.

Then Jack started back. The fitter sat with his legs in the Flame-gunners hatch and sang dirty songs over the I/c. Our driving was careless enough to force a farm cart into the ditch so we had to stop and tow him out. It cost us a lot of cigarettes to soothe the carter. The tank was pronounced fit for action.

We were sorry to leave Wierre when the time came to go and made all the usual promises about writing to the farm where they gave us a farewell supper. Jacques wrote out the words of 'La Madelon', which I wanted for the next town we liberated. In fact, I did write some time later, only to discover that there was no means of postage to French civilians.

We had pronounced as expert opinion that the main trouble with the farmer's car lay in the condition of the batteries and Jacques was to come with us to Marquise to get them charged. He turned up in the morning and we seated him in the front where he was perfectly happy and fascinated, as we expected, by his ability to talk to us all over the I/c. However, his ride was of short duration. We had hardly passed through Wierre Effroy when the tank did its best to go over the embankment into the field below. Jack slammed on the anchors and on raising the engine covers we found oil spouting all over the steering brake drums.

Fortunately, a Jeep from the workshops bound for Marquise cancelled its run and fetched the fitters. Their opinion was that we should be there for hours. Jacques set out on his bicycle, which we had been carrying on the trailer, with his batteries on the carrier. We were still waiting when he passed us on his way home. We sat about and ate and smoked. There was nothing else to do.

The squadron, after assisting in the taking of Cap Gris Nez, had returned to the field at Firques. We entered the harbour to find petrol fires blazing everywhere, by which light the crews were engaged in breaking trailers in readiness for a transporter run up to the Albert Canal. We were needed, it seemed, in Holland, and the transporters were waiting for us on the road.

It was the first time I had helped to load a tank on a transporter and I sat in the co-driver's seat so as to watch. The transporter driver, standing at the end of the trackways, waved us forward. Jack peered tensely through his vision block and jerked the tiller bar[75] occasionally as signalled. The tank shuddered as the tracks clawed at the foot of the ramp and slowly the nose came up: up and up, steeper and steeper, the tank quivering, the transporter trailer jerking and creaking as it took the weight. Then Jack took his foot from the accelerator, there was a sickening moment of hesitation and then the nose sank gently. We rocked, settled, and then crawled forward. The transporter driver held up both hands and signalled finished. The ramps went up with a clang. Jack switched off and we climbed down to help secure the hawsers before strolling back to help the others with the kit.

---

[75] Tiller bar. The Churchill was unique in having a tiller bar like bicycle handles rather than the conventional upright steering levers. It was fitted above the drivers' legs and was easier and more convenient to use than separate steering levers.

CHAPTER 8

INTERLUDE

Peggy was always a nuisance when we slept in the tank, refusing to sleep in her bundle of cotton waste in the pannier when she could disturb someone's blankets. I slept across the toolbox that night and she woke me by licking my feet. So I was up in time to wash and shave comfortably while the transporter crew were cooking breakfast. Their vehicles were Diesel so it was not such a simple job for them to light a fire as it was for us. They had to carry a can of petrol to start it off and they and their utensils got much dirtier than we did. But Diesel soot did not do much harm to the sausages.

Our responsibility was over now the tank was loaded and we could sit back and leave things to the RASC[76]. As soon as breakfast was over the convoy lost no time in getting moving, the driver went through his many gears without a murmur or a jerk and we gathered speed imperceptibly, the tank swaying gently.

It took us a long time to get comfortable. We wanted to see and be seen, but the turret was too high because of the trees lining the road. I finally selected the track guard, with my feet inside the driver's hatch, as the best place.

At first the column was packed close but the long hill rising beyond Marquise proved too much for the transporter in front of us. Halfway up we noticed oil dripping in the road, our drivers started to hoot, and at a lay-by that appeared very conveniently the stricken vehicle halted. We pulled in behind to give assistance, consisting of a brew of tea. There was nothing else for us to do, although the transporter drivers were busy. I lay on the engine deck in the sun all

[76] RASC. Royal Army Service Corps. The general transport arm of the army.

the afternoon and read, except when A Squadron passed, also on transporters. Jeers and catcalls resounded along their column as they saw us, the first casualties.

In Boulogne - our route was conditioned by the disposition of Class 70 bridges[77] - we were held up again by a transporter broken down across the road. For a long time we were driving around the town until we found the Citadel, which gave us our bearings. While the RASC argued over a map, Jack and I bought some rosaries as souvenirs in a little junk shop as we felt we should get rid of some French currency as we were leaving the country and there was nothing else to buy. When we got started again, Shag pointed out the ruins of his chimney but I was giving all my attention to the cooker and a dixie of concentrated soup and so missed a good look at the only tangible evidence that we had taken part in the attack on the town.

Two punctures, fortunately, occurred by the time the soup was ready and we ate it seated on a low stone wall while Jack and the two drivers struggled with the tyres. Jack was very good at this sort of thing on the whole trip. Of course, he was as strong as a horse and I frankly admitted that the transporter wheels were more than I could handle. Shag and Dusty said the same. Even so, Jack and his fellow 'old soldiers' did have a sense of comradeship and a willingness to help out which we younger members of the squadron did not attain. Maybe their age gave them an increased sense of responsibility.

Just as we were about to start off again a fat little Frenchman wearing a black skullcap came up and begged a lift to Les Desvres. It was getting cold so we muffled him in a greatcoat and provided him with cigarettes for the whole way. Most army vehicles were very good about giving lifts.

We approached Les Desvres on a road we had never travelled before. The sun had long sunk below the hills and against the pale mauve of the sky a plain wooden cross was silhouetted, black and stark atop a hill packed with dark pine trees. We crept along the road towards it and its shadow lay grim and forbidding over the valley. It seemed to me the symbol of a stern and uncompromising faith, a cruel

[77] Class 70 Bridges. Classified to take a weight up to 70 tons.

faith that could urge a mob to the excesses of St. Bartholomew's Night. I could feel this enough to make me shiver, even as I admired the artistry that placed the Calvary there.

Between Les Desvres and St. Pol we felt hungry again and it was cold enough, too, for our greatcoats to be welcome. So we pulled up in front of a little café for tea, which we cooked outside and then carried inside to eat. I bartered jam for some eggs and sold some petrol for the transporter crew for about ten-and-six a gallon. Petrol was easily the most saleable commodity in these comparatively unscathed areas of Northern France where there was a glut of sardines and jam.

The transporter crews would buy petrol from the tanks they carried up and sell it on the way back, making quite a steady little income. This particular crew, however, were being careful as, a trip or so before, the tank they had carried had lost so much petrol that it was unable to move off the transporter. Which looked suspicious.

It was too cold and dark to continue sitting on the wings and for the rest of the stage, until we stopped for the night just beyond St. Pol, I dozed in the turret. Jack woke me with the suggestion that we hunt for billets. Civilian households usually made soldiers welcome if they could possibly accommodate them, maybe through gratitude but more likely because we were able to supply many of the goods it was impossible to buy in the shops. Jack's asset in this business was his impudence and my job was to translate his remarks into French wherever possible.

On this occasion we got excellent results. A very pleasant lady invited us in and as there were only two children in the house, one of them still in the cradle, it seemed we would get a peaceful evening. Jack, greatly to my surprise, was very good with babies, making all the right noises. This probably influenced the mother's decision and this ability was obviously going to stand us in good stead.

The elder child was a bit of a puzzle. He seemed more grown up than any of us, for although he was only about twelve in years he had his own carpet slippers, his smoking jacket, and his own particular armchair by the stove. He treated George and Jack as equals and made the rest of us feel very young. He was very much the head of the household - we did not like to ask the whereabouts of his father - and his mother treated him with some deference. I could not imagine him playing soldiers with the other village children who, we saw in the morning, had salvaged British and German tin hats to add realism to their game.

In short, we passed a comfortable, cheerful evening, but in spite of the fact that such complete accord prevailed downstairs we heard the lady of the house bolt her door when she retired. After this we did not like to creep about the upper floor looking for a lavatory and were forced to relieve ourselves out of the bedroom window into the street. Then it was delightful to sink into a feather mattress and wrap cool sheets around us - cool because our shirts were smothered in oil and we had perforce to sleep naked or abuse the hospitality we had received. By entering a civilian house, chatting until bedtime and then going upstairs with a candle, we had managed to escape from the army for a while.

We had eggs for breakfast and got down to the tank in time to move it off the railway line. It was the first railway, or tramline, which we had seen in working order and the tiny engine and carriages looked like toys when they appeared from the depths of the woods and took us by surprise. It clattered to a halt and waited patiently for us, driver and fireman grinning cheerfully at us before giving a colossal blast on their whistle and grinding over the level crossing and away.

George had said something about starting at nine, but by the time we had chatted the baker and got some bread, exchanged some bully beef for apples and rescued Peggy from hordes of children, it was nearer eleven o'clock. The RASC men were in no hurry, anyway, and George could not do anything about them.

From St. Pol to Arras is only 34 kilometres by the main road but there must have been bridges down somewhere for all the morning - that is, the period before lunch - we spent crawling about country lanes, up hill and down hill. I say crawling, and so it was for the most part, but on one hill the brakes failed. We were not worried when our ponderous vehicle began to gather speed but Jack was standing on the running board and he turned round and shouted to us and the transporter swooped round the corner at the bottom at about forty miles an hour. The driver started to change down and luckily the road was fairly straight for the distance necessary for him to bring us to a halt. But it meant more delay while hoses were tightened and the system bled.

Here and there we passed a tank rusting in the ditch, ferns and brambles beginning to engulf it. Somehow, like that, it did not seem out of place or worth a second glance. All the while we were in the hilly country of winding narrow roads and wooded valleys the journey was pleasant. Jack would jump off the transporter at the bottom of a hill, chat with a girl at her garden gate, and catch us up at the top with eggs, tomatoes and apples. George tried to emulate him on one occasion when we had cut some sandwiches for the drivers; only he did not wait for a steep hill but picked a slight incline where the transporter had not changed down much. He nearly went under the wheels and none of us was willing to try after that.

Once we had climbed out on to the plateau towards Arras, where the principal crop seemed to be turnips and the wind was unfettered by hedges or trees, greatcoats soon appeared and we started the engine for extra warmth. For although the countryside was bare and cheerless and the farm workers in the fields just gave one wave and then got on with their jobs, I wanted to see all there was to see and I could study the inside of the turret any time.

We stopped to repair another puncture and while we were huddled over a petrol fire sipping tea a farm cart appeared, stacked with potatoes. This was treasure trove and the carter gave us about a hundredweight for two cigarettes, so we decided to have dinner immediately, with chips as the main dish.

Soon after starting again we picked up two girls who wanted to get to Arras. As they seemed to be willing to pay their way, one of the RASC men joined them on the rear of the transporter under a tarpaulin. The rest of us retired tactfully to the engine deck and watched the white road streaming out in our wake. Occasionally one or other of us would crane up and peer over the turret and see the tarpaulin flapping about and, once, a red face appearing as if gasping for air. They were occupied for a long time.

Women seemed to be travelling. We came across one of our HQ tanks drawn up in the square of Avesnes-le-Comte, repairing a puncture. On board was a most attractive girl who was going from Boulogne to rejoin her family on the Belgian frontier. The driver, Bob Cheney, who was a great friend of Jack's, confided that his crew were cutting cards and the girl seemed to be thriving on it. She stood on the engine deck, quite at home, with her blonde hair tumbling over the collar of an army greatcoat and she smiled at me and I thought she looked lovely and be blowed to her morals, and what a set of roughs her crew looked, and how much better it would have been for her to be with us.

We decided to make Arras our stopping place for the second night, largely because I urged it. I wanted to be able to write home and tell my father that I had been there as well as he, in only slightly different circumstances. So we joined some other laggards parked at the entrance to the town where the roads from St. Pol, Doullens and Bethune made a junction.

As usual, Jack and I secured billets but they were absolutely respectable and we felt that such a town ought to have more to offer. There were lots of people in the streets and lots of shops and cafés open and there was that subtle flavour of vice and the underworld that one sometimes finds in a big town after dark - especially when that town is effectively under military occupation in all but name. Also, the others had promised to get the supper ready and we did not want to get back before all the work was done.

We had mated up with three conscripts of the new French army, who had made most of the enquiries for beds on our behalf and had bullied the civilians into taking us in a way that we could not. We decided to stand them drinks before they returned to their caserne and entered a promising café from which more noise emanated than from anywhere else in the street.

It was not a simple café and I pass over the next couple of hours of which I am not particularly proud. Sufficient to say that Jack and I walked back to the tank, with me considerably poorer, although somewhat wiser for the experience. Obviously, we had to be enthusiastic in making our report and the RASC men, Shag and Dusty, were eager to have a go but George needed more persuasion. It seemed very important that we should get George to go and I told him that he should not miss this opportunity of seeing something of the seamy side of life and it would be of great advantage to him in civvy street. In the end he agreed to go just for the walk and Jack took them all.

It was very cold and I had little appetite left for my supper but I stayed behind and forced myself to eat it. As it was a tin of the unappetising Haricot Oxtail it seemed a fitting penance. We were continually complaining to our Q-bloke about it, for at one time we had never had any other sort of pack for days and it was becoming increasingly difficult to exchange it for something more edible. A further source of complaint was that a compo pack contained rations for fourteen men for one day and we were issued with one every three days: thus we were feeding the equivalent of fifteen men on rations for fourteen. We argued that the Q drew rations in bulk from the RASC according to the number of men in the squadron and thus, every third day, he gained one man's ration from each tank. This would quickly mount up in a squadron of nineteen tanks.

Soldiers are always touchy on the subject of rations and are suspicious of all quartermasters. There seemed good grounds for thinking Q Grace was fiddling as the Qs of A and B Squadrons admitted the justice of the argument and issued an extra pack to each tank occasionally. In C Squadron we held many moan sessions but always received unsatisfactory replies and the matter was never cleared up.

No one was anxious to get up in the morning and a cold, blustering wind did not help in the least. It cheered us up a bit to recount George's exploits the previous evening, when he had been so ungentlemanly as to throw a lady off his lap.

We should not have started as soon as we did if an RASC dispatch rider had not put the wind up our drivers by saying that an officer was coming back to charge anyone found halted after nine o'clock in the morning. Then we were all in a rush to get away. Passing through Cambrai, we doubled back along the main road to Douai and were all asleep when the time came for dinner, at Valenciennes.

By then I had done practically everything, embarrassing or otherwise, in public on the continent, but I had never had such a large crowd in attendance as that which then assembled to watch us cook and eat our meal. My own share in the culinary operations was modest, being limited to chipping potatoes and slicing tomatoes, so I had plenty of time to chat our audience.

Were we going to the Front? But yes, of course. Where had we come from? From Calais. Calais, then, was libre? But certainly; we, in person, had liberated the town. And, without doubt, many of the filthy Boche had died in Calais? Without doubt, we had killed thousands. No, the Boche had not as many tanks as the Anglais. Nor had he une lance-flamme. Voiçi la lance-flamme. But no, the Boche did not like it, naturally. Did we like France? What a question! - but certainly, especially this part.

In this area there was practically everything in the jewellery and luxury clothing line to be had at a price and after dinner we all went shopping. George and Jack, the married men, were in search of silk stockings - Jack, I think, was anxious to make amends. Dusty and Shag, not knowing the dimensions of their girls' legs so exactly, plumped for jewellery. Not having anyone specifically in mind, I did the same and finally paid Jack back in s'Hertogenbosch. Shag, to whom I finished by owing 150 francs, never did get paid.

Leaving Valenciennes, we kept a good lookout for the red and white poles of the frontier post and were elated when we crossed into Belgium. From Valenciennes to Brussels seemed one long street, decorated with flags to a much greater extent than in France, and lined with people whose cheers made the ride more of a triumphal progress than ever. All the Belgian children wore round fur caps decorated with the national colours and Shag and I bargained for them wherever we stopped but without success.

Just beyond Mons we stopped, apparently for the night. One old lady offered billets for five 'correct' soldiers, but we did not like the sound of that 'correct' and Shag and I decided to search farther afield. We had a conspicuous success, as the housewife was plucking a chicken for supper at the moment we called, and feeling that we were in on a good thing we went back to the tank to collect our kit - and found no tank and no transporter. Only a dying petrol fire flickering in an old ammunition case.

As we did not know where they had gone there was nothing to do but wait, and before long George came along and began to lecture us for going off without his permission. So we picked up the fire tin and walked away with George trotting behind ticking like a clock.

The transporter was halted in the square at Maisières, choked up in a mob of civilians through which we had to force our way, swinging our fire tin. Apart from those who were there just to have a look at us and make a noise, a dozen families were fighting for the honour of putting us up for the night. Dusty and I were finally claimed by a quiet old gentleman with a white moustache who reminded me of my father. Shag had been secured by a very snappy lady at one side of the square and seemed very pleased with himself, the RASC men had a billet on the opposite side and George and Jack were next door to me. We all went first to my billet for coffee and anything else that was going.

In every house we visited they would first ask our names and then, for some reason, our ages. Shag looked about seventeen, save for the circles under his eyes, and he was always the 'babby', although actually older than both Dusty and myself. They would never believe I was only nineteen because I never seemed to get a good shave, while Dusty could have been any age between twenty and forty. The evening was very pleasant.

Our last day on the transporter took us through Brussels, where we got mixed up in some sort of procession. There were several bands, hundreds of banners and flags, and all the men were in top hats and morning coats. We were obviously rushing to the front - the transporter had a very musical horn that imparted a nice sense of urgency - and we received a tremendous ovation. George, Shag and I took the salute from the turret but the effect was rather spoilt by the avenues of trees that forced us to keep ducking our heads.

Beyond Louvain - or Leuven - we found ourselves in Flemish speaking country and I was soon to have my first experience of the language difficulty with which my friends had struggled all along.

As we entered Diest a DR from another convoy came dashing up alongside, shouting that the transporter was on fire. It took a long time for him to make the drivers hear and when they finally pulled up we found that three adjoining tyres had punctures and were smoking furiously. This was a big job. We had to take the tank off the flat and while the repairs were being carried out Shag and I went into the town and bought grapes which, at this early stage of the liberation of Belgium, were very cheap.

We had not yet been paid any Belgian money. Some of the shops would take French francs of the British Military Issue, and we had some coins collected in the various cafés en route. We thought they were two franc pieces but found that we had been holding them upside down and that they were in reality fives. We got rid of all the coinage we had - no soldier on the continent could be bothered with coins. In France and Belgium notes below fifty francs were usually ignored in any computation of one's wealth, although fifty French francs was five shillings. In Holland it was worse. A guilder was 1/10½, which put the 25-cent piece at about sixpence. Shopkeepers in Holland always had their prices in odd amounts, knowing that the change in 'kwartjes' would be left lying on the counter.

I was rather attracted by Diest and would have liked to have stayed there longer. The old town wall and moat still survived in part and in spite of the cold there were some men hardy enough to be swimming in the cold, grey water. The narrow, winding, cobbled streets were full of interest, with poky little shops hanging their wares in the doorways. But George could not stop a moment. We heard the horn blaring and had to hurry back and scramble up as our vehicle got under way. That evening the transporter dropped us in a village square just off the main road. There were five other tanks there - it was a gathering of the lame ducks.

There was a fairground covering most of the square and we felt the lack of money keenly. Jack and the transporter drivers got on the roundabout and said, 'Camarade!' and pointed over their shoulders when pressed for payment. They had lots of rides and were hopping about from one horse to another and generally playing the fool but the rest of us had not the nerve to carry it off. There were lots of girls standing around unattached, but here again we were powerless, or the lack of money made us think we were. Eventually we got tired of trying to pass off a mixture of French and German as a language and retired to bed without even trying to cadge a drink in the café above which we had billeted ourselves. The proprietor was not very friendly, anyway.

The next morning we moved up the road about five miles, to Beeringen, and broke down.

* * *

We had drawn the tank into an open space before a café and of course the usual crowd assembled. While Jack diagnosed a leaking oil cooler, Shag and I made a parade of tightening the bogie bolts, which entailed lying down on the ground and struggling with complicated special spanners, which looked rather professional, and which needed doing in any case. The proprietress of the café brought us all glasses of the sweet Belgian 'donker bier', the first we had tasted, which gave us a chance to get chatting and move our belongings into the café. It was pretty obvious we should be there for one night at least.

We met all the family: the parents Emma and Henri, their two sons Fernand and Andre, and the baby Jean-Claude. The conversation was limited at first owing to the mutual language difficulties but it was surprisingly easy to grasp something once we had the context and when the words were assisted by gestures. They were very pleased to hear that the tank was broken down - 'kaput' - everyone understood 'kaput'. What was difficult to get across was how long we were likely to be staying because this was something we did not know.

While we were getting our feet under the table George, too, had been active. He had arranged for the tank to be repaired in the workshops of the Guards Armoured Division, which was situated about two hundred yards from our billet in the great yard before the Beeringen coal mine. They sent an ARV[78] to tow us there that afternoon.

We were fed by the Guards and to reach the cookhouse meant clambering between railway wagons, over piles of sleepers and mounds of gravel and along half a mile of track in pouring rain that was dirty with coal dust. The journey ensured an appetite, which was just as well as, ungrateful as we were, we found much to complain about in the food. After the fresh vegetables we had been able to obtain by barter we were not attracted to dehydrated potatoes and carrots, curried rice and stewed dried apricots.

At nine o'clock the REME held a parade to make sure all their men had returned to work. George would go to this, as he was sleeping in the guardroom at the mine and used to polish his boots. He insisted that we should go also but after the first time we persuaded him that he was disturbing the domestic arrangements of our billet and that it was unnecessary anyway. When we did eventually arrive at the workshops, the first thing was to get a bath, a shave and a change of underwear from the laundry unit that had requisitioned some of the pit head showers. Then we would look at the tank for an hour and buy ice-cream and fruit from the barrow boys on the road outside, for George had managed to arrange for us to draw some money. Also, Shag and I were very busy at first digging the tracer out of an AP shot that we intended to leave with our hosts as a souvenir. On the second day I met a man from my training regiment who had gone to the RTR and whose Cromwell was also in the workshops, so we had notes to exchange.

---

[78] ARV. Armoured Recovery Vehicle. A tank without its turret, which was replaced with towing and lifting gear and repair facilities such as oxyacetylene plant. Normally, each squadron would have one ARV with the same type of body as the gun tanks: i.e. ours were Churchills.

After dinner we always went back to the café to drink beer before going for a wander round Beeringen under the guidance of Fernand and Andre. One afternoon we went to the church, a modern but graceful building of which the inhabitants were very proud. The altar could be floodlit and the caretaker gave us the whole works so that Jack could take photographs.

The local baker, who lived next door and often came in in the evenings, spoke excellent English. It seemed he and Henri had been in the local underground movement and had frequently had their houses searched by the Germans. The usual hiding place for their pistols, Henri said, was in the stove. It was probably just as well that they had never had the need to use them.

As a relief from talking, Fernand played the cornet. His piece de resistance was 'Dorpsmusiek', which carried him through everything else. Several times we visited the local fleapit to see very ancient films. Sometimes they were English speaking but more often we had to do our best with the French and Flemish sub-titles. Henri loved 'coyboy' films.

"Ver-ry good. Ver-ry good," he would say at the end and we would, of course, agree.

But we had no cigarettes. For two days we had been over generous, not expecting to stay so long, and then had to tighten our belts. I had saved a packet of German 'Jan Mart' brand as a souvenir and they carried us for a bit. After a few days, a Jeep coming back from the squadron brought us the first mail we had had for a fortnight and a letter from my aunts contained ten somewhat flattened Woodbines which were much appreciated but did not go far. One day good old Henri came home with his ration, tumbled it on the table, and proceeded to share it out. We had willpower enough to stop this sacrifice, with regret, and after that just had to do without.

Of all our billets on the Continent those at the Café Sport, with the genuine hospitality and kindness of the Moons family, is the place I remember with the most gratitude. Eventually, of course, came the parting. We tried to put it off as long as we could by encouraging

Jock, our usual fitter, to find as many faults as possible. Anyway, it took a long time to get the oil cooler from base at Diest. We were becoming used to meeting nice people and then passing on but they did not want to understand that we could not stay indefinitely. The war was over so far as Belgium was concerned and the problem now uppermost in their minds seemed to be the value of their currency. However, our last evening was a jolly one with too much beer - that 'donker bier' was very nice but it just went straight through. Henri, who was a clog maker in his spare time, gave us a pair each as souvenirs and very decorative they were.

The morning was bad. While the rest of us packed Jack collected the tank and George and brought them up to the café. Emma cried, the children cried, Henri was very miserable and so were we. We took Fernand and Andre in the tank to Bourg Leopold, for their school had just reopened and as the tramline at Beeringen had not yet been repaired they would otherwise have had to walk. We dropped them outside the gate just in time and I lost sight of them surrounded by a crowd of admiring schoolmates.

* * *

Our instructions were to follow 'Club Route Up' to Nijmegen. All the main routes were named and had signs every few hundred yards which were illuminated at night. In Normandy there had been 'Neagle', 'Macdonald', 'Rathbone' and other famous film stars. In Belgium and Holland there were 'Club', 'Heart' and 'Diamond' and, in the Canadian sector, 'Victoria' and 'Maple Leaf'. In Germany they switched to precious stones, 'Emerald', 'Ruby'. 'Onyx' and the like. Only occasionally towards the end was unimaginative numbering adopted - '240' and '355' being the only two I call to mind. It would seem to be impossible to go wrong.

From Hechtel to Valkenswaard in Holland 'Club Route Up' was the main road. For miles on each side of the border was an expanse of moorland studded with straggling plantations of fir trees. It was raining and the whole aspect was desolate. On one side of the road an

RAOC[79] depot lay in the mud, huge piles of ironwork, sleepers, Bailey Bridges, pontoons, bricks and cement bags untended and seemingly in hopeless confusion. Opposite, two Thunderbolts lay in the heather. Deadened by the rain, the tarnished aluminium of one was no brighter than the olive drab of the other.

A little further along was a REME workshop, also bogged down in mud. There were countless wrecked vehicles, most of them rusty - tanks, armoured cars, trucks, motorcycles, all the litter of mechanised warfare. A Jagdpanther[80] nestled amid the fir trees, its mottled camouflage making it invisible until we drew level. The long gun drooped dejectedly. Four neat little holes pierced the side and externally they were the only signs of damage.

Then came the frontier post and we were in Holland. The road was lined with burnt-out Half-tracks. In the ditches, on the moor to either side, lay Shermans, brewed up, overturned, turrets blown off. The Guards Armoured Division, busting on for all they were worth to rescue the paratroops round Arnhem, had neglected to watch the flanks for Eighty-eights. Just along the road were four of these weapons, breeches blown off and barrels burst by the German gunners. There were more in the ditches where they had been driven from the road. Four stood in a clearing, muzzles pointing to the sky. The Guards had certainly run into trouble.

We were getting very wet, for the short waterproof jackets we wore were not sufficient to prevent the rain driving through the hatches into the turret and soaking our legs. So we felt miserable and must have been a demoralising sight even so early as Bourg Leopold,

---

79 RAOC. Royal Army Ordnance Corps. The 'supply' corps for guns, ammunition and other support fighting equipment.

80 Jagdpanther (Self-propelled Gun - SP). This 'Hunting Panther' had an 88 mm. gun with limited traverse mounted in the raised hull of a Panther tank chassis. The Germans made great use of SP's, which were cheaper to produce as they had no turret and, with their lower profile, were more easily concealed for their anti-tank role. Those I came across, in addition to the Jagdpanther, were usually 75 mm. on Mark III or Mark IV chassis.
The only similar British vehicle I saw in action was the 17-pounder mounted on a built-up Valentine chassis. This seemed a very good vehicle as the Valentine, although obsolete as a gun tank, was most reliable. The RA also used the Sexton SP as mobile artillery: this was a 25-pounder gun on a Grant chassis.

where crowds of infantry reinforcements watched us pass with flattering interest.

So we stopped at a village to brew tea and warm ourselves and got talking to some officers in the Pioneer Corps, to whom we explained our situation. They were very sympathetic and we were directed to the cookhouse and stocked up with bread, bully, tinned milk and tea.

I have said that the system of routing was simple and thorough; you only had to know the name of your route and you could not go wrong. Shag was asleep in the turret, Dusty in the front. Jack was too busy to bother with signs and I thought George could cope with it. We rattled into Valkenswaard, the first town in Holland liberated by ground troops and in the big square in the centre of the town the routes diverged and we were following 'Hat'. George said afterwards that there was a sign

"CLUB ROUTE UP FOLLOW HAT ROUTE UP"

but I had not seen it. Jack kept on driving without comment and George seemed to know what he was doing.

We refuelled at a Yankee petrol dump just outside Heeze. It was situated at the end of a long lane in a clump of pine trees and we were surprised that George knew anything about it. The Yanks did not seem worried about an order to draw petrol and were a queer crowd altogether. One of them asked me if this here was a tank and when I assured him that it was, he supposed it was one of those Tigers. I said no, it was a Churchill flame-thrower. British? Naturally, what else did he expect? He said he did not know the British had any tanks. I said we had so many we did not know what to do with them and that our Churchill was the best tank there was. When I told him the weight he appeared impressed and almost convinced.

In fact, we did not form a very favourable opinion of our American allies. They did not seem to know or care anything about the war, and all they could think about was pistols. We had no German Lugers but could have sold our Thirty-eights ten times over. One sergeant offered me two wrist watches and ten English pounds for mine. It was even harder to refuse when another offered a superb pocket watch with flowers enamelled on the face. But while we could lose practically anything else and get it replaced there was a strict check on pistols.

We left them in their wood, cut off from the world save for chance visitors like ourselves, and pushed on down the road. It appeared that we were heading for Weert and Roermond but we were all very cheerful, as George now admitted that we were lost. Then a Yankee MP stepped into the middle of the road and asked us if we knew the Germans were only five hundred yards ahead and that put a different complexion on George's blunder. Jack said it only needed some big bug with a few stars to come along and we'd find ourselves in action and not know where or why.

So we turned and went back. George became more and more worried and the rest of us more and more pleased at the prospect of extra time on the loose. But soon I saw an RHQ[81] sign and so did George. I tried to persuade him that he had got it wrong, by which time we were well past and he had to stop the tank and run back to check. Then we tried to tell him RHQ would not know the location of C Squadron but he was adamant. So Jack had to reverse and we turned down a by-road.

We reached the outskirts of Gemert and RHQ was stationed in a cluster of farm buildings at the end of a muddy track about half a mile from the road. Jack parked at the entrance and we lit a petrol fire against a wall while George went to report. When our wall started to crack and send bits of brick flying we judged it time to look for billets.

The 15th Scottish Division had just pulled out of the line and the village was full. Jack and I tried a smattering of Flemish acquired at Beeringen but to no avail. As most of the houses had troops crowded round the stove we were able to believe the negative gestures. In any case, we were not very keen on sharing a billet with the 15th Scottish, which was known as a bullshit division in which the infantry had shave parades before going into action.

81 RHQ. Regimental Headquarters.

The tank stood in a sea of mud and the weather was too bad for a bivvy. Jack and I waded down the street, envying the infantry we could see through the windows sitting around glowing stoves. Then we met the local priest. He spoke English and we spent the first night in a bare room under his roof. Jack was very particular in making his bed down so that he lay along the boards and although this sounded silly I found that it really did make a difference. But this billet was too far from the tank for comfort and the next day we squeezed into a house at the end of our track that was already packed with REME.

Dusty and I went up to RHQ in the morning as I wanted some distilled water for the batteries. We found all our acquaintances there fooling around on first parade in best battle dress, belt and gaiters, while we were unshaven, extremely dirty, and dressed in tattered denims - it was a glorious moment. We stood and watched until the parade was nearly over and then continued on our errand before the RSM[82] was free to check us. Fortunately, RHQ moved out the same day. Still, we had got our back mail, piles of it, which was one good thing.

RHQ had not known C Squadron's location, as we had predicted. Our tank was again showing signs of exhaustion, so we stayed at Gemert while the fitters came over and worked on her for two days. George went about listening to rumours and the rest of us had leisure to compare our position with that of the troops of the 15th Scottish, and were gratified to learn that what we had heard was only too true. And we went to an ENSA[83] show.

Dusty and I had gone the first day. The town was packed with MPs and staff cars flying large priority flags. I had never seen one of these before and was astonished to see Dusty suddenly salute. I got to attention and Dusty explained that the MPs would nab one like lightning for not saluting, especially as we looked just about as scruffy as possible.

---

82 RSM. Regimental Sergeant-Major. The senior NCO in the regiment, reckoned to be able to frighten the life out of anyone below the rank of Captain.

83 ENSA. The voluntary Organisation of show-business personalities which provided live entertainment for the Forces.

Captain Barber had again been to see us in his Jeep and we had managed to borrow some Dutch money from his driver, Bish. I also borrowed an army handbook on the Netherlands which contained a useful selection of words and phrases and we could now make our hosts understand most of what we were saying - I had got fed up with being inarticulate, anyway, and had written home for a 'Teach Yourself Dutch' book. Sooner or later we were issued with a handbook for the country we were in, dealing with the civilians and the way we should behave towards them. Apart from the vocabulary there was a lot about the history, geography and constitutional framework of the country, the German behaviour after they had occupied it, and an impressive list of 'Do's and Don'ts'.

On the evening of the third day I commanded the tank on a test run and returned with the fitters reporting everything OK. George was waiting in the twilight, muffled up in his greatcoat. A cheerful glow from the windows of our billet was reflected in the grey mud outside and I sheeted up and hurried into the house. George, it appeared, was waiting for the Jeep bringing us C Squadron's location and was afraid he might miss it. We rather hoped he would.

However, in the morning we moved to join the squadron at Nistelrode, a village north of Eindhoven and not far from s'Hertogenbosch. On the first stage of the journey, along a good road to Helmond, a tank transporter tried to overtake us - rashly, for it was not a modern vehicle. Our tank, pepped up by the fitters, responded nobly, while George and I kept our eyes to the front and encouraged Jack. The transporter crept alongside, fell back, crept up again and then fell away belching steam. We were all very pleased, even George.

Helmond, a maze of narrow streets and flimsy bridges over the canals, was choked with traffic. We hit a bridge in the centre of the town but escaped before the MPs could descend on us.

George had an irritating habit of nattering over the I/c whenever vehicles were passing, even upon a broad straight road where there was plenty of room and no reason for Jack to swerve. By contrast, over a dodgy bridge or through narrow streets he would sit tight and say nothing. We had a lot of this behaviour after leaving Gemert and Jack, getting fed up with descriptions of whatever officer happened to be passing us in a Jeep, took off his headset to give his ears a rest. In consequence, when George and I both shouted to him to stop he took no notice and a cartload of furniture being pushed by a Boy Scout littered the pavement. He stopped then.

So far as we could see, the boy was OK. George got down, went back to him and asked if he was all right. The boy did not understand and this appeared to exasperate George who started to shout his query and got very red in the face, while the boy shouted back at him and kept pointing at his furniture. We were all highly amused but it cost George a few guilders. When he returned to the tank Jack asked him if the boy was all right and got no reply.

We passed through Geldrop. The church with its green dome and twin spires was a landmark for miles around. Then across a maze of tank tracks for miles and miles until a yellow and black German notice board proclaimed:

"NAAR NISTELRODE 1 KM."

The village was plastered with

"DIVERSION"

and

"NO ENTRY"

signs in an attempt to simplify the winding streets. There was a burnt-out Cromwell on a corner and our sign leaned against the rear.

The squadron was harboured in an avenue of birch trees, a sort of lane leading from the village to the fields without being elevated to the dignity of a road. There were some farm buildings on our left and the scout cars were harboured in the yard. The yellowing leaves drifted down and spread over the tanks, or danced violently in the air every time an engine started. The sun was shining brightly but winter was on the way.

Our tank halted behind the others as there was not room to pass and join our Troop. No one took much notice of our arrival and Dusty and I cooked dinner. Afterwards, the Fitters came along to refit our Flame Gun as Dusty was not happy with it. Before they had half finished there was a sudden order to move. The other tanks were reasonably ready but we were caught completely on the hop. However, we piled all our kit in at the pannier doors somehow and then it was decided that we should continue the work on the Flame Gun and when it was finished the Fitters would lead us to the new harbour.

Half-track and tank were drawn up back to back so that when the job was done, and we had had tea and a smoke, we left by one end of the avenue and the Fitters by the other, intending to meet on the road. Our way was the longest and when we did get on the road the Fitters were nowhere in sight. But George said he knew the way and we plunged into the tank tracks leading away from the village. We came to a fork and there was a long argument which ended by our taking the right fork.

We drove deeper into the country. The sun had gone down and the sky was dark save for yellow and orange streaks low in the west. The soft brown mud of the track merged into the heather and the gorse bushes and it was difficult to see our way. A cold wind swept across the open plain. From a scrap of meadow a milkmaid, her face dim, struggled home with her pails and we waved to her and felt nearer to civilisation. Everything was very peaceful and even the noise of engine and tracks was muffled. We had seen marks of trailer tyres in the mud but when we came to a crossroad they were lost. George and I walked a little way along each track but found no sign so we turned left and then right and stopped among some woods. The engine died and stillness closed in on us. George then admitted he had no idea where we were.

German throat cutting patrols were supposed to be very active in Holland. I began to think about them. George, with Shag this time, went off to look for marks of trailer wheels and the rest of us sat down in the tank, closed the hatches, and listened hard. I started on a bar of chocolate and the others cursed me for making a noise when I unwrapped it. We speculated as to the likelihood of George and Shag finding their way back to us in the dark but they returned after half an hour with nothing to report. This was not surprising as it was now pitch dark and they were afraid to show a light. We woke up Jack and moved on.

Presently we met a Jeep without lights, making heavy weather in the mud. The three occupants were also lost and, to cheer us up, reported seeing what they thought was a German patrol creeping through the woods ahead of us. From then on we watched every bush, loaded the Besa and had the safety catch to 'FIRE'.

At last we came to a bridge over a canal and beyond the bridge a cottage with chinks of light showing through the shutters. We rattled over the bridge at top speed and it was as well that we did for as we jolted by I got a closer look at the weight classification sign. What we had taken for a seventy-ton bridge was in fact scheduled to take seven.

The cottage was occupied by an RA Signal Troop and they had a spare hayloft in a barn built on to the dwelling. George wanted to put a guard on the tank but was overruled. He got his own back by asking me to pick up the squadron at six o'clock in the morning, when they would probably be netting. I had been sensible enough to get a weeks supply of code signs before the squadron left us at Nistelrode and he knew it, so there was no excuse. The men in the Artillery telephone exchange promised to call me on time.

They did and I shivered my way out to the tank. The sheets were wet and stiff and dew dripped in at the hatches and my teeth chattered as I switched on and waited for the set to warm up. Presently I heard Jack searching for tins to make a petrol fire. He could not just dig a hole and pour in petrol as the soil here was almost pure sand and the spirit just seeped away.

While drinking my tea and feeling much better I heard the squadron very faintly. I answered at the end and called up again straight away, giving my position and asking for theirs. But something was wrong with my set again, as it kept fading out, and I got half a message and asked for a repeat and they got half my query and I missed their request to say again. In the end, somehow, I got our position across and was told they would send something to lead us in.

This done, I had another go at the set. The artillery sergeant was very helpful and gave me replacements for all my valves and it was something to do while we were waiting. Just after dinner Paddy came along in his Jeep and stopped for a cup of tea. He was looking for his echelon which was on the loose no one knew where but at least he had news and advice to give. The squadron was moving up to attack two villages and he thought we ought to make in the direction of s'Hertogenbosch. As there was no sign of anything coming specifically to pick us up and we were fed up with hanging about we decided to do this and soon entered a village which I was unable to identify, parked beside a barn occupied by a platoon of the Queen's Regiment, and planned to spend the night there. George seemed to know what he was doing, so we did not question his decision.

The Typhoons were bombarding a nearby village with rockets. It was an impressive sight although a bit trying on the nerves when they passed low overhead and we did not know whether they had got rid of their rockets or not.

At teatime the Fitters visited us, were unrepentant for having deserted us at Nistelrode, and gave us a position where the squadron would probably harbour after the action. We spent the evening playing pontoon in the front room of the house next the barn. As the infantry were doing a guard George was saved the labour of trying to get his crew to mount one.

The next morning we moved through the village. Ever since Calais we had been running on an offside track with a hole in it big enough for me to put my fist through. It had seemed strong enough but, taking a corner sharply, the strained metal parted and the bogies ran off the track.

The first task, obviously, was to brew up. Over a mug of compo tea that was hot and wet and had no other recommendation we discussed the hopelessness of our situation and where we should spend the night. For once we were in agreement with George in wanting to get back to the squadron as soon as possible, for we had not been with them long enough to draw our rations and were running short of tea in particular.

About that time I read an account in a paper of the hardship we were bearing so gallantly and the fact that we had to endure a tea-sugar-milk mixture was a feature that called for emphasis. However, made properly and with a good bit of looted sugar added, it was possible to get a result that was almost like real tea. There were considerable differences of opinion as to the proper way to make it; some crews stewed the mixture at the boil for some minutes; we always whipped it up in a mug, shot it into the dixie as soon as the water boiled, and then considered it ready. It did not make a lot of difference.

I was not very fond of tea. Or at least I was not prepared to put away such large quantities as my companions considered necessary. My abstinence assisted the ration to last its three days. Later, I joined the Baker crew and there it was not enough for tea meant everything to the commander, Steve O'Neill, and we had to hide the ration in order to make it last unless there happened to be a packet of 'fresh' tea from England.

So we sat on a convenient tree trunk, drank our tea, and looked at the tank. The road was made of bricks and all save the last two bogies had dug deeply into the surface. While we were studying the wreck a Dutch girl came along and Shag produced Peggy as a means of attracting her attention. This always worked and we learned that her name was Mimi, or near enough that, and that she was eighteen years old. Jack had a glitter in his eyes which George saw and immediately began to emphasise the need to get to work. We invited Mimi to come to tea and bring her sister. She came and, of course, the sister was aged about eight.

At length George persuaded us to start work and I got all the tools together - the track punch and puller, crowbar, sledge and service pins. The idea was to dig away the road so that we could lower the track below the level of the bogies and then slew the tank over into position, when we would be able to make the track with a new plate and the service pins. It was a long and backbreaking task and the sun blazed down and we were all set in lazy ways induced by the last few weeks. During one of the frequent breaks Shag and I explored the village with Peggy - she attracted more girls than we did - but Mimi seemed to be the only girl for most of the village was in ruins and such houses that remained were bursting with troops. The main road was busy, too; trucks, Carriers, antitank guns all speeding towards the front line not so far away.

During the evening we tried to get dug in at various houses but the villagers were reserved and if they did not resent our casual invasions at least they did nothing to encourage us to stay. We were beginning to understand that the Dutch were not going to take us at face value, as had the Belgians, and that friendships would not be the product of a few hours acquaintance.

In this particular case there was not much lost by our inability to cadge a bed as it was long after midnight by the time we had mended the track. Even then we had to use the steering brakes to hold the track fast while we joined it. This emergency procedure was used because of the late hour and one member of the crew had to stand on the decking for the duration of the work with a Methyl Bromide bottle at the ready in case the brake linings caught fire. When the job was complete we were not particular where we slept.

We had whipped two immense tarpaulins from the workshops at Beeringen - a poor return for their hospitality but I do not suppose they were missed. Thus we were able to erect a very roomy bivvy and could use the engine sheet as a floor, so that what remained of the night was peaceful, the rumble of guns serving effectively as a lullaby.

We expected the Fitters Half-track to be searching for us in the morning and were up early to make a hasty breakfast but it did not appear. Near our tank was a large house and a church and we started at the church and collected a sack of ripe pears from a tree in the graveyard. Thence to the house. The garden was a tangle of apple trees, tomatoes, potatoes and onions and we filled another sack without any difficulty. Dusty and I were interested in the tracks of some Cromwells which had been in action in the next field but we soon got back to business and entered the house. Maps and pamphlets in a well-stocked library proved - or seemed to prove - that the owner was pro-Nazi. Having lost our scruples due to this research we removed plates, cutlery, saucepans, frying pans and a number of other items that promised to be of use. As we left we saw some of the locals in the garden with sacks and some of them were entering the house as we passed by in the wake of the Half-track.

We were just in time to catch the squadron before it moved. From the sandy clearing among the pine woods the first tank was already lurching on to the track as we drew up behind the others. Sherry's tank, I noticed, was short two bogies. Major Duffy came hurrying across to meet us and George jumped down and saluted. The Major grasped his hand and pumped it enthusiastically and although I could not hear what he said above the mutter of our engine, no doubt it was something about the prodigal son. Our holiday was at an end.

CHAPTER 9

S'HERTOGENBOSCH

The Normandy smell - the sickening odour of burnt and decaying flesh, the bitter stench from the blackened shells of buildings. Dead cattle littered the fields. A grey-clad figure lolled out of a foxhole clasping the twisted wreck of a machine gun. A Sherman at the roadside, hatches gaping, gun cocked enquiringly, a neat hole pierced in the front of the turret. German rifles, Spandaus, tin hats, gas masks and other equipment, littering the verges and piled in the ditches. A rough wooden cross, or the broken stump of a rifle, with a tin hat and the name printed in indelible pencil, marked the graves. All this bordered the country lanes leading towards s'Hertogenbosch, supposed to be the pivot of the German defences and the capture of which would open the road to Tilburg and Antwerp. That much we had been told, although our exact task was not yet decided and we had not been briefed.

We took a right angle bend very sharply and hit a 15-hundredweight truck which had been concealed by a high hedge. George got down to apologise and Jack did his nut; firstly, because George had failed to see the truck, secondly, having hit it, he had been so foolish as to stop. Of course, it was difficult for Jack, the tank having been designed to drive on the left-hand side of the road. I scribbled the number of the truck on the top of the turret in case we were involved in claims and counter-claims and kept quiet for I, too, had failed to see the truck. Privately, I thought the tank looked much neater with the right wing gone as well as the left and Jack, who did not care for neatness, had opposed an attempt on my part to remove it some time before. Jack was more concerned with its value in keeping dust and grit out of his eyes, having declared the celluloid shield that fitted into his vision block to be a menace and flung it away a long time ago.

At length we got out along an open stretch of road, flat land on either side, and ahead of us the darkening sky was dotted with black puffs of smoke. Someone came up on the air saying we were under observation and I retailed this information for the comfort of the crew. Shag, who had been sitting on the back bin, wriggled his legs into my hatch and he was just in time. There was a crash, a great mass of smoking and splintering yellow flame and we bumped our heads getting inside the turret. My hatches clanged to.

The shells continued to come over at irregular intervals. George was fooling with his mike, again complaining that it was u/s,[84] and with my single periscope I had a very hard task to guide the tank through a mass of trucks, motor cycles and German prisoners caught in a village street. More by luck than judgement we did not hit anything.

The run was not a long one and, still closed down, we drew into a sunken field just off the road, bordered by a high hedge on our side and, towards the Germans, a dyke and then a lot of open country. A few hundred yards up the road one of our tanks was rusting, knocked out in the attack two days previously with the loss of two lives.

The shelling stopped as it grew dark but the officers, particularly Captain Shearman, kept running about cautioning us not to light fires or smoke as the whole area was under observation. Tubby Faulkner, one of the squadron clerks, and Paddy, had come up in a scout car to distribute the NAAFI ration and everyone was in a good humour. Paddy put up with a lot of cracks about Ireland that would have got the jokers into trouble had we not been expecting an action. And Ted Currie of 11 Troop had killed a pig the previous day which the Fitters had cut up and were distributing. Our share came to several large steaks and Jack having promised to get up early in the morning and cook them in the only right way it seemed a good time to go to bed.

I was dozing. There were a great many bangs but I knew there was a battery of 25-pounders behind us and did not worry. The bivvy

[84] U/S. Unserviceable.

shook furiously and I only swore and turned over. Then Jack shoved his head under the flap and shouted that we were being mortared.

He vanished. There was a lot of shouting and more bangs. I dived for the rear of the tank and squirmed underneath. My hand landed in a sticky mess, I recoiled, banged my head, and fine dirt from the belly of the tank poured inside my shirt. Someone panted up beside me and by the light of the flashes I recognised Shag. The crash of mortar bombs rose to one continuous roar, petered out and then there was complete silence all of a sudden and I could hear my heart thumping.

We lay still for some minutes more and then people began to stir. There was the clang of a hatch being thrust open. Jack came ducking along the side of the tank and knelt silhouetted against the sky. Having ascertained that we were OK, he said he was going to sleep in the tank. We said we were staying put, despite the dung and the dust. So we got our blankets under the tank and wriggled into them somehow. Every time we touched the tank's belly we got a shower of dirt, but at last we got settled and next thing I knew someone was calling me for guard.

The moon was brilliant and imposed silence. Shag and I walked to the head of the column and back, taking ten minutes by Shag's alarm clock which he had picked up in Boulogne and which was proving useful on such occasions as neither of us had yet managed to acquire a wristwatch. In the other direction we turned the corner of the hedge to where the other half squadron was parked. Two dark figures in greatcoats who were leaning on the front of a tank seemed uncertain whether or not to challenge us and, in fact, did not.

There was time for a short chat and then we strolled back to our tank. It was all so quiet that Shag suggested that we move our beds back to the bivvy and this task passed some time. Then we went up the line again, the alarm went off and we hastened to call Jack and Dusty. The rest of the night was uneventful.

In the morning, cheered by the sunshine, we moved out to the fine broad Rijksweg that runs from Nijmegen to s'Hertogenbosch and halted in the village of Heesch. There was some talk about the village girls being out in force but I stayed sulkily in the turret correcting my net. They had blamed me for the loss of Peggy, who had wandered away during the night and we did not know that the echelon had picked her up until we met them in s'Hertogenbosch. But my occasional sulks never lasted long and when we left Heesch I was on the turret again and laughing at Shag who said he had lost his heart to some girl he had talked to for five minutes.

Entering the outskirts of the town, the suburban houses were modern but every roof had a hole, the windows were shattered and doors sagged open. The trees were splintered, tangled telephone wires sprawled on the pavements, a German truck stood with its nose through a fence. Beyond was a field kitchen and a dead horse that some civilians were carving. Then a field gun and a German soldier, his face a sickly grey, lying on his back on the grass dividing the twin carriageways. All down the street was littered the wreckage of an aeroplane; the engine had ploughed into the tarmac, bits of wing and fuselage were scattered for half a mile, and the tail assembly with the black and white stripes on the rear fuselage, comparatively undamaged, pointed to the sky from a front garden. I pronounced it to be a Typhoon and rocket rails on a piece of wing confirmed this.

A harbour had been selected in this suburban area, an oval grass patch with the road running round it and streets entering it at right angles. At one end a school had been turned into a dressing station and ambulance Jeeps were constantly coming and going. The less seriously wounded made their way on foot, their bandages bloodstained and muddy. Some troops of the Welsh Regiment who were digging foxholes in the gardens explained that the area was still under mortar fire. Across the main road Shermans of the East Riding Yeomanry were gathered in a square like ours and we noticed that the crews were sticking pretty closely to their tanks. There were lots of troops moving along the road and confusion was caused by an AVRE carrying its Bailey Bridge. There were lamps strung between pylons across the street and the AVRE demolished each as it came up and scattered the troops marching down the verges. We heard the noise and all ran down to watch it pass - of course the crew were enjoying every minute of it.

We stocked up with saucepans from the nearest houses - we were always losing or breaking our kitchen utensils and it was a good thing they were easy to replace - and pulled up the paving stones and lit fires in the holes to brew tea. Every so often a mortar came over and we had to drop everything and get under cover. There was something particularly unnerving about mortars - on reaching safety I invariably found myself sweating, even if I had run only a couple of yards - and sitting about with nothing to do but wait for them did not help matters.

We stayed in the square all day but pulled out at night to a field a few miles out of the town. As we dipped through the gateway I wondered how we should ever be able to sleep, for the tank sank heavily into what seemed particularly soggy mud, but as the tracks flung dust into my eyes I realised it was extremely fine sand. We churned in among the bushes on the far side of the field and then had to keep flashing our Hellesen lamps to prevent collisions. I tried to be clever and rig a light from the wireless but by the time I had found a lead long enough the need had passed.

The sand got everywhere. We had sand in our blankets for days, in the bully beef we had for supper, in the tea, in our boots, caked in our socks. But it made a soft mattress and Shag and I were reluctant to get up for guard. I mislaid my beret and although Jack and Dusty were fuming outside I could not go on guard without that - I hated losing things at any time and it was doubly important on waking from a heavy sleep.

We were on the last 'stagger'[85] but one. Dew coated the patches of rough grass and glittered in the cold moonlight. Gunfire rumbled in the distance. It was just cold enough to be refreshing, so that the time went quickly watching the traffic on the road. Although it could not be called a good guard, for that would be a contradiction in terms, it was better than most.

13 Troop was the first to move in the morning and, since we considered ourselves the crack Troop, we argued from this that we

[85] 'stagger'. A guard period. I have no idea why it should have been so called. 'On stag' to be on guard.

were going into action. At least, as was generally admitted, we had the best officer, and the other Troop that had landed on D-Day, 15, had been broken up when it was decided to have four tanks in a Troop so that the distinction gave us some sort of claim to seniority.

At the first halt we found several 88 mm. shells lying in the ditch. They were a tremendous length but so light that I should have thought that they did not contain a full charge had they not been so well balanced. As the loader, I was very interested in them, of course. The job could not have been an easy one inside the turret of a Tiger but then the way the German tanks worked on the continent, lying up until they could fire at point blank range, meant that the first shot was usually all that was necessary.

We entered the town, passed our harbour of the previous day, crossed two canal bridges, the second of which was a very patched up job, and reached our forward harbour. This was called 'The Triangle' from the shape of what had once been a green park. Now the turf was rutted by tanks and splotched by mortar bursts. In one corner a 17-pounder and crew were dug in under an elm tree. Empty compo boxes, tins, ammo cases, paper and cardboard littered what must once have been a pleasant interlude to the narrow streets entering on two sides. On the third the remains of the town moat stagnated beneath huge grey stone bastions, overgrown with duckweed and fringed with reeds. Beyond the moat the flat, dyked country, indistinct under a faint blue haze, extended in unbroken contour save for a church spire on the horizon.

We stood about under the elms and waited for something to happen. Stirred by the exhausts the brown leaves drifted lazily about the tanks. The artillerymen told us that a civilian had been killed the previous day by a mortar and that the place was still liable to that form of attack.

Chung waved for me to take over the wireless watch just as the order came to pressure up. As I climbed to the turret the trailer began to groan and wheeze and give every indication of imminent explosion, which was usual. Each trailer had its own particular combination of weird sounds and on the flame course at Creully we had been cautioned against taking any notice of them.

On this occasion, however, Dusty darted from the bottles at the rear and screwed frantically on something inside the front hatch but in spite of his efforts it continued to hiss loudly and he stood back and looked hopeless. Jack came and flung a spanner in at the pannier door. The trailer was 'diss'.

The Able tank was in like difficulty and all the commanders were having a little conference. George came back with orders to stay put while the others flamed a canal bank not far distant.

Of course we were disappointed but there was a compensation and as the other tanks moved out, playing havoc with the young trees and the telephone wires hooked to them, we buried a couple of Besa boxes in a rut, filled them with petrol, and stood waiting for dinner to cook.

Then there was an ear-splitting whistle. Someone shouted 'Get down!' and Dusty kicked me in the face as I followed him under the trailer. Then we made a run for the tank. I moved pretty quickly, for splinters were ripping through the branches overhead, but Dusty's speed was phenomenal. His hatches banged shut as I grabbed the gun muzzle to haul myself up on to the tank. For some reason this struck me as supremely funny but there was no time to stand and laugh at him.

We had been talking to three RAF officers who had come up in a Jeep to view the front line. As they were Typhoon pilots they had not been very impressed, understandably, by all the dangers attending the ground forces, until that moment. So we were very pleased to have them all jammed together on the toolbox in the front compartment. They also seemed highly delighted - I suppose they felt they were beginning to get their money's worth. Two Dutch civilians had been hanging about, watching us cook dinner, and we had them in the turret.

Shag had his alarm clock hanging by a hook near his periscope. The mortars came over regularly and we timed them. After a bit we were able to predict the arrival of the next bomb and thus to impress the RAF who, in the front, could not see the clock. Our experience, we said, enabled us to 'feel' them coming.

While this afforded some innocent amusement for a time, we became worried about our dinner which was boiling high behind the trailer. After much persuasion Dusty agreed to rescue it. He was the best able to go as the mortars were falling mostly on our right and he could slip through his pannier door straight to the ground in the shelter of the tank. He burnt his fingers and I scalded myself bashing a hole in a tin of M & V.[86] The meal was an uncomfortable one and by the time it was finished the mortars had stopped. The RAF climbed into their Jeep and made off. The Dutch were just as quick and we found a few minutes later that they had taken twenty of Shag's Woodbines with them. This seemed a poor return for our hospitality but the temptation must have been great.

Although everything was now quiet the sudden onslaught of the mortars had made us chary of emerging from the tank and it was a relief to be ordered back to the suburban harbour where the Fitters could repair the trailer and we could await the return of the rest of the Troop in comparative safety.

Sherry's tank - or rather, Steve's commanded by Sherry - was the first to return. Jinx Brown, the gunner, had an annoying habit of 'creeping' on the power traverse in order to see more through his sight. This trick would infuriate the commander but it saved the lives of the turret crew on this occasion. The tank had been crossing the end of a road and an 88 mm. shot, fired from an SP at fifty yards range, had ploughed right up the side of the turret wall. Had the turret been in the correct position it would gone smack in the front and in like a knife through butter. As it was the driver put his foot down, the operator pumped out smoke, and they escaped before the Jerry could get a second one in. We heard later that the infantry had

[86] M & V. Meat and Vegetable mixture - a sort of stew which was generally well-regarded.

revenged us by knocking out the SP by indirect fire with a PIAT[87] and very pleased we were to hear it.

We broke into a house that night. Having neatly removed a pane of glass from the centre of a front door and operated the Yale lock, I found Sherry had just entered by the back window and claimed the house for his crew. But there were plenty of houses and although the one next door had already been looted we finished it off.

Everyone was sorry about this when the owner came back the next day and he was such a nice old chap that we put back as much as we could without his seeing us. Some things, however, we had to keep. I had one anxious moment when showing him over the tank, one of his scarves being draped over the Seventy-five. I just had time to stuff it under the wireless before he was beaming at me over his spectacles. I felt pretty small just then.

We were so contrite that we fed him, his son and his son-in-law, for the duration of our stay. This repaid them in some measure and got rid of some of the huge stock of concentrated soup which we had accumulated. They cooked us pancakes, we providing the flour and they the apples - the son-in-law, in particular, was an excellent cook. Dusty and I took it upon ourselves to provide coal for the community from a house just around the corner. We had one awkward moment on the third trip when a woman entered by the front door and gave us only just time to get out of the window, but we had a good stock by then.

On guard that night, Shag and I walked the streets until the tiles rattling down from the roofs and the occasional whine of a shell or mortar drove us into a billet where a roaring and red-hot stove provided tea and toast. In this atmosphere the hour passed quickly and the tanks looked after themselves.

The next day we moved up again, determined to have a good go. Although our trailer was still u/s, Sherry said we could come in as a gun tank and the only one disappointed was Dusty since there had

87 PIAT. Projector, Infantry, Anti-Tank. The British equivalent of the bazooka, firing a 'hollow charge' which increased the penetrating power of the missile.

been no time to dismount the Flame Gun and replace it with the spare Besa.

As usual, we fooled about all morning and afternoon, so that it was already dusk when we passed through the town, crossed the Afwaterings Kanaal and approached the railway line behind which were our objectives. Of these there were three, but the last one was not essential so Sherry said he was going to leave it alone if we met any difficulty.

Crossing the railway line was the worst part. We jolted and lurched over the embankment, the tracks clanging and clawing at the rails. All the kit in the turret fell about our ears. I had a large amount of loot stowed in my corner by the wireless set and it was soon rolling on the floor with spare smoke bombs, tin mugs and mess tins. George had his head peeping out of the cupola and he said that the Seventy-five cleaning rods were working loose. Presently we heard them being churned to matchwood in the tracks.

Ahead of us an M10[88] stood beside a house, some infantry sheltering behind it. The Shermans in front of us were belting away at a factory out in the flat and it was burning furiously; the roof had already fallen in and the flames streamed up without any impediment. I envied the Sherman loaders - the American Seventy-five was easier to handle than ours as the breech opened at the side whereas on ours the round went in at the top.

We all swung right on to the road and Shag traversed the turret to the left. The Shermans drew level with the first of a row of houses and the leader put a round into it at point-blank range. Through the drifting smoke we saw four German soldiers stumble out of the front door, their hands grasping their collars. We surged up past them and loosed off.

The scout car was asking for 'situation', for we were out of touch with the CO and the scout car was his intermediary, but no one bothered to answer. It was load and fire as fast as we could go. Then to the Besa, the belt whipping out of the box. Another box in the pan

---

88 M10. American Tank Destroyer. A cross between an SP and a tank.

and away again. I was supposed to watch each round. What a hope; I could only ease the belt into the breech and trust to luck.

"See that window - the big one?" yipped George.
"Yep."
"Put an HE through it, then!"
"Stand back, then!" Shag's invariable warning.

The gun slammed back, ran out, a clang and a clunk and another round was in the breech.

"See that chimney?'
"Yep."
"Knock it down, then!"
"Stand back!"

The turret was full of fumes. The fan whined. Dusty kept coughing. My eyes were streaming.

"I don't think there are any Jerries here," I said.
"Doesn't matter," laughed Shag. "Look at those tracers sticking in the wall. Ain't they pretty?"
"Jolly nice. See if you can do it."
"Are those Dutch civvies, George?"
"I think so. Better leave 'em alone, then. Look at 'em running."
"They're a silly lot of bastards to be here at all!"
"That was the second objective," said George.
"Give it some Besa, Shag."
"Fire this HE first."
"Put it through that window, then!"
"Stand back!"

We saw no more Germans and soon it was too dark to proceed further. Sherry gave the order to retire and we moved back to fill up with petrol and ammo before supper, moderately well pleased with ourselves.

* * *

Two more days were spent in s'Hertogenbosch but the fighting was over. We had a church service and a booze-up. There was a bath expedition. And we were busy selling cigarettes. These had now reached a standard price, a guilder for ten, which was considered reasonable as it was only 300% profit. Haricot Oxtail and concentrated soup sold well, too, for it seemed as if the Dutch had had nothing to spend their money on for the last five years.

For the bath we had to go to Oss, a journey of about fifteen kilometres. The morning was bitterly cold. Harry Garrity of 12 Troop was wearing a very flamboyant scarf and was much chaffed, but our looks became envious when we were in the back of the open truck and hurtling along the main road. Our features were blue by the time our destination was reached.

A dirty marquee stood under a canal embankment and there was also a smaller tent, a boiler and a pump. The marquee was divided into two; the smaller part was a dressing room, the larger with pipes hanging down from the roof. The duckboards were slimy, the water tepid, and the wind swept in at the far end and right through. Most of us decided to stay dirty.

When we returned there was a church service, presumably of thanksgiving, for those that wished to go, and in the evening a 'Do' at the top of the erstwhile dressing station. I was not fond of beer and would not have gone at all but that the NAAFI ration was being distributed at the same time. But although I came away early there was already a lot of beer on the floor and the 'Do' was as successful as such functions usually are.

The next day we moved out along the Nijmegen Rijksweg to the village of Heesch. Again it was bitterly cold and in spite of all our scarves (for everyone had followed Harry Garrity's example) it was with faces raw from the sting of grit and biting wind that we left our tanks parked under the trees at the side of the road. George said something about there being a Troop billet but we were not very interested in that and I entered the nearest house, that of a baker.

I was making every effort to learn Dutch but the old woman to whom I spoke let fly such a torrent that I had to let it go by and start again from the beginning. After a quarter of an hour of repetitions I was placed in possession of the front room, on the understanding that the family would use it in the evenings but we could sleep there afterwards. I accepted just in time to beat another tank crew who had hastened there on hearing that there were girls in the house.

It was privately agreed that there would be no room for George, who always seemed to cast a damp on a family party, and he accepted the situation readily, arranging to sleep in the billet of another sergeant. So everyone was satisfied.

The girls were very nice. Jack confined his attentions to Maria, the eldest, and Dusty and Shag gave me a free run with the youngest, Wilhelmina, or 'Zussie' as she was called. So we had an enjoyable stay.

The second day was All Saints Day and Zussie had a holiday and wanted me to go to church with her. 13 Troop was at two hours notice to move but Jack promised to fetch me if this came to anything. So I went and it was well worth it. Even I could understand the warning of hellfire waiting for any Dutch girl so misguided as to step beyond the pale with a British soldier and as we were at the back and the church was crowded - in fact, there was standing room only - I could be entertained without being too much in the limelight.

The collection, however, was embarrassing. I had paid Jack the money I owed him and all I had left was a two and a half guilder note, and I was not going to give that. My pocket contained a lot of Belgian coins, some buttons, a toffee and two .38 rounds. When my turn came I thought I would get away with it by putting my hand into the bag empty and bringing it out as if I had given something. But the sidesman pushed the bag back at me and jiggled it up and down on the end of its pole and I blushed, felt acutely uncomfortable, and gave him an assorted handful from my pocket. I hope the priest was pleased with it - the toffee and both the rounds were included.

Zussie and I went to an ENSA show in the afternoon. I saw later that this particular team had been the first to give a performance to British troops in Germany, for the leading lady was stout enough to recognise in the photograph. It started off well enough with a couple of Dutchmen playing accordions, but the rest of the entertainment was very poor. The only bright spot was a heated exchange between the comedian and a member of the audience who was courageous enough to voice the discontent we all felt. The comedian, when he lost his temper, was not very funny at all.

In the evenings the family seemed keen to have singsongs. Every soldier knew 'Obadiah', they taught us 'Sarie Marais' and were pleased to find that we already knew 'Dorpsmusiek'. I liked the mournful Dutch songs best and there were plenty of them. On the second night we considered the question of a souvenir. I suggested an AP shot as we had a spare. Dusty suggested a shot of flame in the back garden. In the end we left Peggy. The family promised to look after her well and we felt, anyway, that it would be cruel to keep her on the tank through the winter. But when I visited Heesch later I was told that she had been stolen by some Canadians. I was not very satisfied with that story and have often wondered if that family really wanted to receive a dog as a present.

Shag and I were on guard the last night. We walked in the middle of the road, from the wreck of a 17-pounder Sherman Firefly[89] at one end of the village, past the house of the quisling burgermeister who had decamped with the Germans, to the burnt out Sherman on the Oss cross-roads where there were some Dutch Resistance men on guard also, although they could not make us understand why. The orderly officer made his rounds, in pyjamas with a greatcoat thrown over them, and we challenged him correctly so everyone was satisfied. Then Shag's alarm went, we hastened to call our relief, and so to bed.

---

[89] 17-pounder Sherman Firefly. A standard Sherman modified by the British with an enlarged turret to take the 17-pounder gun. Designed to stiffen the Sherman regiments and successful in this.

CHAPTER 10

MEIJEL

We left Heesch on a bright November morning, the sunshine offsetting a bitter wind. Through Uden and Nistelrode the AVREs were on the road as well and the narrow streets were jammed with tanks. One rumour had it that the Germans had broken through south of Helmond, while another said that it was we who had broken through. Through Veghel and all along the road to Helmond each village was filled with trucks and tanks of every description, nose to tail under the trees.

Helmond was full of traffic as always but we got through without trouble and continued eastwards. Ours was the last tank in the column and I had just finished waving our echelon by when we came to a jolting halt. I turned to see the Able tank in the ditch, almost on its side with one track off.

The crew were scrambling down and we learned that Reggie Webb had been driving and in his anxiety to give a Canadian convoy plenty of room he had failed to notice the ditch on the other side.

The convoy was now pulling on to a very narrow verge for a break. The tank was in the ditch and looked like staying there for some time. The combination of ditched tank and parked trucks blocked the road. There was no time to come to an amicable arrangement with the Canadians, for a staff car arrived with a lieutenant-colonel in a hurry and a temper. We were near enough to hear the consequent altercation. The colonel ordered the convoy to move. The lieutenant in charge of the convoy refused. He said he had orders to dine at half twelve and he was damn well going to dine at half twelve. The colonel asked the name of the unit and the lieutenant said it was the Canadian Army and he'd be damned if he'd take orders from any bloody Britisher given in that tone.

We thought this was a jolly good show. The colonel stormed up and down the line but the Canadians just took no notice of him. We kept very busy in case he should think to direct his anger at the cause of the trouble. George stood in front of our tank and saluted every time he came by.

In the meantime the driver of the staff car had got friendly with the Canadians opposite the disabled tank. They moved a lorry forward two feet. The addition to the gap was sufficient, the staff car squeezed through and drove down to where the colonel was raging at the lieutenant. We saw him no more and five minutes later the convoy moved on.

There was nothing we could do to help the ditched tank so now we could get past we did so and promised to report its predicament when we caught up with the squadron. This we did at Vlierden, where the tanks were harboured in a turnip field behind some houses. As we dipped into the field the tracks sank deep in the soft black soil - the first indication of what winter would mean for our heavy vehicles and for us.

As in every Dutch village there were swarms of children. We were parked at the bottom of a garden and those attached to the house clamoured round the tank to invite us to sleep indoors. We were only too pleased to accept and I carried in the blankets and did other odd jobs while the others replenished the petrol tanks. 11 Troop had got another pig - they seemed lucky with pigs - and our host cut it up for all of us that evening. So we all had pork for supper, in company with most of the village, and sat down to the accompaniment of aeroplane engines passing leisurely overhead.

"Moef? Moef?" The family pointed upwards. "Moef vliegers?"
"Nay, niet moef vliegers," I answered. "Engelse vliegers."
"Ah! Engelse vliegers! Goed! Goed!"

The children, who had begun to get alarmed, calmed down at this. I congratulated myself and there was a tremendous crash nearby. The family made a dive for the cellar, while we ran for the back door. I stopped to put out the lamp and when I got there only Jack was visible, leaning against the door post. He said that Shag was under the Half-track and Dusty, we found, was under the kitchen sink.

The aeroplanes seemed to be going round in circles. There was a whistle and for a moment we did not catch on and stood looking at each other. Two flowers of fire blossomed in the field across the road. It was our turn to jump down the cellar steps. More bangs followed us. The family were clustered together, praying for all they were worth. I could not make out if it was Dutch or Latin but 'Maria' figured frequently in a continuous drone in which the children's shrill voices mingled with the deeper tones of the parents to produce an effect which was extremely depressing. Jack said he had had enough of it and went back upstairs.

I fetched some blankets for the children and then joined him. Scared or not, there did not seem much use praying about it and in any case we had our dignity as British soldiers to uphold. However, by the time I was upstairs again the explosions had ceased and the sound of the aeroplanes was dying away in the distance. Over towards Germany a brilliant yellow glow filled the sky where it seemed our bombers had been active. In fact, I suspected that some had got off course and that I had been right in speaking of 'Engelse vliegers'.

Our people were emerging from tanks and other places of relative safety. Everyone talked at once. Someone had taken a header into a patch of stinging nettles and spoke accordingly. Another man - a member of a tank crew - related how he had found the echelon all in one hole with their tin hats on, which was sensible enough but seemed very funny to us. For a bit I watched the fire spreading and gradually lighting up the whole sky but apart from that the entertainment seemed to be over. I soon returned to the house to help the others coax the family out of the cellar and back to their supper.

We were all in bed in the front room when Sherry came in with George to brief us for the forthcoming attack on a wood near the village of Meijel. Each Troop was to flame a certain sector of the northern side of the wood. The Germans who fled before our onslaught would be dispatched by a battalion of the Guards Tank Brigade which, executing a dashing left hook round our flank, would collect any honour and glory that happened to be lying about. It was all rather vague - the days of sand tables and lots of maps seemed to be over, although there were supposed to be alternative plans in case the opposition differed from that shown by the intelligence reports. Details of this were sketchy. The Germans were supposed to have a lot of heavy artillery beyond a canal to the east of the wood and an Eighty-eight was situated in a cluster of buildings, marked 'hof' on the map, to the west. It looked like being a case of suck it and see.

* * *

By first light we had stowed everything, I had netted the set, and we had extricated the tank, not without difficulty, from the turnip field. The infantry had been on the move for some time and the narrow road was lined with sullen, plodding foot-sloggers, all with their leather jerkins turned inside out, Bren or mortar ammunition hanging in front and a pick or shovel behind. They showed a little interest in us but it could hardly be called enthusiastic, for they were mainly concerned with keeping out of our way, especially at those points where we had to pass broken down units of the Guards Tank Battalion. It was the first time we had worked with the Guards, of whom we had heard little good, and judging by the number of their tanks fallen by the wayside we should have little opportunity of noting their prowess on the field of action.

SP guns, assault guns, all varieties of tracked and wheeled vehicles stood about in the lanes and clearings, lurched over in the ditches, half buried in bracken. We came to a Bofors battery that was being used as ground artillery and was laying down a barrage to cover our approach, the gunners capering about their weapons in their shirt sleeves despite the cold. A little farther and the line of infantry swung sharply from the track and plunged into the woods. A machine gun battery kept up a furious clatter. The tanks in front were closing down. I did the same, but George continued to sit on the flap of his cupola and I had to keep tugging at his leg to persuade him to come down.

We swung violently to the right, narrowly avoiding two Guards tanks who had tried to go left and had got into the ditch. Now we were out in open country, strung out along a narrow track leading towards Meijel. Owing to the stiff going the Guards in front were held up and we halted to wait for them to get sorted out.

Ahead of us a farmhouse was on fire. On our right bare heathland stretched away to the woods from which we had emerged. To the left little copses of stunted trees and bushes, and here and there a farmhouse or barn, dotted the pasture land away to the raised embankment of the canal.

It was not long before the German guns of which we had been warned, One-O-Fives or One-Five-Fives, got our range and from then on they plastered us. The farmhouse burst into flames once more and was soon blazing merrily. We increased the distance between the tanks and still the sparks flew. The front tanks laid down smoke which made us cough but did no good. An infantryman sheltering by a trailer was killed. One of our drivers was hurt when a periscope was flung in his face and it was decided to change him for the co-driver on the CO's tank. This was a difficult operation as it appeared the CO was not willing to open his hatches to make the exchange before the other tank did and vice-versa. The bickering that ensued provided amusement that was badly needed.

Some Guards tanks, coming up late, had trouble in passing us and managed to ditch themselves. The Flails, or 'our flogging friends' as they were called in what must have been a futile attempt at security, being wider, had even greater difficulty and preferred to hit us rather than get bogged.

Everyone was getting very browned off. The waiting was bad enough in itself but the shellfire was incessant and the news disheartening. The Guards were losing a lot of tanks, most being bogged and then brewed up at leisure by that single Eighty-eight. All day long the crews were walking, running and crawling back past our column or dodging through the field on our right to escape the shellfire.

The Second-in-Command of the Regiment came up in his scout car but had difficulty in talking to our CO as neither of them wished to put their head out. In the end the car was parked slap alongside the tank and they conversed by wireless.

The wireless was also the medium for a lot of idle chatter among the officers on the subject of tea. Someone said he had just made a brew. Then another capped it by saying he was just drinking his second. Then a third sang 'I like a nice cup of tea in the morning'. One of the operators switched to the A-Set 'accidentally' and made cracks about there being one rule for men and one for officers and this brought them to their senses.

However, it turned our own thoughts to the subject of something hot and wet and Jack unearthed the cooker and filled it. This was done on such occasions by disconnecting the lead from the petrol tanks to the Flame Gun and Jack must have been careless for when he struck a match a sheet of flame swept over the toolbox and into the turret. Jack and Dusty set up a terrific shout and Shag grabbed the Pyrene and set it off. The fire was extinguished almost immediately but the Pyrene fumes choked us and tears were streaming down our cheeks. The fans were not up to that job, we did not dare open the hatches, and we spent ten very uncomfortable minutes before the gas dispersed.

Just afterwards, and while our eyes were still smarting, we got news that German infantry had been seen crossing the canal. Shag traversed left to cover the area but could see nothing, although the news and the excitement of looking for a target cheered us up a bit. It was said later that Paddy Scallan, given the information, had looked up the map reference and found it to be two fields from where he was parked with the echelon. He bolted out of the Half-track, gave one yell, and they were all on the move within a minute, which we said was a record.

Traversing the turret lead to unpleasantness between Shag and George, for Shag complained that his view through the sight was blocked by a barn and George, for reasons known only to himself, refused to let him move. An argument ensued, ending by George threatening to hit Shag and Shag begging him to do so, just once, go on, and see what would happen. The rest of us said 'children! children!' and they calmed down but it left a nasty taste.

We could not see any Germans but there was great activity among Bren Gun Carriers and ambulances in that direction and we surmised that there must have been some fighting. Other Carriers, nearer us, were now salvaging sheets of galvanised iron from a ruined house and arranging it as protection from the shell bursts. For the German gunners were still working with a will. Our trailer suffered especially, for our personal kit had been stowed securely but we had taken far less trouble with the parking legs and handling bars. But despite the fact that we sat on that track all the day long and the shelling never let up for a moment, no tank received a direct hit.

General Mud had won his first victory. The Guards had felt his power and while we had not risked our even heavier vehicles in his clutches we now had a good idea of what to expect in the future. Nevertheless, we were all very cheerful on the way back, for it was relief enough to be able to get the hatches open. HQ Troop, of course, led the way, which was in itself a source of amusement. When we heard the Major calling the cooks to get a brew ready for the tank crews we realised that we had had an arduous and nerve-racking day and that we were important people who should rightly be served by the lower orders in the echelon. So we sang choruses over the I/c all the way back to Vlierden.

CHAPTER 11

WINTER

We were not, of course, aware of what was going on in the upper reaches of the British Army but from mid-November it seemed we were being put into cold storage. We moved first to the village of Someren, on the Bar-le-Duc canal south of Helmond. A false alarm put 13 Troop at two hours notice to move soon after we arrived but this petered out and we settled down to forget the tanks for a bit. To this end we were immediately issued with tank suits - christened 'zoot suits' - which we had first seen worn by AVRE crews on top of Mont Lambert and which it was now our turn to receive.

George was excellent at getting things. As I think I have said, he had quartermaster's blood in his veins and our whole crew was equipped with zoot suits and leather jerkins while other crews had only commanders and operators so clothed. The new garments were wonderful creations, all zips and pockets, with hoods, and very warm.

Apart from the primitive sanitary arrangements usual in rural Holland the billet was satisfactory, although a trifle crowded as the whole Troop had to cook, eat and sleep in the large loft that appears to be the usual top floor of most Dutch houses. My corner contained a pile of onions, which the owner would have been wise to have moved as I have always been partial to cheese and onions and we had plenty of the anaemic processed cheese that needed livening up.

I repaid our host with cigarettes. It was worth a cigarette to watch him accept it. He would look at the tin and I would hold it patiently. He would consider, stroking his chin and looking as if he really was not sure. Until at last:

"Um. Ja. Dank U wel."

And he would select one with care, as if they were not all the same.

He and his two old sisters were very reserved at first but thawed gradually as they realised that we were all harmless. After three days we were invited to use the warmth of the living room if we wanted to write letters. We had to remember they were very old people and every day we chafed at the top of the stairs, wanting to get at our dinner but not liking to go through the living room while they were saying grace. This invariably lasted for ten minutes so it should have engendered an appetite.

There had been vague rumours that the business regarding Captain Douglas-Home at Le Havre had come to a head and at Someren we had our introduction to our new Colonel. Although I had only known the old one by sight I found it easy enough to join the others in reviling our new CO. We held a parade for him and he gave us the usual pep talk about the 141, which did not create a lot of enthusiasm as he could not be expected to know anything about us but what was told him. Then he went on to tell us about himself. He was, he said, a professional soldier but that did not mean he believed in bullshit.

I do not know what he classified as bullshit but everything he wanted us to do was put under that heading by us. As an example, he wanted all the grease nipples to be highly polished. If the tank was clean outside, he said, he could take it for granted that the inside was up to scratch. This, of course, was enough to condemn him. My tank, like all the others, looked one huge pile of rubbish outside, as it was good policy to hang everything expendable around the turret and along the sides, but the Colonel could have eaten his dinner off the turret floor. If the tank designers had done their job properly and given us spaced armour the untidiness would not have been so necessary. In addition, if they had realised that crews have to live in a tank as well as fight in it then perhaps they would have provided enough stowage space for the crew's possessions. Finally, accepting lack of steel as an excuse for the absence of spaced armour and the exigencies of the service as the reason for the paucity of stowage space, then the man in command of a tank regiment ought to be aware of the defects of his vehicles and realise that his men were doing their best to remedy them.

When the Colonel did inspect the tanks he could not see the bogie nipples as they were under the mud. However, he did lift the tarpaulin on our trailer, which we thought was safe enough as Dusty had spent all morning polishing the controls. He ran his finger over the decking and complained of dust. Major Duffy looked fit to burst. Sherry had a very straight face. The Colonel walked on, tapping things with his stick. "Dust it!" snapped the Major and scampered after him.

If the main purpose of the visit was to raise our morale - and the way we were organised we could not think of any other task for the Colonel - then I fear it was a dismal failure as he left everybody, including the officers, very depressed. But apart from that episode there seemed to be a sincere desire to let us have a rest. Liberty trucks ran into Eindhoven every afternoon and left again at ten o'clock. I went the first day, we lost our way coming back, and it meant missing tea so I did not go again until the opening of a canteen in Eindhoven removed this difficulty. Then the only objection that remained was the journey. Going was not so bad but the return, cold and tired, seemed to last hours. And getting lost, which was frequent in the early days, was not funny at that time of night.

On these occasions the quieter sort would attempt to sleep, hampered by those of a more active nature who insisted upon relieving themselves over the tailboard or singing. Apart from modern dance tunes there were Christmas carols and hymns, of which the favourites were 'Holy Night' and 'The Holy City', and soldier songs such as 'Roll Me Over', 'Ringarangaroo', 'She Was Poor But She Was Honest' and the paraphrase of the regimental march, entitled 'Knife, Fork, Spoon', which started:

'The Buffs, the bastards, have gone away,
They've left the girls in the family way.'

By the time we reached Someren we had usually exhausted our repertoire and in apathetic silence would tumble out of the trucks and squelch wearily down the muddy lane to our billets. Perhaps there would then be time to fry a tin of M & V and make down our beds before the electric light was shut off at eleven o'clock.

Taking everything into consideration I generally preferred to spend a quiet evening in the billet and savour to the full the pleasure of being lazy. There were letters to be written and several people in the Troop now had books to swap. Also, we had all grown very fond of pancakes, in the tossing of which I became quite adept. But the great thing was that the evening lasted longer than if I went to Eindhoven.

Bath trucks were run at frequent intervals and would have been more appreciated if the distances involved had not been so great. There were two bathhouses at Helmond and one at Asten, none very good, but at Eindhoven we could get a first class shower in the public baths. In Helmond and Asten the water was inadequate and erratic and the sheds were draughty but we could get our underwear, shirts and socks changed. In Eindhoven we could not get clean laundry but each man had a separate, tiled cubicle, the water was always just right and the cloakroom heated.

One Sunday, our last at Someren, Steve O'Neill and I skipped church parade and 'poodled' to Heesch. I cannot remember why Steve elected to come with me, for he had no business in Heesch and there was some risk of his losing his stripes if we were caught, but anyway we got a lift to Helmond and out to join the Eindhoven-Heesch road at Veghel. We were fortunate on the outward journey, it being daylight and the Canadian sector and the Canadians were very good about lifts, but coming back it was cold and dark and we had to walk long distances.

Just below Uden we were picked up by an Airborne Forces Jeep, minus windscreen and hood as usual, and we gradually froze into our seats and even our teeth refused to chatter. Just south of Uden was a very dramatic road sign reading, on four successive boards:

"DO YOU VALUE YOUR LIFE?
-IF SO -

- FOR CHRIST'S SAKE -

-GO SLOW!"

Our driver passed this at 60 mph and maintained this speed all the way down through Veghel and St. Oedenrode to Eindhoven and out to Geldrop, where we left him.

We had a drink and thawed out in a café near the peculiar church that was a landmark for miles around and congratulated ourselves on getting so near home so quickly. I sketched a menu for supper and Steve made amendments - he could always improve on anything. Then out into the moonlight once more and almost immediately we stopped a 15-hundredweight truck driven by an RSM who said he was going through Someren.

Steve got in front beside the driver and I climbed into the back. At first I did not take much notice of our route, but we passed through Heeze and then I began to sit up and get worried, for we went through another village and I knew there were none between Heeze and Someren. And the broad main road that stretched out behind us, straight for miles and glistening white in the moonlight, was totally unfamiliar. I expected a turn off to the left that would bring us into Someren from a different direction but when we turned right along a winding marsh road I was certain we were off course. Several more miles and then the truck stopped.

I heard the driver say, "Here you are!" and jumped out. The truck drove away as we inspected a sign. Somdonk!

We entered a café to get our bearings and found ourselves to be four kilometres from the Belgian border - our supper was a long way off. So we drank our beer in a hurry and started to walk again. There was not much traffic but we did get a lift to Valkenswaard from which it was only a short walk to Heeze. Then we made a fatal mistake, for instead of waiting for a truck on the corner by the village we started to walk. Out along the narrow, dark, tree-lined road, we waved cigarette butts every time lights approached but no vehicle would stop. Indeed, they all increased speed as soon as they saw us.

Neither of us knew the road well and so, naturally, it seemed longer than it was. The roadside trees and the dark woods beyond them stretched for miles without a break and began to get on our nerves. Steve doubted if we were going right but we could not think where we had missed our way. The occasional houses seemed to be deserted for no shutter showed a gleam of light. At one a Carrier and a couple of trucks were standing in a yard but there was no sentry and we could not make anyone hear. Just as we were wondering if we ought to turn back there was a blaze of light down the road and our liberty trucks swept past, coming back from Eindhoven. Like the others, they refused to stop, but the sight of them renewed our energy and in half an hour we were snug in bed and dreaming of the supper we were too late to cook.

Brussels leave was now organised and had started for us as soon as we settled at Someren. My turn came towards the end of November. I had hoped to go with a member of our crew but this did not work out and I mated up with one of the Fitters named Dave. The idea was for us to be taken in squadron transport as far as Bourg Leopold and from there Brigade would look after us. But something went wrong and when we reached Brigade the Brussels truck had left. This suited Sergeant Franklin, who was in charge of our Studebaker, very well, and it pleased the rest of us to have our own transport all the way and so avoid hanging about for connections.

Dave and I had rooms in a very comfortable hotel in the Rue Montoyer. But 48 hours was not long enough to enable us to appreciate it to the full, for we could not make ourselves feel at home in that short period and by the time the strangeness of privacy had worn off the leave was finished. We changed our money, explored the red light area between the Rue Neuve and the Boulevarde Adolphe Max, rode on the trams free and hunted for suitable souvenirs. A bit of sightseeing and that was about all.

On the following Sunday, November 25th, I had planned to visit Zussie again, but on that day we moved to Oerle, a village on the other side of Eindhoven. It was the first occasion on which we had worn our zoot suits on a road run and we soon realised their value; the only trouble was that with our bodies kept so warm the coldness of our hands and feet was all the more apparent.

Oerle was a miserable, muddy village but trucks still ran to Eindhoven so we could get out of it. The first night there was a terrific tick because no trucks had been laid on and those with girls in the town had made all their arrangements to meet them. After this there was no problem. I used to go more regularly now to collect and send letters to Zussie, via her uncle, who occasionally travelled to Heesch. Then to the theatre which was attached to the Phillips works, or to the pictures where there was the choice of the Garrison Cinema usually showing Betty Grable or a Dutch house with English sub-titles to very old films. It did not pay to walk around the town - at least, there were unpleasant stories of British soldiers being found floating in canals. Apart from that, every few yards one was accosted by a Dutchman wanting to buy cigarettes. This was annoying and also it was considered unwise to sell cigarettes casually in the street as both the Dutch police and the MPs were rumoured to be using plain clothes to trap the unwary soldier.

At Oerle we painted the tanks. The intention was to change from our khaki to the olive which the Americans had always favoured and in which our new vehicles were arriving. It was rather difficult to follow the mental processes of someone who could order all tanks to be painted and provide only half enough paint and no brushes. However, it was in line with my experience at the Training Regiment when we had to tear off the grass with our hands because there was nothing with which to cut it except one pair of scissors and General Montgomery was expected the next day. We did our best with engine cleaning brushes and with some tanks khaki, some green and some half and half, drove down to Meerveldhoven on the main road and loaded on transporters.

We were to return to Belgium. The run down through Aalst and Valkenswaard to the border was bitterly cold and we sat inside the tank and shivered, emerging only to take the salute at villages. When it got dark I tried to sleep in the co-driver's seat but it was impossible so I tried to take my mind off my freezing feet by paying attention to our route.

Jeeps had an annoying habit of refusing to dip their headlights and the transporter crews were much troubled all along the road. So on one occasion all the transporters waited until the offender got close and then switched on immensely powerful spotlights in succession. He lasted about halfway and then got mixed up with the tramlines at the side of the road and as we had also experienced this lack of courtesy everyone was highly delighted.

We unloaded at Waterscheeuw, in the Belgian province of Limburg. The night was pitch dark and it was raining cats and dogs. The transporters rattled away as soon as they were free and the tanks closed up to await laggards. This took a good time although casualties did not seem so common now as on our trip up from France. We thawed round the roaring fire in a café. The elements outside were forgotten in the warmth and steam and smoke of the tiny bar but when the order to move came we felt them all the more.

The rain in perpendicular sheets reduced visibility practically to nil. About one tank in three had lights in working order and the rest had to rig the spot, cutting a shaft through the rain to silhouette the mass of the vehicle in front. The fuse blew as soon as I switched on ours and I had to fumble about in the turret replacing it, the only light the dim glow from the festoons, my fingers numb to the bone, while every time the tank lurched icy water cascaded over me from the turret roof.

I had torn my zoot suit along the right shoulder - they tore easily - and the wind and sleet seemed to select this point to concentrate in their attack on me. It was a miserable journey; but at last, cold, wet, tired and hungry, we drew into the open space beneath the walls of the Winterslag coal mine. The tracks sank deep in the mud. The wind tore at the sheets and it took a long time to secure them. A faint voice in the darkness declared its willingness to show us our billet and we were only too pleased to drop everything and follow.

A day to recover. I changed my wireless set again, having to argue with the signalmen in order to retain my vibrator unit[90] that saved the drain on the batteries but which was not always fitted. I cleaned the turret. Then we were on the move again, our route being through Genk, Bilsen, Maastricht and Heerlen to Nieuwenhagen on the Dutch-German frontier.

George had gone on leave to Brussels and his place was taken by that Sergeant Franklin of HQ Troop who had accompanied me there, one of Jack's old cronies. This made the run pleasant in one respect as no harsh words passed between driver and commander. Also, I was in a good mood as I had overheard George telling Franklin that he had a good operator and need not worry about my side of the tank.

Otherwise the journey was far from pleasant as the weather gave us no respite. A snowstorm blew up as we reached Genk and drove directly in our faces. By the time we reached Maastricht it had turned to rain. When darkness fell a biting wind took over and was worse than either.

A bridge that was supposed to be finished but was not held us up for a long time while a twenty-five mile detour was mapped out. It was here that Dusty had a narrow escape from a nasty accident. We had removed the centre section of the track guards as a precaution against the turret being jammed by their being buckled by mud and the fact that a large portion of the track was thus laid bare was new to us. Dusty was standing on the uncovered part when the order came to turn round. Jack heard the order via the filter-through to the I/c and started forward. We all shouted together and he stopped just in time. Dusty's foot and ankle, caught between two track-plates, had been dragged beneath the remaining section of the guard. An inch or so further and the bones must have given. As it was we had to reverse to free his foot and he escaped with a sprain.

We had got about another mile on our road when Sherry's tank hit an electricity pylon and brought it down. The wires fell across the

---

[90] Vibrator Unit. Only fitted on some 19 Sets, it reduced the drain on the batteries when the set was on and was, therefore, a desirable fitment.

wet road and blue sparks flew all over the place. Why Sherry and his crew were not electrocuted I cannot explain.

While awaiting our turn to cross the long pontoon bridge over the Maas at Maastricht we hit an American ambulance but it was on the commander's side so Jack kept quiet. Indeed, Sergeant Franklin had taken George at his word and left me to pilot the tank while he sheltered from the weather. However, he should have given me a hand in a traffic jam - I had been reading the big notice blazoning the details of the American unit which had built the bridge, how long they took to do it, and how many yards it was from shore to shore so I did not see the ambulance. However, little damage was done.

There was another long halt just after dark while Sherry went ahead to recce the road. We made tea in a house below the embankment and spent a long time over the map trying to determine our position. As no one could decide for sure it was no use looking forward to bed.

An advance guard had been sent to secure billets and when we got into Nieuwenhagen about two o'clock in the morning the job had been done properly and the Dutch were waiting up for us. All the way from Winterslag I had been fighting the weather with the thought of something hot and a warm bed to follow. Now we met the Dutch family and they had hot drinks for us and we smoked and chatted and no one felt the least inclined for sleep.

This was our first experience of being stationed actually on the frontier between two countries and we were surprised at the way the races were intermingled. German was the second language and the coal mine was shorthanded because it had drawn a lot of its labour from across the frontier prior to our invasion. However, some of the German staff still remained and no one seemed to think that worthy of remark. One crew of our Troop was billeted in a house where the husband was away - he was a German Panzer Grenadier. Two German children hung about our tank all one day and we gave them work greasing the bogies. Apparently they had nowhere to live and for a bit we were quite worried about them, but they seemed happy enough and the moment for doing something for them passed.

A large number of American Negro troops were stationed in and around the village. Both they and the civilians were greatly excited by the rumour that an SS officer was roaming the countryside after dark. A phantom figure indeed, and the Americans turned out in force every night and shot at every moving object they happened to see, so we had to stay indoors. Thus circumstances were not favourable to getting to know the Americans well, which was a pity as this was our first meeting with a Negro unit. However, during the daytime we liked them well enough.

We lost Sergeant Franklin, although the Americans had nothing to do with that. I was testing the power traverse. The drill for this was to go round each way slowly to make sure there was no obstruction and then to whip round at top speed. I did the slow bit and then Sergeant Franklin, who had been standing on the engine deck, must have stepped forward, for as I jammed the spade grip hard over he gave a tremendous yell, I stopped the turret, and he had his foot caught between the armour and the exhaust stack. The ankle appeared to be broken so he was rushed to hospital and the war was over before we saw him again. No one thought I had done it on purpose but of course they all said I had.

The squadron stayed at Nieuwenhagen for several days although the job for which we had been sent there had fallen through. It was said that it had involved breaking through the German lines and staying behind them for twenty-four hours. At the officers' briefing the infantry commander wanted the leading tank to go down the centre line (a straight, main road) with luminous paint on the air louvres! As if we were not easy enough to see without that! It was further rumoured in 13 Troop that Major Duffy had tried to swing this job on to one of us.

"One of your tanks, Mr. Sherriff."
"No, sir, not one of my tanks."

However, it blew over. We all had good baths in the mine at Heerlen. When the Germans opened their offensive in the Ardennes we heard that Nieuwenhagen had been overrun by a subsidiary thrust.

The author whilst on leave in Brussels, Nov. 1944

Churchill Crocodile

"Colin Campbell" 'C' Sqn I Lothians coming back to rally at Le Havre

Le Havre - assault team forming up

AVRE's of 222 assault Sqn. R.E. near S'Hertogenbosch

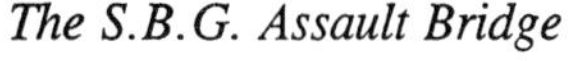

The S.B.G. Assault Bridge

Churchill Crocodiles stand by as houses in S'Hertogenbosch are cleared in October 1944

Crocodile (Corporal Robb) of 'C' Sqn. 141 RAC. flaming across canal at S'Hertogenbosch on 24th Oct. 1944

Artist's impression of conditions in the Reichswald.
Crocodiles ploughing through mud and rain.

British armour approaching the banks of the Rhine

Presentation of awards to 'B' Sqn 141 RAC. by General Simpson, Commander 9 US Army

The Ram Kangaroo

17-pounder gun on Valentine Chassis.

* * *

The village of Bergeijk lies just off the main road from Eindhoven to Belgium, near Valkenswaard, and became our main base for much of the winter. So we had time to get our feet right under the table.

It was a large village and we were the only troops there, so each crew got a house to itself. Ours was in the Broekstraat and the tanks were in a field just across the lane at the bottom of the garden so everything was very convenient. We had the usual loft for our bedroom and of course spent the evenings with the family - again, as usual, a large one. The inhabitants of the country districts of South Holland are extremely prolific but I never came across a village with such large families as those of Bergeijk. A dozen or fourteen to the household was quite normal and we could never remember all their names or even which ones belonged to us.

One reason for the high birth-rate must be the power of Roman Catholicism, for the priest was certainly an important man in his parish. For instance, I could not imagine an English parson censuring the morals of the village girls from the pulpit, and mentioning names at that.

At Bergeijk the priest came in one night when we were all gathered cosily round the stove and quietly enjoying ourselves and warned the eldest girls to be on their guard against us. Lena, the best looking one, translated for us after he was gone and we were very mad about it, especially as we knew he could speak English. We thought he should have told us what he was doing so that we could have had our say. And at Heesch the priest questioned Zussie as to my intentions. He was more tactful than his colleague and visited her when I was not there. But I felt a bit less friendly towards Zussie when I found that she accepted such interference without annoyance.

The great majority of us, especially when in such billets as at Bergeijk where we were all known and treated as part of the family, never had any idea of doing the wrong thing by a Dutch girl. The priests may have carried on in the same way when the Germans held the country but we suspected that they had not and therefore regarded their interference with all the more indignation.

In any case, at Bergeijk we had very little chance of getting the girls on their own as they had far too much to do looking after their menfolk. These always seemed to be around and how most of them earned a living we could not understand. Occasionally the elder boys would go into Eindhoven and spend a couple of days working on the aerodrome there. While others would stand about the road with shovels presumably employed by the equivalent of our Rural District Council. But such casual labour could not have been sufficient to keep twelve people.

However, it seemed quite usual for the ordinary working man to carry the equivalent of a hundred pounds in his wallet. Of course, they could have saved a lot during the Occupation when, presumably, there was regular employment and very little to buy. Now there was a large 'zwarte handel' stocked by us. Apart from food, soap and cigarettes we were a source of even greater profit for black marketeers as we had leaves to Brussels and could provide Belgian currency; and a few kilometres down the road was the wide open frontier of Belgium, where every luxury was to be had at a price. Naturally, the rate of exchange recognised in the squadron as being fair was considerably different from that laid down by the authorities.

At a humbler level, the mess orderly's job was greatly simplified. If there was anything left over from a meal - and there was always plenty of curried rice if nothing else - he divided the dixies among the horde of children always clamouring at the back door of the cookhouse, whence they were borne away in triumph and returned spotless. 'Niet in de winkel, alles in kokhuis'.

The Dutch were badly off for food for, of the countries we liberated, they seemed to have suffered the most. But they always invited us to share their supper - usually pancakes with a huge lump of bacon in the centre - and afterwards we had to set to and cook our own and then invite the family to share that so as to be all square.

The one commodity we could not immediately supply was coffee. Their 'surrogaat' coffee did not resemble the real thing even in appearance, let alone in taste. Some was composed of brambles and nettles, some of a chemical substance looking like liquorice. If the family preferred tea they could buy a mixture the shape and colour of cough lozenges but which did taste almost like the real thing. Every morning our landlady had it ready for us and we crowded round the glowing 'kachel' and took it as a necessary stimulant before attempting the quarter-mile walk through slush or biting frost to the cookhouse. Needless to say, we watched - or threatened to watch - our cooks and quartermaster very closely but could never get any proof of black market activity.

In the middle of December the Germans caught the Americans napping in the Ardennes. Rumour was at once active and while we shrugged our shoulders and said it was only to be expected of the Yanks the Dutch were distinctly uneasy. The Germans were reported to be dropping paratroops in British and American uniforms and many of these, of course, landed near Bergeijk - every evening there were tales of Germans seen, caught, or attacking our transport. I should hate to think that the Dutch had swastika flags hidden under their mattresses ready to hang out if necessary, as we heard was the case in Belgium, but they were very perturbed about the whole affair. After continual success all the way from Normandy I suppose this reverse assumed greater prominence by contrast.

We had assumed we would spend Christmas at Bergeijk and had collected a sum of money and the squadron's NAAFI ration of chocolate to give the children a party. The Ardennes offensive upset this, for two days before Christmas we got the order to move to Blauberg in Belgium. I was left in the trailer party as Dusty was celebrating Christmas in Brussels.

About this time it was decided that it would be an advantage if we possessed our own means of towing trailers, instead of having to rely on the goodwill of medium artillery regiments, and a party had been sent to exchange our assorted three-tonners for some heavier American HARs.[91] These were not due in Bergeijk until Boxing Day

[91] HAR. 4-wheeled heavy American lorry, powerful enough to tow our trailers.

so the trailer party had a very dull Christmas with little in the way of jollification.

Under Sherry's leadership we made the best of a bad job and the chocolate and boiled sweets were bartered for the means to make some semblance of a Christmas meal, but without drink or music or the room to make a row we were rather hampered afterwards. We could sit around the 'kachel' and yarn but our comfort was spoilt since the Brigade Major had been round and after his visit we had to mount a guard on the trailers, which hitherto we had not done.

We had a lucky escape there. The truth was that Bob Williamson, the co-driver on Sherry's tank, and I, happened to be near the trailers when the Brigade Major came. We had been out in the fields to fire Bob's P35[92] automatic, which he was carrying in his hand, while I was wearing my .38. When we caught up with the squadron a stinking report had been sent in stating that the Brigade Major had been around the trailers for half an hour and had seen no sign of a guard. Sherry demanded a written apology and Bob and I were produced as having been on guard at the time of his visit. I think the Major knew how the land lay but he could not disprove our story that we had been on duty for half an hour and that the Brigade Major had only been there for two minutes, if that. The fact that we had both been armed gave credence to the picture we painted. Sherry got his apology.

By the time the trucks arrived it was getting dark and we had to endure a long ride south with the countryside in the grip of a bitter frost, in typical American wagons with canvas hoods and no doors. The halt at the Bourg Leopold canteen was necessary to restore our circulation and not just desirable.

NAAFI had come a long way since it opened in Caen with a cup of tea and a packet of biscuits after an hour in the queue. The establishment at Bourg Leopold sold cakes in unlimited quantities as well as all the necessities and comforts retailed by NAAFI in England such as soap, razor blades and boot laces. The Americans patronised the place as well as our troops and they were greatly attracted by our

[92] P35. The Walther 9 mm. automatic pistol, the most modern German sidearm.

zoot suits. If the weather had not been so cold it is possible some of us might have yielded to the fancy prices offered.

In Blauberg the tanks were drawn up in the school playground and we had commandeered the school. Our room had a tiled floor but was strewn thick with trusses of straw and in the centre a stove roared dangerously red-hot until it was almost impossible to bear the atmosphere. The Troop spent an afternoon sawing up logs for it.

As we were only in Corps Reserve and our forces were now coping in the Ardennes there did not seem much chance of our seeing any action. On the first evening after the arrival of the trailer party we had a special Christmas Dinner laid on for us and the Major came along and said that the newspapers required us all to have turkey and he hoped we all liked it. The next day Mr. Bottomley took photos of us all, by Troop and by crew - considering it was December they came out very well.

We went back to Bergeijk for New Year's Day and it was then that the Luftwaffe made a last attempt, if not to regain mastery of the air, to make things more awkward for us than had been the case during the last few months.

We had had a sort of first parade and were strolling up the lane to start work on the tanks when the first lot came over, a formation of twelve at about five hundred feet. We thought they were Hurricanes at first, then they passed leisurely overhead and the black crosses were visible in the sunshine.

We got swiftly into the shelter of a copse as the formation suddenly split up and circled the tanks. There was no shooting, however, and after an inspection they turned and raced for Eindhoven. A few moments later there was a stutter of flak and the crash of exploding bombs. A thick pall of oily black smoke rose in the sky. Rumour stated maliciously that the RAF had been caught with their trousers down and had had hundreds of machines destroyed on the ground; that the Germans had hit a petrol dump; that they had hit the main ammo dump for the area.

However, the RAF got enough fighters into the air to get their own back. A Messerschmidt crashed in flames into a field a quarter of a mile away. Others raced low between the treetops, flat out for their own country. All morning the air was filled with cannon and machine gun fire above the whine of engines. Shag got out the Bren Gun but we told him not to be such a fool as to attract their attention. As the day wore on the sky became full of our own aircraft and the Germans came no more.

There was not much to do on the tanks save for the driver but now Jack always insisted on having my help. We two had always been on reasonably good terms but I felt that he had a faintly contemptuous attitude towards me. This vanished when we came back from Nieuwenhagen. Jack was very cold and tired and Dusty could not drive a Churchill so I offered my services. Jack took my place in the turret and I was on my mettle. He must have been anxious but I drove carefully and found my gears - not easy on a Churchill - and presently he was telling me to speed up and chatting away and I knew I had passed my test. I was very pleased and more so when Jack said, "I never thought you had it in you, Smudger." After that all trace of contempt vanished. It was always, "You can bugger off, George - Smudge and I will see to this!" and "Do you think this will be best, Smudge?" and so on. All very pleasant. However, apart from the periodic checks, bleeding, draining and renewal of the oil filter elements, we had little work.

On the whole the winter passed pleasantly enough. UK leave was laid on now and one night there was a grand draw for the January dates. I was not eligible as I did not come over with the Regiment but Shag was lucky. We were now laughing at B Squadron, who had snatched a 48[93] when they called at Portsmouth on the way from Brest to Ostend by sea. They told us that the chance had come as a complete surprise and that they had all had to go on leave in their working clothes. As these were an interesting combination of British, American and German uniforms the MPs on the railway stations had all gone mad. But they had all got their leave and because of this the allotment for the Regiment was initially given to the other squadrons. January leave was determined by draw, as I said, but in February all

93 "a 48". 48 hours' leave.

the D-Day blokes went and from then on the procedure was complicated and we were too busy to wonder how the dates were fixed.

There was an occasional church parade and we held another for General Simpson, commander of the US 9th Army, to give medals to members of B Squadron for their work done in co-operation with the Americans at Brest. After the parade we had kinder things to say about the Yanks. There was nothing ornate. We were drawn up on three sides of the village square and on the fourth side was an American flag slung between two trees, behind a kitchen table with a blanket draped over it. The General arrived on time. He drove up in a Jeep with three other officers - unlike the procedure at an inspection by Montgomery at which I was present where, although it was summer, he drove up in a saloon with a highly polished Jeep behind ready for him to stand on to have his photo taken. We had spent all the previous day scrubbing our belts and gaiters but General Simpson declined to inspect the Regiment saying, loud enough for all to hear, that he had seen us in action. His speech was merely to thank us, without any bullshit, and he apologised for keeping us so long standing in the cold. He and his staff, in tin hats and raincoats, were a pleasant contrast to the polished brass and blanco of high British officers. He looked a workman - they appeared to have made others work.

* * *

Since September I had been filling my post as wireless operator adequately, if not with distinction. I liked being on a tank and was not worried by not receiving the extra three pence a day to which a trade test would have entitled me. It was very annoying, therefore, to be told that the authorities considered a trade test to be essential. My friends said it was the military system and it was no use moaning about it.

Major Duffy had given me permission to go to Heesch on the Sunday and it was not until I got back late that night that a casual study of the notice board outside the squadron office informed me that with three other operators - Ginger, Jimmy Judge and Jack

Washington - I was to leave for Montague in Belgium at 0800 the next morning.

264 Forward Delivery Squadron treated us with all the deference due to men who had seen action and in our barrack room in the local school we became something in the nature of oracles, which was very gratifying. The snow was on the ground so we had an excuse to wear our zoot suits all the time, which lifted us out of the common herd.

Unfortunately, the Delivery Squadron was run on Training Regiment lines and it irked us to have to wait for the five minutes at the end of each hour in order to be allowed to smoke. Also, before break each morning there was PT. Directly we heard this Jack Washington and I developed bad feet and limps and used to fetch the tea from the cookhouse while the rest cut capers in the snow. On cloudy days the Germans sent V1s over, aimed at Antwerp, and they were almost a welcome diversion - we were all terribly bored.

The town was not nearly as gay as a Belgian one ought to have been. There were cafés, but the Belgian girls always seemed to be accompanied by their mothers. So most of our money went on sweets and fancy cakes. Since we were not allowed to buy foodstuffs and there were MPs on duty on all the cross-roads the operation of getting in and out of shops unseen was very difficult. Especially as the MPs had little to do but stamp their feet and look around.

Jack Washington was the only one to get fixed up with a Belgian girl - being a territorial he naturally had more impudence than the rest of us. We only did one guard at Montague and after we had walked along the lines of Flails and Kangaroos and seen they were all there we spent the rest of the two hours comfortably in her house.

At the weekend Jack wanted to go to Eindhoven to see a girl there and I wanted to go to Heesch. The Orderly Sergeant advised us to put in passes for Brussels for the Sunday, which our friends would draw in the morning, so we fixed this and left for Holland on the Saturday afternoon, after dinner.

We soon got a lift to Bourg Leopold and could have gone right through to Eindhoven but Jack wanted to stop off to buy some brandy. However, we were lucky again and found a Jeep going all the way and parted there after fixing a rendezvous for the morrow. It was getting dark. I did not know Eindhoven very well and spent some time finding the right exit. When I did get on the road not one vehicle would serve and in despair I boarded a Canadian truck bound for s'Hertogenbosch, intending to try again there.

We came to a fork. I was not certain, but I felt that for s'Hertogenbosch we should have turned left and that the right fork which we had taken led to Heesch. Of course, I said nothing and presently the Bailey Bridge at Zon confirmed my suspicion. We drove through Nijnsel and familiar landmarks stood out in the glare of the headlights: the line of burnt out Bedfords in the ditch; the Panther in the middle of a field; the huddle of overturned, blackened Shermans close by; the two SP guns on the outskirts of St. Oedenrode; the canal with its colourful barges at Veghel, the road always under repair south of Uden; the French R35[94] tank just beyond the maze of Nistelrode. At last the cross-roads at Heesch where I thanked the driver and directed him down the Rijksweg to s'Hertogenbosch.

The next evening I was back in Montague. Our friends had neglected to draw our passes but we sneaked them from the office and handed them in half an hour later, so no one was the wiser.

---

94 R35. The Germans used a lot of captured vehicles. This one was an old French tank with poor armament and armour and was probably in use as a road block.

CHAPTER 12

INTO GERMANY

We were two thirds of the way through the course and beginning to remember our morse. This was the most difficult part of the trade test as we never used it operationally and it got rusty quickly. We were also getting used to the Delivery Squadron and were friends with all in our barrack room. Then one evening we had all gone to bed and were talking when the Orderly Sergeant came in, asking for any Buffs. On admitting our identity he told us to get our kit packed as we were going back to our squadron immediately. The truck would be round in half an hour.

This was good news and the lateness of the hour was more than offset by the impression made on our companions. We must be needed urgently to be sent for with so little warning. However, there was little time to enjoy the admiration of our classmates, for the truck turned up on time and by daylight we were in Sittard, a town of Dutch Limburg near the German frontier. We saw some members of A Squadron there and heard that they had had casualties from shellfire. They seemed very depressed and certainly the cold, bleak, snow banked streets were anything but cheerful.

C Squadron was harboured in the village of Merkelbeek, the tanks being drawn up in the square and whitewashed to conform with the heavy snowfalls of the past few days. The snow had fallen, partially thawed, and frozen. The tanks were travel stained and rusty, littered about with old compo boxes, water cans, empty bottles, buckets smeared with whitewash and empty jerricans, and sheeted up as if they had not been touched for days. An old mattress had split open and the stuffing lay kicked across the snow. The place was deserted save for a child dragging a sledge piled with firewood. The only other sign of life was a bedraggled crow roosting in a withered tree on the corner of the square which every so often gave a melancholy squawk.

When we had located the office and announced our return we found everything topsy-turvy as so many people were on leave. Jack Rodaway was driving Sherry, while George was commanding Steve O'Neill's tank with Shag as wireless operator. Neither George nor Shag was happy about this: Shag was a gunner and hated wireless sets; George wanted an operator who was ready to help him guide the tank.

I was equally discontented at not having a tank and started to persuade Shag to change places with me. He refused at first and George, who had an interest in the exchange, explained that Shag was afraid something would happen to me, when he would feel to blame. I thought this was rather nice of Shag, although he would not admit it to be the case. However, when I promised to be extra careful he gave in and I had my old place.

George was the same as always but our new crew seemed a good one. I knew that when Steve came back from leave he would take over again and I knew how good he was, from Le Havre. So I asked Sherry to let me stay in the crew and he agreed. My position was not legalised until we entered Germany proper a month later but it is from Merkelbeek that I date my association with the 'Sandwich' crew - Ted Denman, driver; Len Brown, Flame Gunner and his brother Gus, or 'Jinx', the gunner; and, of course, Steve O'Neill, commander.

The snow and subsequent frosts had made the roads like glass and in consequence fifty tons of tank and trailer was never more than half under control. The whole squadron would be slipping across the road, into ditches, trees, banks and each other - an erratic procession that quickly became chaotic when I had my first experience of this aspect of winter travel on the run from Merkelbeek to Gangelt, a small town just inside Germany.

It was the first time we had entered the Reich by design, although one of our tanks claimed to have done so in error at Nieuwenhagen. There were big notices:

"YOU ARE NOW IN GERMANY - BEHAVE LIKE CONQUERORS"

and:

"THIS IS GERMANY - BEWARE OF SPIES."

It seemed a bit un-English and in any case, both were rather unnecessary as the countryside was absolutely deserted and the little girl who waved to us from the Dutch frontier post was the last civilian we saw before our return to Holland.

Beyond the frontier was the usual waste land and straggling pine forest, with foxholes under the trees roofed with freshly cut logs. The road was typical of all on the German frontier - narrow and badly made as if the Germans had lost interest. The whole vista was softened and dimmed under the snow and a stinging wind swept powdery drift in our faces.

In quieter times Gangelt must have been quite a picturesque country town with a massive archway, a relic of the town wall, guarding the narrow streets where the houses fronted directly on the road without the interference of garden or pavement. One large building was still occupied by German hospital staff and red cross flags drooped from the windows. It seemed queer to see German uniforms unescorted.

The rest of the town was inhabited by the crews of Five-fives and Bofors which were sited in the fields around. Ted and I took one of the little four-wheeled handcarts that seemed peculiar to Germany and went to the nearest gun site to beg some ammunition boxes which, welded to the turret, were the ideal receptacles for rations, blankets and loot of all descriptions save the valuable.

We had taken over some new houses just outside the town on what, had it been a better road, would have been termed a by-pass. Behind the houses a large area was marked as an Allied minefield. When Ted and I returned the crews were busy patching windows, throwing out unwanted furniture, lighting the stoves and generally making the billets as habitable as possible. And comfortable they could be made although, however large our fire, we could never get rid of the dank atmosphere of disuse and decay.

A little further up the road was a Tank Battalion of the Grenadier Guards and we went to inspect their Panther tank which was in its original colours save for a big white star painted on the offside quarter of the turret. I had seen one intact on a transporter at Bourg Achard, when I was in B Squadron, as well as many wrecks, but I had never before had the opportunity of getting inside. It was rather like the Sherman with the steering columns together between the knees and turning in the same manner as the American tanks by braking one track - greatly inferior to our epicyclic[95] gearbox and steering system. Still, the Guards said they could get 45 mph out of it and the gun, of course, was a winner. The Germans always covered their tanks with a thin layer of cement known as 'zimmerit' and the Guards said it was to counteract sticky bombs although we had always thought it was just for camouflage.

Since January 16th our troops had been advancing steadily from the Maas into Germany, village by village, the aim being to gain a base from which to cross the River Roer and enter the Rhineland. 12 Corps had three divisions and an assortment of 79th Armoured Division equipment. By now, January 21st, the 43rd Wessex Division had taken Breberen and was fighting in Schierwaldenrath and around Birgden.

Sherry came to brief us just as the tea was made, as he well knew. We left the dinner to cook itself and gathered in the biggest room, sitting on the beds and rickety chairs while Sherry stood as near as possible to the dim light filtering through the snow-blocked windows to enable him to see the map.

---

[95] Epicyclic gearbox. The Merritt-Brown gearbox fitted to British tanks had the great advantage that, when steering, power was transferred from one track to the other without loss. In contrast, German and American tanks steered by braking one track and lost power thereby. The only disadvantage to our system is apparent in the text, the unexplained behaviour on icy roads.

We had two objectives. Firstly, the villages of Pütt and Waldenrath: Pütt to be burnt to the ground, Waldenrath only singed unless the infantry called upon us to do more. With us were the Grenadier Guards' Churchills, Flails of B Squadron of the Westminster Dragoons, and infantry carried in Kangaroos of A Squadron, 1 Canadian Armoured Carrier Regiment. Our second objective was the larger village of Straeten for which we had the same assistance. Sherry was not expecting a lot of opposition and picked a haystack, marked on the map as occupied, as his especial target. He could not give us any dates or times and no one had any questions apart from these so we were not kept from our dinner for long.

Len had been helping Sherry's crew drape white sheets round 'Sidcup', my old tank, which Sherry had taken at short notice and which had not been whitewashed. About two o'clock he came in with definite news. Reveille was to be at midnight, we were to move off at one-thirty and be on the start-line at seven. As the start-line was only about four kilometres away this seemed an excessive allowance of time but Ted reminded us that the roads were pretty bad.

With the prospect of a night march we went to bed but I could not sleep. People were moving about and talking. A cooker was roaring in the next room. Someone was whistling by the Bofors gun under the window. The dim, cold light of the winter afternoon accentuated a feeling of unreality, a vague uneasiness always present on such occasions. The table, the broken chair, the compo box, were shadows against the peeling wall. The huddled shapes under the blankets stirred and muttered occasionally. I dozed, woke, read for a bit and dozed again.

It got dark. Len suddenly sat up, put on his boots and went out without saying a word. Presently he came back with a dixie full of stew. Ted lit a candle and after the stew it was impossible to sleep so we packed our kit and went downstairs to the room where the artillerymen had a stove going.

Around midnight there was movement in the rooms above and we could hear people putting on their boots and stamping to get their feet warm, coughing, rolling blankets and packing cookers and compo boxes. Outside, a brilliant moon shone on the snow. An engine was ticking over somewhere. The strains of music came faintly from an RA billet.

We stowed our blankets and went back in the warm. The artillerymen said they did not envy us. Len had made some tea in which they joined us and we sat round the stove drinking this and chatting spasmodically. About one o'clock, Ted and I roused ourselves to go out in the cold again, he to warm up the engine and I to test the I/c. There were a lot of little things to do at the last moment. A half tin of tea mixture to stow away where it would not spill; my mug to be hooked under the water-runnel outlet pipe of my hatch; the plates to be jammed between the wireless set and the turret roof where they would not get broken; my small pack to be squeezed into the corner above the smoke bomb bin; George's headset to be put where he would not stand on it when getting into the turret. One by one the engines started. Len and Jinx stood talking at the front, George on the track guard. Sherry came floundering across in the snow. Were we all right? Yes, we were. The front tank started.

We got on the road and then the fun began. The tank slid into the verge and my air louvre got hooked in the wing of a scout car. I told Ted to go ahead and damn the thing but we just dragged it with us. Ted stopped and the tank performed some complicated manoeuvres that finally rid us of the car but landed us in the ditch. Now George's air louvre hugged a telegraph pole. We charged ahead and the pole gave way, falling across the turret. George and I ducked just in time and the catches snapped off as my hatches clanged shut.

We disentangled all the wires and got back to the road at last. A right angle bend was the next obstacle. One tank had already slipped over the verge and was nearly on its side in the ditch. Our tracks beat furiously on the icy surface, unable to grip, clanging and jangling at twice the normal speed. The gearbox was playing all sorts of tricks and at one moment the right-hand track was stationary while the left-hand went backward although the tank was in a forward gear.

I had to stand to the wireless but George, Len and Jinx jumped down to drag bales of straw from a nearby barn and litter the road.

They tore down doors and fences, brought chairs and tables from the houses. The tracks spewed splinters of wood but the tank only slid nearer the ditch. I told Ted to reverse and he could do this as the ice was torn and then Len and Jinx concentrated wreckage and straw at one point. The tank lurched forward, the tracks beat ineffectually for a moment and then gripped and we swerved and skidded round the corner. The tanks behind churned through a garden, blazed a new path, and rejoined the road further along.

Overhead, red and gold tracers curved against the sky, paling in the beams of the artificial moonlight that now replaced the natural. There was a distant rumble of guns. Infantry walking and in Carriers were dark blotches against the snow.

In order to avoid minefields the way was north through the hamlet of Vintelen and round the back of Langbroich to the start line. It was now across country, along a narrow track beaten by hundreds of vehicles before us. To either side the landscape was blurred and deadened by drifted snow. Carriers clustered among farm buildings. At one point infantry were settling into Kangaroos. A scout car lay in the ditch, a Carrier trying to extract it. Our track wound through the fields, occasionally striking a piece of gritty road but mostly between high snow banks that at times reached to a level with the turret.

Then there was a wide open stretch. As far as we could see to right and left were tanks: Churchills, Kangaroos, Valentine 17-pounder SP guns manned by the Artillery and working with us for the first time, our own Crocodiles. All lined up among the cabbages.

It was ten minutes to seven - it had taken us five hours and twenty minutes to reach the start line. Len and Jinx got down to pressure up. I checked my set and went over to 'Sidcup' to warn the operator about certain peculiarities of the vibrator unit fitted in that tank, then hurried back to take the cover from the muzzle brake and bomb thrower, unlock the gun from its travelling position and unlock the turret. Sherry moved from tank to tank, having a last word with each crew, then ran back to his own tank. I put an AP up the spout. Len tested the Flame Gun. There was a hiss and a jet of flaming petrol shot out.

Len got up and beat out that which still burnt on the glacis plate and signalled that everything was all right.

Then the whole line surged forward. Behind each dim shape churned a great plume of snow. We closed down and George started to give directions.

"Driver right... Driver left... Slow down, Ted... Speed up, as fast as you can. Follow Mr. Sherriff."

"Shall I warm the Besa?" asked Jinx.

"Yes."

Machine gun tracers gleamed in the sky. Little ripples of flame wreathed the gun muzzles. From the exhausts, glowing cherry red, belched blue flame and smoke to mingle with the flying snow. The speed, the bounding of the tank, the whip of the belt through the Besa, were all exhilarating and I was glad I was there.

A dark cluster of trees and houses loomed ahead on the skyline, the tracers curving towards it. I saw the tank ahead lurch violently to the right.

"Is that Pütt?"

"No. That's - I don't know. Laffeld, I think it must be. It's taken anyway."

We swerved south, away from the Churchills of the Guards who were using their main armament. It was fast getting light and we saw that a steep bank broke the downward slope. It was scored with tank tracks and George, instead of making his own, elected to follow another tank. The tracks tore round and round and the tank shuddered and sank back. The engine died suddenly. We were bogged.

Ahead a rosy glow spread in the sky and tinted the snow. The other tanks were flaming Pütt. We swore at our bad luck in missing it. Then Jinx reminded us that we were sitting ducks if the Germans counterattacked.

Three Guards tanks were standing beyond the summit of the bank, firing towards Pütt. I volunteered to ask them to give us a tow, got down, floundered across to the nearest, and clambered up to the side of the turret. The commander, peeping from his cupola, looked surprised to see me standing beside him, as well he might be, but said he was too busy to help us. I swore at him and the whole Brigade of Guards but it made no difference, so I ran to the next tank and there was an officer. He said that the first tank must help us and I said he would not. Then a mortar came over, flinging up the cabbages a hundred yards away, and I gave it up and scuttled back to safety.

George was queer about explosions. We said he studied Jane's strip[96] in the Daily Mirror so much that he had been convinced he would merely lose his clothes and sustain no bodily harm. The rest of us had no such illusions and got under cover at the first whistle but George pottered about outside. He was now talking to the crews of two Valentines that were about to attempt the bank and we saw one of the artillery men look at us and shake his head. But at least they tried. George hitched the towrope, Ted revved the engine, the Valentine strained. It was no use - the Valentine stood on its tail and did its best but it was just not up to it. The mortars were now dropping all over the place, near enough to shake the tank and strike sparks from the armour yet George, miraculously unscathed, was still fooling about outside trying to persuade the Guards to help us. Despite our shouts and swearing at him he took no notice.

But it all ended in the most prosaic way for the mortars quietened down after a bit and the three Guards tanks, after George had worried them enough, backed up and dragged us over the bank. We lost no time in getting underway again towards Pütt.

We did not know we were crossing a minefield as we had been too tired the night before to study the minefield trace for the area. A broad waste of pitted, rutted, cratered and frozen ground interlaced

[96] Jane's strip. Probably the best-known of all the strip cartoons appearing in any newspaper. Jane was an extremely attractive young lady whose adventures always resulted in her losing most of her clothes although she usually retained some items of underwear. In that more innocent age it was, of course, regarded as somewhat daring and was much studied.

with winding trenches, it was difficult going. Crossing the trenches we feared for the safety of the kit piled on the trailer and with reason; when we checked up the tin box containing Ted's blankets was missing.

Both villages had been taken without much trouble and the Germans were now busy making life as precarious as possible for the new occupants. Shells and mortars - as usual, particularly mortars - rained down on Pütt, but the fall was pretty constant and where we stood to one side was quiet enough.

One of our tanks had broken a track on the minefield and we drew alongside just as the crew finished repairing it. The driver hopped into his seat, started up and, instead of staying put in comparative safety, the tank drew forward. How the sergeant in command escaped with his life I do not know, for he was standing right by the front wing when the next mine went up. He ran round in a circle, his hands to his face, then dropped.

"Bob's hit!" shouted George. "Quick! The first aid box!"

Len handed it out smartly and George ran across to where his crew were clustered round the stricken man. To give George his due he went across the minefield with no thought for his own safety but the rest of us stayed put. There were enough already round the wounded man and there were plenty of mines although we had been lucky coming over to the village. We heard later that the Engineers lost so many men in trying to recover vehicles in the area that they had to give up their attempts and just leave them to rust.

By the time an Ambulance Jeep had arrived to take Bob Everest to the dressing station everyone had got tired and the war was now being prosecuted in a very desultory fashion. Half a dozen Typhoons were leisurely attacking the environs of Heinsburg. A few casual mortars dropped in the ruin that was Pütt. The Guards Panther, away to one side of the village, fired occasionally in the direction of the German lines. The infantry were making themselves comfortable under their Carriers. Overhead, three Flying Jeeps circled lazily among the flecks of clouds.

In the front of our tank Ted and Len took the opportunity to examine the contents of a Five-five box, blown off a Guards tank and picked up by us. It contained two suits of battle dress, a set of blankets and a looted eiderdown, so it had certainly been worth the trouble of salvaging it.

An Australian War Correspondent had bogged his Jeep in a crater just behind us and asked for assistance. Like a fool I volunteered, as did odd people from the other tanks. From inside the tank everything did seem quiet. Outside, the mortars landing in Pütt sounded louder, more often and more lethal. There was machine gun fire now and the incident of the mine had made me chary of putting foot to ground. I sweated and strained at the beastly Jeep and expected to be blown to smithereens at any moment but it just stuck in the crater and the wheels spun round and we could not do anything with it. Then George shouted that the master switch had gone again and would I come and fix it and I blessed him and made my apologies to the Correspondent. He did not take my name to put in his paper.

The master switch had played tricks before and I sat on the turret floor and tapped it with a hammer before starting to take it to pieces. Then with a roar an aeroplane zoomed low overhead and the whistle and crash of a bomb blended with the rush of sound. Machine guns chattered. There were shouts, drowned by the noise of the aircraft as it came round for a second attack.

"It's a Thunderbolt!" cried George. "He must be after the Panther."

"Never mind him! Shut them bleeding hatches!" I yelled.

He looked down at me and grinned.

"Frightened, Smudge?"

"Yes I bloody well am, you silly bastard! Shut them bloody hatches!"

"Shut the hatches!" barked Len.

Fortunately, it seemed the Yank had only one bomb and he soon went away, but after that we were continually on edge when the Typhoons came over. They were still concentrating on Heinsburg, going down in long power dives, trailing smoke from their exhausts, little puffs appearing behind them as the rockets shot ahead. Now the flak was very heavy and one Tiffie was hit halfway along its dive and just disappeared. We stopped saying we should like to be up there, but it did not seem to discourage the others.

Presently we started back along the track through Waldenrath. Ahead of us the Flails were having a busy time and the mines they set off were big ones. The Flail commander was giving all his instructions over the A-Set and very complicated they were. These tanks always worked in troops of five and I should imagine it was difficult to manage so many.

It was a glorious day, more fitted to early autumn than mid-winter, for the sun gleamed in a pale cloudless sky and the snow took on a renewed brightness from its rays. I was very surprised to find it to be only two o'clock, not remembering until then that we had all been up since midnight.

Waldenrath was deserted and we parked along the western side of its square. The houses were mostly marked,

"DANGER! BOOBY TRAPS"

in pink chalk, but some of us entered such as were not in search of loot while others went after chickens. Since we had been reminded about booby traps I had a long pole with which to test the safety of any article I fancied, although there was not much lying about.

Then we were ordered to move back to Stahe on the road between Gangelt and Geilenkirchen. Between Waldenrath and Schierwaldenrath, the Guards Panther, in a hurry, nearly had us in the ditch. We had been carrying a water can on the hot gearbox decking without knowing that it was empty and it chose the moment when the Panther was alongside to blow up, right in the ear of the Guards driver, and he nearly hit us.

My operations on the master switch had given only a temporary respite from trouble. We crossed a narrow bridge over a frozen dike and turned left into the main street of Schierwaldenrath and it went again. Luckily there was room for the rest of the squadron to pass but I could see nothing to give me a lead in the twilight of the turret. Then an HQ tank stopped alongside and Mr. Grundy shouted a question. I was still scrabbling about on the floor of the turret and George's voice blasted in my ear.

"It's the master switch again, sir," he shouted, forgetting that the I/c did not connect with the other tank.

I grabbed my mike and roared back and he removed his headset to receive the map reference, while the rest of us conferred and I scraped a dirty terminal.

It was night before we got in and the sky was hard, the stars bright and very close and the frost that despite the sun had never seemed far away all day was now upon us. We were dog-tired and every routine job - filling up with petrol, changing the gas bottles, getting out bedding and food - was done in a sort of daze. Ted and I were last to leave, having remained to sheet up, and loaded ourselves with our blankets, a frying pan, the compo box, my pistol and his Sten.

A constant succession of cigarettes had left a filthy taste in my mouth but here was food at last. We could smell it as we clambered up the rickety staircase to the loft of a barn. A candle cast a glow on a heap of straw filling half the room. The rest of the floor was littered with broken glass, scraps of paper and general rubbish. The roar of cookers dulled every other sound and the smell of stewed steak and concentrated soup rose from a dozen points. Len had ours ready. Ted and I wolfed it down, scraped our straw into shape, and I was asleep before he had finished making his bed.

* * *

Reveille at 0500 hours. Check net at 0530. Move off at 0630. Word goes round during the night and each crew hears it as they go on guard.

As usual, I am down at the tank before the others, who remain to pack the kit. It takes some time to remove the stiffened sheets and erect the aerial but inside the turret the atmosphere is comparatively snug. I switch on the lights and warm up the wireless, find my notebook containing the daily code signs, the Unicode (rarely used) and the Slidex[97] (never used), and provide myself with a piece of paper in case the command operator gives a special order of answering. That is all for the moment, so I light a cigarette and raise myself to look out of the hatch.

The crew are coming down the road now with their boxes and bundles. Someone throws some kit on to our track guards and shouts for me to pack the blankets. Len leans through my hatch and tells me that Ted is cooking sausage and beans in the billet and that I am to go down and get it as soon as I have finished netting as they want to pack up. I wave him away as the tuning call begins to come over.

It is getting light by the time we have got everything out of the billet and warmed the engine, and ourselves in the exhaust fumes. Dark figures flounder through the snow between the tanks. Little jets of blue flame from the exhausts stab the twilight. Voices are muffled under the roaring engines as the warm-up is done as quickly as possible.

George swings himself aboard with the news that 13 Troop are in reserve at the moment and then the leading tank moves on to the road, barbed wire from the fence tangled in its tracks. There is a halt while the crew get busy with wire cutters. We follow in our turn, jolting down through the snow bank and swinging in close behind the others. The track is just wide enough for the tanks and the snow piled on either side prevents them from sliding.

---

97 Unicode and Slidex. Two types of code for messages and positional references. As stated, they were never used as there was never time, even if we could remember how they worked.

We enter a village, and I look for the name but cannot see it. From George's map I judge it probably to be Birgden. It is now quite light and the first mortar bursts among the ruins to the left of the HQ tank in the van.

Jinx, who is always anxious and always muttering over the I/c, pesters George to close down. I have already closed my hatches and wipe the moisture from my periscope. Ted swears at a Jeep cutting in front of him. More mortars burst nearby. Ted says he is closing his vision block and it is now up to George and I to guide him. His two periscopes are too close to the ground to give him much of a view.

There is chatter on the air about the mine which Mr. Bottomley, now 11 Troop Officer, has exploded with his trailer. He is unlucky, for many vehicles have passed over it before him but now his trailer is leaking and useless and, what seems more important, he has lost his spare compo. We see it lying in the ditch but decide it is not worth the risk of salvage.

A little farther and we have to leave the road to avoid a mined patch. The diversion is deeply rutted and Reg Webb, who has been following us, reports that he is bogged. He is about the last D-Day commander left and we speculate as to whether he is furious or relieved. He has not yet had his leave so we think the latter.

We have now passed through what I take to be Waldenrath and are rolling along a road bordered on the right by shattered trees and on both sides by a steep embankment.

"Shall I warm the Besa?" asks Jinx.
"If you like," agrees George. "Traverse right and have a bash at that wood over there."
"Coming through, Jinx."

I pass the belt and he fires a few rounds. Then the gun jams, as it frequently does before it gets warm. Jinx traverses front to avoid the gun hitting a tree and starts to clear the jam. I throw out a Besa box that has got crushed. Then Sherry calls up and I acknowledge the order for us to go in with 11 Troop while he joins 12. So much for being in reserve but it is what we all hoped and expected.

The tanks in front speed up. The infantry are down in the ditches and shell holes now. The trees and bank have petered out and away to our right is a flat snow-covered field marked on the map as the Heidenderfeld, and in the distance a black cluster of trees and buildings.

"Is that Straeten?" I ask.
"I think so," says George, peering out of his cupola. "Pull right, Ted, and follow Mr. Sherriff."

I switch the Seventy-five safety catch to 'Fire' and through my periscope watch the tanks in front all jumbled together - Crocodiles, Guards gun tanks, Kangaroos - and all zigzagging.

"Have a go with the Seventy-five, Jinx," I urge.
"No, wait a minute!" cries George.

I turn back to my periscope and then there is a tremendous crash and everything blacks out for a moment. Then I find myself back against the wireless. The turret is full of blue smoke and flying glass and things are falling down all over the place. My hatches are wrenched wide open and it is instinctive to reach up to close them but they will not shut properly. I grab at the Bombthrower but it is loose in its mounting and all the screws are falling out. There is a gaping hole where once had been my periscope.

"Smudge is hit!" cries Len, peering up at me.
"Are you all right, Smudge?" asks Ted.
"I think so." I feel around and seem OK. "For Christ's sake - let's get out of here!"

Ted begins to turn right and I find my mike and report. The wireless is working, at least.

"Hullo, Fox Three Baker. I've been hit - can I go back? Fox Three Baker, over."

"What hit you?" asks Sherry. "Did you see it?"
"No. We don't know."
"What is wrong? Where are you hit?"
"I've lost a periscope, lights, fan and - a small weapon."
"Roger. Go back."
"Wilco. Out."

I switch to I/c and speak to George, who has not said a word since we were hit.

"You all right, George?"
"Yes. Yes, I'm all right. Carry on as you are, Ted."

We all had the utmost confidence in the tank and, apart from that, once the hatches were shut the noise and confusion outside was cut off and we were a little world on our own. Now I can see daylight and the illusion of being separated from the battle is shattered; the reality is all the more terrifying in its suddenness. The little hole in the turret roof is only six inches in diameter but it saps my morale completely. Normally I never worried about mortars or any similar weapon hitting the tank - they would just set the sparks flying. Now, I think, if one lands on the roof I'm done. I want to get away from Straeten just as soon as I can and the others, apparently, feel much the same.

The Heidenderfeld is mined, of course, but we reach the road safely and urge George not to stop in Waldenrath, which is still under fire, but to go to the village beyond. If the CO asks any questions we will say that the redcaps kept moving us on to get us out of the way of the traffic.

The road itself is now clear of mines and the Flails which have done the job are standing by some ruined houses at the entrance to the village. 'Sandling' is still bogged on the diversion and Reg stops us to ask for a tow. Of course George cannot refuse his request although the job is a difficult one as it entails reversing over the sticky patch and the trailer keeps swinging from the straight. And there is no help from me, for I still feel very shaken and keep my seat in the turret. George, most tactfully, struggles on and says nothing.

The job is done at last and with Reg heading eagerly in the opposite direction we lose no time in reaching Birgden where it is safe to get out and we can assess the damage.

* * *

There was a deep groove across the fan cover and a chunk taken out of the Bombthrower housing, via my periscope which, of course, had disintegrated. This was all to be seen from the outside and from the size of the groove we judged the gun to have been a Seventy-five or Eighty-eight and congratulated ourselves on the fact that it had not been a few inches lower.

Inside, the ledges of the turret were thick with powdered glass and pieces of twisted metal. The festoon lights dangled picturesquely, the fan hung by one wire, the Bombthrower held itself together somehow. My hatches had been bent back with such force as to wrench the hinges and could not be closed, while the welding at the corners was cracked. We could not understand how this effect had been achieved by what was really a glancing blow. All in all, it was not so bad as it might have been and the tank was still fit for action if necessary.

We had parked in a space in front of an archway between two houses which led to a yard at the back of one of them. In the yard was a brazier and a shed held a pile of coal bricks. It did not take long to get the brazier going and melted snow began to drip from the arch. Len and I fetched chairs and a table from the house while Ted cooked a second breakfast - bacon, sausages, beans and fried bread - an extra special one in celebration.

Jock Wyper, an operator from 14 Troop, appeared in the road as we began and joined us at table. His tank had brewed up, he thought, but he was not very clear as to exactly what had happened. There had been an order to bale out and he had done so but had seen nothing of the rest of his crew. The Kangaroos had been unloading nearby and he had dodged among the infantry and then made for the road as fast as he could, assuming the others would do the same.

After breakfast I felt much better and stood on the corner to watch the columns of prisoners coming back, an oddly clothed assortment. Our own infantry were moving up along the other side of the road, leather jerkins worn inside out, spare socks tucked in their belts, the inevitable pick or shovel hung in the back of their equipment. Presently a scout car came down the road, slowly enough to enable me to get back to the tank and warn the others that the Major was coming.

George immediately flapped in case there was no tea but there was plenty and I managed to find a clean mug. Major Duffy was very cheerful. He came up to the brazier rubbing his hands and accepted the hastily proffered mug as a matter of course. He said that the infantry commander had been most enthusiastic about the flame-throwers and that the Regiment had got all the credit for the capture of Pütt, Waldenrath and Straeten. We were very pleased about this, as it was usual for the Guards to collect any praise that was going and this time it seemed we had done them in the eye. We all talked at once, gave our CO another mug of tea, George told him of our misfortune and he climbed on the tank to view the damage. His view was that we had been very lucky as he had heard that there was an SP around - which was something we had not been briefed about.

He went away after that. About eleven o'clock the rest of the squadron came back, all very cheerful after a successful action. We had a brew ready for our Troop and they told us about Jock's tank, which had returned with the rest. It seemed that the same weapon that put us out of it had taken a crack at the 14 Troop tank. The crew had baled out and then found that only the link was hit and the tank itself was unscathed. There was enough smoke to cover them so they regained their vehicle, although worried about Jock's disappearance, and brought it out.

We stayed in the village while the squadron rested and breakfasted. The houses had been knocked about a good deal and also the civilians had taken everything of value with them. Len and Sherry found a bicycle each and rode races until Len's front wheel buckled. Then he joined the rest of us in searching the houses and struck lucky immediately, finding a tin of cigarettes from someone's compo pack.

By this time a squadron of Canadian Kangaroos had arrived in our street and from the systematic way in which they occupied the houses it was obvious they were going to stay for some time. The thud of mortars could still be heard in the distance and we were not sorry to hear that we were going back to Gangelt as soon as there was room for the column on the road.

We returned to Gangelt that evening. Ted had a row with the HQ Troop sergeant, Sergeant Perry, who had given him some blankets to replace those Ted had lost. Ted swore that HQ Troop had taken the new ones given out by the Q and passed old ones on to him, but he could not prove it and the whole affair was most unpleasant. Ted was always fussy about his blankets.

He and I were on guard in the small hours of the morning. Muffled in our zoot suits, we huddled round the glowing brazier of the MP on duty at the cross-roads. Over towards Heinsburg the sky was illuminated by searchlights and tracer curving towards the German lines. The snow glistened chill in the starlight and although the fumes from the brazier were stifling it provided light, warmth and company, and we stayed close to it.

The squadron was to move out in the morning, leaving us behind to effect repairs. George was going in command of another tank and, much to Len's disgust, a Flamegunner was needed as well. Snug in bed, I listened to the roar of engines and the clank of tracks dying away in the distance and savoured to the full the pleasure of being idle while others worked.

I awoke again about ten o'clock to learn that the welders wanted all the ammunition removed from the tank so that they could get on with their work; since a nasty accident at Bergeijk had given one man bad burns they had always insisted on this precaution. A very reasonable one, indeed, but I cursed them for it as I struggled into my clothes and went downstairs into the biting air. My hands were numb long before I had finished passing the rounds up to Ted, who was piling them on the track guards. Then we doubled back to breakfast, leaving the welders to get on with the job.

Ted and I amused ourselves during the afternoon by setting off an alarm flare which I had picked up. We thought it might be designed to explode, so ran out the full length of the wire and then tugged. It fell off the post to which I had attached it, gave a sharp pop, and diffused a faint pink radiance over the snow. It was so pretty that I wished I had picked up more and made a note to look out for them in the future.

On the evening of the second day the new 'Tech. Q', Staff Sergeant Hemingway, paid us a visit. He enjoyed the reputation among the tank crews of being a very hard man indeed and ordinarily was welcome nowhere, but he could give us news. The squadron, after spending two days killing chickens outside the village it was supposed to take, was now harboured just on our side of Geilenkirchen. The route to join up lay through the scene of the first battles on German soil, through Stahe and Gillrath to Bauchem. He told us that the sooner we got started the better.

In the face of that we consulted Eddie Eldridge, a lance corporal who in some way had been forgotten by the squadron when it moved out the previous morning. He was not very clear how that had happened but we were not curious and as the senior rank he would command the tank. We decided to start.

The tank slid about a good deal but that was only to be expected, and all went well until we were through the straggling ruin that was Gillrath. The road then made a sharp bend to the right, steeply cambered, at the bottom of a hill. It took us about half an hour to get round that corner and then, about ten yards up the hill, we got stuck on another slippery patch. Fortunately, there was very little traffic on the road and we stuffed fencing, ladders and doors under the tracks and finally got her moving again. But about halfway up the hill swung to the left and the tank slid into the bank. More branches and fencing and gates went under the tracks only to be churned out in splinters while the rear of the tank dug itself further in under a notice reading,

"MINES IN VERGES!"

and the trailer was twisted so far round that we were afraid the link would snap. The left side of the tank was nearly down to the air louvre. We stopped for a smoke.

We told Jinx to make a brew while we had another go. Eddie, who was a driver by trade, told Ted to rev like mad and not to touch the tiller bar. Ted let in the clutch with a bang. For a moment the tracks clawed ineffectually, while we frantically threw bits of wood within their grip. Then the tank rocked, started forward, checked and slowly mounted from the rut. Eddie shouted for Ted to leave the tiller bar alone. The tracks clanked and crashed on the frozen ground but the tank was going up the hill. We ran in front shouting and cheering Ted on. The tank slid into the verge again until the furiously revolving track bit in a flurry of snow and mud and shot her out in the middle of the road, to repeat the performance over and over again.

At the crest of the hill we drew off the road and held a consultation. Jinx had the cooker and the dixie but it seemed too much trouble to get a brew going on our own. We decided to approach some artillerymen who were occupying the buildings of a tileyard and we were in luck as they made us free of their rations. They had a roaring fire going and we stuffed ourselves with tea and bread and jam and sat and smoked afterwards without a care in the world.

It was hard to get away. All along the main road to Bauchem it was cold, and grit and low branches stung our faces. Snow draped wrecks of Shermans lay on the verges, heeled over in shattered orchards or blocking alleyways between buildings. Further evidence of the fury of the fighting was provided by Bauchem itself, a dead village, rubble covered by snow. Few houses had escaped complete destruction. In fact, only half a dozen buildings at the far end, nearest Geilenkirchen, were fit for habitation, and were shared by our squadron and a troop of Flails of the Lothian & Border Yeomanry.

In our own house only the ground floor was intact and it was a tight squeeze to get the Troop in. Even then I could not get to sleep in earnest as I had only an hour before my stagger. I went out to join a representative of the Lothians just as a squadron of AVREs coming from Geilenkirchen thundered past along the road, no lights showing and not a sign of life in the turrets. It was a grim and purposeful procession, indicative of our armoured might and the readiness with which it could be switched to the area where it was most needed.

Watching these, swapping yarns with the Lothian, and criticising the antics of a 14 Troop Crocodile, another late arrival, made the time pass quickly. The Crocodile had been trying to get through the gate into our field when I went on guard and was still hard at it when I went off.

CHAPTER 13

INTERLUDE

No one hurried us in the morning and we were all able to get a very necessary wash and shave before breakfast. Then my crew was ordered to stand by to move with 14 Troop officer, Mr. Carroll, in command. He was a new arrival in the squadron and not greatly liked, so we were glad when the move scheduled for ten o'clock was cancelled and instead the news went round that we were released and were to leave the sector altogether.

The rest of the Troop had built a huge bonfire, the principal combustible being a moth-eaten divan from our billet, and we left our tank to go and warm ourselves with the others. It was soon evident that our beautiful zoot suits had one failing - they were inflammable. There were a good many sparks flying about and mine was the first to catch. A big area was burnt out of the right leg before anyone noticed it. The fires were persistent, too, for each little spark had to be destroyed separately as, if one spot was left, it spread rapidly.

I have mentioned that the squadron had been occupied during the previous two days in shooting chickens. The highlight of the action had been when, with the fowls clustered on the side of a railway embankment, half the squadron had been along the top shooting down and the other half along the bottom shooting up. If we were to believe the accounts, only a miracle had prevented a higher mortality rate among the squadron than among the chickens. Len, at the expense of a slight nick on his ear of unknown origin, had secured two bodies as his share and these were hanging from the B-Set aerial base.

The main road from Geilenkirchen back to the Dutch frontier was free from snow, which was not surprising considering the thousands of vehicles that had used it since the falls. In its place was grit which the tracks flung into our faces. The ditches were filled with the wreckage of British and German equipment. The fields were torn with tank tracks, amongst which I distinguished the unmistakable sign of the Tiger. To aid the scores of Five-fives dotted about the countryside, the artillery were bringing up huge American guns: monsters with barrels and carriage on separate transporters.

After the emptiness and desolation of Germany, it was a relief to cross the frontier and see smiling Dutch faces on every side. Even the brown-frocked monks laughed when they saw our chickens and at Merkelbeek we got a grand welcome. One crew had brought a great sofa back for their family, carrying it across the turret, and others had beds, chairs and tables.

We knew that our stay would not be a long one and when Reg Webb informed me that I was on guard that night it was certain that we would move on the morrow. It always seemed to work out that way. Also, they had decided to mount a proper guard and collected us all together in the cold, unused little café on the corner of the square. Confirmation of our fears followed swiftly. In the morning we were to run to Winterslag, load on transporters, and on the following day be taken back to Bergeijk.

I was particularly sorry about the guard as the last evening in our billet had promised to be a jolly one. There were four extremely handsome girls and relations had not been too good at first, for which we blamed the artillery who had preceded us. Ted, whose sister sent him the words of the latest dance tunes as they came out, had offered to copy some of them as the family had heard no English or American music for five years. Christina, the eldest girl, said she did not want soldier's words. This put Ted in a fury and he laid down the law at some length, greatly taxing my powers of translation. Apparently I made them understand that the Baker crew of 13 Troop was a good many cuts above the artillery, for their distrust disappeared after Ted had calmed down. Although George nearly spoiled it by coming in soon afterwards and trying to get a kiss from Teresa. Which was very unlike George and he could not have acted out of character at a more unfortunate time.

The whole village turned out to see us off in the morning and although we were sorry to leave the run was a good one as the wireless produced a lot of tunes we knew. The roads were still extremely treacherous but we had only one moment of difficulty when an air louvre threatened a bay window on a sharp corner.

We got into Belgium, crossed the Albert Canal, and then had a halt. The sergeants were now getting a bottle of whisky each per month and George, who was always generous, passed his round. This increased our sense of well-being as we bowled merrily along the straight main road, all singing at the tops of our voices and suddenly the tank made a run at the ditch. Ted jammed on the brakes, we slid and the grass verge brought us to a halt.

The Fitters always brought up the rear in their Half-track and were always a good way behind as they usually had something to sell, or buy, or scrounge, that delayed them. By the time they arrived we had confirmed our suspicion that the left-hand final drive had broken. This was a workshop job.

About fifty yards ahead was a row of houses with an open space in front and we decided that we ought to get the tank up to this as we were partially blocking the road and a traffic sentry was necessary.

Attempts to move under our own power only brought the tank nearer to the ditch, so George went to a breakdown point along the road and got a Scammell[98] tractor. This, too, had difficulty as the road was so slippery that when winching operations began the Scammell only dragged itself towards the tank.

On the opposite side of the road, alongside the usual tramline, lay heaps of slag deposited by the tiny coal-burning engines. We plied the shovels, spreading the road with cinders and heaping them about the wheels of the breakdown wagon. This gave enough grip to move the tank and started a slide which finished with the air louvre against a tree. It was not a big tree but it had to be felled before we could shift the tank again, and after two hours hard work she slid neatly down the road camber and parked herself as required.

[98] Scammell. Our heaviest wheeled recovery vehicle.

I had already visited a house and cooked dinner there. When it become apparent that we should have to stay in Eisden - that was the name of the village - for one night at least we moved in with our kit.

We liked the mother and father and their two children, Johan and Katerina, immediately. Luckily, I had had a properly iced Christmas cake sent me and this was soon carved up. It seemed the children had never seen anything like it before.

The mother was expecting a third child and her sister, Marthe, came to stay with her every night. Marthe was a school teacher in Eisden, twenty-six, could speak a little English and was extremely attractive. We all became rather keen on Marthe.

George broached the subject of a guard. It was like him to think of something like that just as we were settling in so comfortably. Ted was very short with him - it seemed George was fated to subjection by his drivers. Then I suggested that a hurricane lantern, suitably draped in some red material, would meet the case and that, no doubt, he could obtain one from an MP post I had seen a few hundred yards back down the road.

George, surprisingly, thought this was a good idea and went off on his errand. While he was gone we approached the Fitters - who had commandeered the kitchen and were frying enough pork to feed a Troop - with a view to their taking George back to the squadron with them. They agreed and George himself made no objection. Indeed, the best argument in favour came from him - he said he ought to report the condition of the tank.

The Fitters departed at last. Len had gone with the trailer from Merkelbeek, which left only Jinx, Ted and myself in the house. We had the front room downstairs and our host was busy making mattresses of straw and lighting the pot-bellied stove that was the only article of furniture in that room. 'De moef', he explained, had requisitioned everything else. The evening was very enjoyable. We removed our boots and put our feet up on the stove in the approved manner, got very friendly with Marthe and went to bed late.

However, we had to get up early in the morning for the final drive, we guessed, had only broken through lack of oil. If the Tech. Q came along and discovered that, Ted would be on the mat. So the first task was to locate the filler plug and find that we had guessed right. Then, leaving Jinx to fashion a funnel from a piece of old tin, Ted and I went off in search of oil. We had not far to go for some Shermans of the Northamptonshire Yeomanry had drawn into a field along the road during the night and while we could not get C. 600[99] we did get between three and four gallons of another sort, judging that as long as oil was visible it would not be examined too closely.

With elaborate precautions the final drive was filled, the spillings wiped up, the cap and sprocket rubbed with dirt and snow. I hid the drum in a truck standing on the tramway. This done, we could face the Q. with confidence if he did turn up.

On going back to the house for a wash and a shave, we found that our host had laid out his own razor, soap and lather brush for our use. This touched us, for we knew how short of such articles the civilians were. We took care that he was plentifully supplied with shaving soap before we left and, needless to say, used our own kit then. Apparently it was necessary for us to sit down to shave - he insisted on that part of it.

In the afternoon, just as it was getting dark, the tank was towed down to the workshops which were stationed in Eisden village proper. They wanted us to sleep in what had been a café but it had a black-and-white tiled floor and was cold and cheerless; as we had left our kit back at the house, permission was given for us to remain there. We had tea and walked back.

It was dark, cold and snowing. Jinx was moaning about the distance so we thumbed a Utility Van and piled him into it with such kit as we were carrying and with instructions to take care of it. It was very necessary to give Jinx clear instructions about anything he had to do.

---

[99] C. 600. One of the standard oils used by the tank.

When we got in, he had thrown our kit on to our beds anyhow and I could not see my greatcoat immediately. He supposed he must have left it on the van, and that was all his expression of regret. It was no use swearing at Jinx for he was just not with you a lot of the time. I was very sorry for the loss of the coat, which was a good one with bakelite buttons that saved me a lot of trouble. However, when we got back to Bergeijk Ted told the Q. that it must have been lost in the box with his blankets and as these were 'lost in action' I got a new coat without any trouble.

At last Tech. Q. Hemingway appeared and we definitely came to dislike him for he told the workshops that our tank was urgently needed in the squadron. As a result the workshops spent all night on it and on the third evening we got the unwelcome news that the tank was ready to go and a transporter ready to take us. So we packed our kit, leaving our two chickens which we should have had for supper at the disposal of the family, and said our farewells. Having loaded the tank successfully, we traversed the turret to the rear to get more room and squeezed together on the engine decking, covered in blankets. The engine deck was all right for two but three was a crowd. The inside man could not sit up as the Seventy-five was over his head and he could not lie down comfortably because of the deck fittings. The outside men, apart from the discomfort of the wind whipping round the turret, could sit up at the cost of their feet getting colder and colder.

I pulled a blanket over my head and slept in snatches. Jinx was in the middle, being the smallest, and he grumbled all the time. Villages and towns were still - there was not a gleam of light in any window, no traffic, the purr of the transporter's engine and the creaking of the springs were the only sounds. The countryside was snowed under, which made the route seem strange, the road stretching away behind us as a ribbon of black across the desolate landscape.

So we were thankful to see the windmill by the broad stretch of road that was our unloading point at Bergeijk. The work went smoothly, a muffled shout in farewell was heard from the transporter, and then we sidled past and entered the village.

The road was a mask of ice. The tank slid to each side, slid skew-wise, bumped a house, demolished a telegraph pole and felled a young tree before we coaxed her on to the track into our field. There stood the other tanks, looming against the snowy hedges and swathed in tarpaulins. It was too dark to hunt for our trailer so that was left to the morning.

The engine died and the smell of burning cloth rose from the engine deck. Our blankets had been put into a Five-five box and left there and they had been singed. I laid them out to cool and then felt for the German water bottle hanging by the wireless set and passed round the rum. In the billet the family had heard the noise we made and hot coffee was ready for us.

CHAPTER 14

THE SIEGFRIED LINE

The German offensive in the Ardennes was given as the reason for the delay in clearing the land between the Maas and the Rhine. Our operations from Gangelt had been to give the US 9th Army a foothold for a push northward and now the Americans were ready to move. At the same time 30 Corps, operating as part of the Canadian 1st Army, was ready to push east and south of Nijmegen to clear the Reichswald Forest and, reaching the Rhine at Xanten, to join up with the Americans there.

That part of the main Siegfried Line, with which 30 Corps was concerned, ran from north of Kleve to the Goch area, but there were subsidiary branches to the north and east. However, German troops were thought to number only two divisions, with little armour. Five British and Canadian Divisions were to be concerned in the initial assault, not counting the troops of the 79th Armoured Division that were attached, as usual, to each. 51st Highland Division would clear the South Reichswald and move along the road from Gennep to Goch. 53rd Welsh Division would clear the Reichswald. 15th Scottish Division would pass through the Siegfried Line, take Kleve, and move northwards. 2nd and 3rd Canadian Divisions were to watch the left flank and clear up any pockets north of the Nijmegen-Kleve road, which area was flooded. From then on further movements would be assisted by the 3rd British, 52nd Lowland, 43rd Wessex and 4th Canadian infantry divisions and the 11th and Guards Armoured Divisions. It was hardly fair to call it a Canadian show.

As far as my part was concerned, for the kick-off 15th Scottish Division had attached to it Crocodiles of B and C Squadrons of 141 RAC, a regiment of Flails, the 22nd Dragoons, AVREs of 81 and 284

Assault Squadrons, RE., and Kangaroos of 1st Canadian and 49th Armoured Carrier Regiments.

* * *

Our friends at Bergeijk assured us that we should leave on February 5th, which shows they had good sources of information. They also said that we should be back within a fortnight; so the information they obtained could not always be taken as being correct. We had been warned of an impending move, being particularly cautioned to keep our mouths shut, but it was all round the village just the same.

As well as an increased emphasis on security, the authorities were taking more trouble over traffic control. It seemed that we could only move in the back area at night, so that our departure from Bergeijk was fixed for 22:00 hours on the 5th. This information was first given me, confidently, by Lena. Obeying instructions, I told her she must be mistaken, at which she laughed and when we started to pack our kit, of course the so-called secret was out. Once more we were to experience the sadness of parting from generous friends whom we were never to see again.

We were to travel via Eindhoven and s'Hertogenbosch to the concentration area at Nijmegen. Ted and Len, with many more of our Troop, were going on leave the next day and did not accompany us. I was making up a scratch crew with George and Jack, Fred Bass from Sherry's tank as gunner and 'Slim' Bridge, a newcomer to the Squadron, as Flamegunner.

The night was pitch-black. To help matters, we were ordered to run without lights but this was soon found to be impossible and such tanks as still retained their head lamps switched them on. Even then the darkness seemed to press in on all sides, imprisoning us in our little world of the tank. Ahead was a yard or so of road and a darker shadow that was the ditch and that was all we could see.

After a bit the staff car ahead of us - we were the leading tank - switched on its sidelights and the rear light gave us a lot of help. But to offset this there was a DR, 'Yorky', also with a rear light, between us, and he roamed from side to side, distracting Jack, who needed every ounce of concentration. Jack kept swearing. Then the tank surged forward, right up behind the DR, and we had almost hit him before he realised his danger. He spurted to safety and Jack swore again - I think he really meant to have him. Anyway, at the first halt Yorky came back full of complaints but was met by such a storm of abuse that even his dialect was stifled. We had no more trouble - he dropped back to the rear of the column.

There were other worries - a night run under such conditions was a nerve-wracking business. We drove beneath avenues of trees, every low branch plucking at us and the worst of all looming out of the darkness to sweep us off the turret but never materialising. Through sleeping hamlets, mazes of twists and turns where the tank seemed to be going round in circles and the streets seemed to get narrower and narrower while we wondered if we would end up in the canal. Over flimsy bridges, a lamp at each end and no more to be seen but the dim outline of the railing an inch from the air louvre and the dull water rolling below.

As always at night, Jeeps were a great nuisance with their blazing headlights. Encountering the first of these just before Eindhoven, we remembered the transporter crews and every tank got out its spotlight. The next offender received a concentration of light full in his face, shot past us with a foot to spare, and finished on the verge with his headlights dipped. Why Jeeps had to behave so discourteously I cannot understand.

However, by the time we got through Eindhoven the night had cleared a bit and we could see reasonably well. The road to s'Hertogenbosch was straight as a rule could make it and the countryside inexpressibly dreary and desolate with flat, dyked heath land dotted with silent pine woods. Having so little to take my attention I chanced to look behind and saw a Hellesen lamp being flashed on the following tank and smoke pouring from our offside trailer tyre. I grabbed my mike and called to Jack to stop. The rest of the squadron rumbled past as we jumped down. There was an overpowering stench of burning rubber. The trailer tyres were run-flats, but not as flat as that. A great spike was driven into the tread.

The Fitters halted behind us, tumbled leisurely out of their Half-track, and stood around with their hands in their pockets. The most they could do was to promise to send back a spare as soon as they caught up with the echelon. Then they moved off without waiting for a brew so as to keep ahead of B Squadron, which could be heard on the road. Presently the tanks passed, the huddled figures in the turrets regarding us without much interest. It was then about two o'clock in the morning. The moon was up, but a thick mist was creeping slowly along the dykes towards the road.

We had no jack, but the road was bordered with flat paving stones and we took up some of these and jammed them under the trailer. Then we dug a hole beneath the wheel. By the time this was done a truck had come back with a new wheel and to make the change was the hardest task of all.

The change was complete about five o'clock and we started off again. The mist had come down thickly and the few trees stood out above it like ghostly sailing vessels upon a silver sea. The road was covered and from his seat Jack could not see a yard unaided. We had to use the spotlight, cutting a path through the fog and throwing gigantic shadows upon the grey eddying wall.

Now we were safely behind the squadron it was decided, at my suggestion, to stop for breakfast at Heesch and in spite of the fog Jack pushed the tank as hard as he could so as to get there before eight o'clock when Zussie would have to go to work. Houses and trees came out of the fog and vanished again. A sign, tacked to a tree, attracted the spotlight. There were plenty:

"SLOW! BAD BUMP!"

"SLOW! NARROW BRIDGE!"

"DANGER! BAD BENDS!"

or simply:

"DIVERSION"

And the repetitive:

"MAPLE LEAF UP"

every few hundred yards.

S'Hertogenbosch was a maze of twists and turns with hundreds of signboards which we had no time to decipher. Corners leapt out of the fog, the engine screamed, gears clashed and clanged, the tracks groaned and shrieked as we swung round, crushing the kerbstones. Then over the canal and along the road to Heesch. The Dutch did not seem to have done much to clean up the town. We passed our former harbour and there was still bits of the crashed Typhoon in the street. The German field kitchen was still there. The body in the grass was gone, though.

Dawn was cold and hazy, with grey storm clouds hanging low over the pine woods. Several tanks were broken down along the road. Their crews were busy cooking breakfast and took no notice of us. Jack did well, because it was exactly eight o'clock when we passed Heesch church, the spire of which had long been visible.

The family were all very pleased to see us and we had a good breakfast with them. I assured Zussie that I would be back in a fortnight - perhaps. 'Perhaps' was an indispensable word in all our dealings with civilians because, obviously, we could never be definite about our movements. So 'peut-être' in France became 'misschien' in Holland and was to become 'vielleicht' in Germany, and very useful words they were! As it happened, it was as well I qualified my statement for that was the last time I saw Zussie.

When we had finished waving goodbye I got down into the comparative dryness of the turret and tuned the wireless to catch a recording of 'La donna é mobile' followed by Mary of Arnhem's[100] husky and attractive voice.

Turning the dial brought a man repeating, "Hullo Box I for Item. Hullo Box I for Item. There are no messages for Box I for Item." We could not understand this but Fred suggested it was meant for some resistance group and that seemed the most likely explanation.

The Rijksweg to Nijmegen was a broad main road in good repair but covered with sticky, slimy mud and in no time our faces, hands and clothes were caked. George had no rear wing on his side and the centre parts of the track guards were missing anyway, so that in no time his battle dress was ruined, for he was not wearing a zoot suit. He had to get a new uniform when we caught up with the echelon. However, the route was straightforward: no diversions, no bumps, no Baileys. We had only to follow the Rijksweg until we reached the Grave bridge.

Coming from a country where there are few large rivers, and from a part of that country where there are none at all, continental bridges always fascinated me. I do not know what I expected to see but the monstrous structure of grey steel girders at Grave, span after span receding into the distance, gaunt, grim and bare above the featureless countryside, seemed unreal and almost uncanny. It was as if a giant Meccano set had been laid out at the bottom of the garden and left there in the rain. Gliders were standing about in the fields around, relics of the first push into Holland and with their rotting fabric and broken spars they added to the impression of abandonment.

It was drizzling as we climbed the approach to the bridge and we stopped there to adjust sheets over the front hatches and extend them as far over the turret as we could. The crew of a Bofors gun placed below the embankment were curious about us and we attempted to find out if they had seen any of our tanks. However, it appeared that to them one tank was much like another.

[100] Mary of Arnhem. This lady played us music and tried to convince us that the Germans were going to win the war and that the Americans were letting us down in all sorts of ways. She always sounded very pleasant.

Nijmegen, as we approached the town, was plastered with signs:

"DIVERSION"

"ALL CORPS TROOPS REPORT HERE"

"NO ENTRY"

"ALL CONVOYS REPORT HERE"

and so on. Then there were the more imaginative efforts of the Canadians who far surpassed their allies in the art of erecting signs. One huge board invited us to:

"SPEND YOUR HOLIDAYS IN THE NIJMEGEN SALIENT
MODERN FLATS (MUD)
ALL WITH HOT AND COLD WATER (MOSTLY COLD)
LET US PLAN YOUR VACATION FOR YOU
THERE ARE EXTENSIVE TOURS TO BERLIN AND BEYOND
AND LARGE PARTIES ARE ESPECIALLY CATERED FOR
ALTHOUGH BABIES IN ARMS CANNOT BE ALLOWED."

There was a lot more but we had not the time to read it all.

No one knew anything certain about Crocodiles, although far too many people had seen them and if we believed all we were told they had been passing all day in every possible direction. The rain was now coming down in torrents. We parked the tank near a sign reading

"INFORMATION POST"

with a large arrow giving a choice of three forks and while George went to find it, the rest of us took shelter beneath the overhanging front of a petrol station.

He was gone a long time and I entered a house to make tea. I suppose the inhabitants of Nijmegen had got used to British soldiers - in fact, the 49th Division had been in the town since its liberation and was now known as 'The Nijmegen Home Guard'. At any rate, there was no running out to look at the tank, nor urgent invitations to 'kom binnen bij de kachel'. The lady who finally admitted me had a gas stove and I plonked down the dixie and turned up the gas. She protested that the gas had to be turned off at midday and, anyway, she was only allowed so many inches, or whatever it was. I said 'nix verstaan' whenever I could get it in, until the water boiled, and gave her a cake of soap which, at the current rate of exchange, left her with no cause for complaint.

When I got outside with the steaming dixie, I found that George had returned and although he had no definite location there were a lot of suggestions and possibilities. The most likely place appeared to be Bergendaal, on the Arnhem road and we decided to try this place first.

After several attempts to find the right road, the one we took eventually led steadily downhill, through thickly wooded country, and quickly degenerated into a muddy track winding past countless vehicles parked wherever space was available. I do not know how many tanks were massed at Nijmegen, although I heard later that the contribution of 79th Armoured Division alone amounted to 560 tracked vehicles; anyway, there seemed to be thousands. One squadron area would be a hive of activity with men carrying ammo boxes, jerricans and compo boxes, others probing under lifted engine hatches, still others heaving at a bogged truck. In the next area all the tanks would be sheeted, bunched in the space the size of a football pitch, gun muzzles thrusting from beneath the enveloping tarpaulins, a disconsolate figure wreathed in tobacco smoke huddled on the lee side.

We could see water gleaming through the trees and it dawned upon us that we were approaching the vast inundated area north of Nijmegen. We had heard vague reports of this. Some said the Rhine had burst its banks, others that the German had deliberately flooded the area. Probably it was a bit of both and we had no wish to get too close to it.

Half a dozen AVREs were parked near the bottom of the hill, their crews bundling fascines on to a sledge. We stopped to consult them - at least they were in our Division. Ahead, the track curved out of sight among the woods and there were no more vehicles to be seen.

George enquired about this and the Engineers admitted that they were the most forward tanks in the area.

This was confirmed by an infantry sergeant who happened to be passing. He then informed us that the forward positions of his company were dug in just around the corner and that from there on the open country was under observation. We were preparing to turn when an Engineer officer ran up to us and did his nut with George. Apparently an artillery barrage had been laid on specially so that he could bring his tanks down without detection, and here we were making a hell of a racket and letting the Germans know that tanks were about.

George, to his credit, stood his ground. He pointed out that there were no warning signs, that hundreds of people had seen us and made no attempt to stop us, that if we had not stopped his own men would have been quite content to see us go by. Tactfully, he refrained from expressing the opinion that probably the Germans knew perfectly well that tanks were present. All in all, we felt he won the argument and once we had the tank turned we lost no time in getting away.

Back into Nijmegen. I was very tired and could hardly keep my eyes open. I remember watching a dog run across the road, barking at the tank. It did not come from anywhere, or go anywhere; it was just there, barking, and then vanished. Then a scout car shot by us and halted at the kerb. An arm waved peremptorily from the hatch. We drew in behind and Major Duffy descended stiffly to the pavement. The squadron was harboured in one of the suburbs of Nijmegen and we were no more than ten minutes run from it.

The main street of this suburb was occupied by the Scots Guards. Their Churchills were being loaded with extra ammo - they even had 2-inch Smoke bombs strapped outside the turrets - spare compos, twenty-four hour packs, boxes of tins of self heating cocoa and soup. All these preparations indicated a big push and breakthrough with no prospect of a speedy return to civilisation and would have impressed us had we not believed the Guards to be nothing but a bunch of show-offs.

In a nearby field Buffaloes[101] of the Royal Engineers were being unloaded. Tables and chairs, beds and mattresses, emerged from the roomy interiors to make way for field guns and tractors that stood waiting.

Our own tanks lined two small streets. Nearby, a Bailey Bridge mounted on a Churchill chassis, from which it could be lowered by a hydraulically operated arm, occupied the front garden of a large house. Flails of the 22nd Dragoons were parked in an adjacent avenue.

One advantage of having so many units in such a small space was the spreading of duties. The Scots Guards, typically, did all the 'staggers' except at mealtimes when we and the 'Dinky-Doos' patrolled the area.

After spending an uncomfortable night in a school already overcrowded with guardsmen we secured a house of our own near the tanks. In the school, the Guards had taken all the rooms on the ground and first floors, which left us only the lofts. Ours was particularly dark and gloomy and, coming in late, our crew had missed the best positions. My own bed was in a corner by a rafter, I had to use a candle all the time and water dripped into a bucket at my feet. When we moved to the house we were still cramped but it was snug and warm, with electric light and thick felt covering the floor.

Having sorted out our domestic arrangements we set about replacing the temporary trailer wheel. To start well, the new wheel got away from us and bowled down the road. Fortunately, it finished up against a tree that withstood the shock. We lugged it back to the trailer and were sweating to raise it into position when an officer, looking very important, came marching down the street and demanded to speak to the Troop Sergeant. Since Reg Webb was on leave George held this office. The newcomer explained that he was Officer

[101] Buffalo. The Buffalo LVT (Landing Vehicle, Tracked) was an American amphibian, driven in the water by its tracks. It was very lightly armoured so it could not be considered a tank. It was also very noisy and somewhat unreliable mechanically. It could carry 30 infantry, or a Carrier or 25-pounder, so it was a very useful assault vehicle across muddy ground or, of course, rivers.

I/c Camouflage, 30 Corps, and that when flying over the area that morning he had had no difficulty in distinguishing our tanks. He was quite pleasant about it and asked us to improve our camouflage more as a request than a command. As we could not remember seeing any German aircraft since New Year's Day it did seem more cautious than perhaps was necessary but George promised that we would do the best we could within the limits of being able to work on the tanks. This seemed to satisfy the officer. He went away and we returned to our wheel.

Major Duffy held a briefing in the school that afternoon. The squadron filed in and lined the walls while maps were being pinned up and the Major studied his notes. After a brief speech couched in his usual disjointed sentences touching upon security and camouflage, he discovered a pair of twins in his audience, Milner by name, who had recently joined us. So there was an interval while he asked their names and enquired if they were ever mistaken for each other.

Returning at last to the business in hand, he informed us that over the next fortnight we were all in for a very rough time, with little sleep, lack of food, heavy opposition and any other discomforts that could occur. We were attached to 15th Scottish Division which was to breach the Siegfried Line and capture Kleve. It was essential that the operation be launched as a complete surprise and be carried out as speedily as possible. Delay might enable the Germans to move two parachute regiments which were holding a more northern sector. Should the attack be successful and Kleve fall according to plan, then the war would be over within a month.

Although we had had many evening discussions of our plans for after the war this was the first time anyone had given us an idea of a date, even though it was coupled with a proviso. I do not think many of us believed it would all be over as soon as that although no one thought of failure, given the impression of overwhelming strength assembled around Nijmegen. In any case, success and failure were concepts too definite to be assessed at our level, unless it was something like Arnhem or the Falaise Gap where the result was apparent to all.

On the rare occasions when I thought about the matter at all I recollected that if anything went wrong I should not have to take the can back save in one sense which, despite my fright at Straeten, it was no good worrying about. So waiting to attack was never the strain I thought it might be. Normal life went on, except that we had more leisure than usual as the tanks were fit and there was no more to be done. We lounged about the billet reading, writing letters and playing cards. I remembered that my father told me that in the 1914 - 18 War he always spent every franc he had before going over the top, in case he was unlucky. Perhaps this philosophy was adopted by the card-players. If it was, it was the only preparation made.

* * *

The Troop briefing given by Sherry was merely a repetition of what the Major had told us, with the addition of more important details such as times of netting and moving off and order of march. All kit except blankets, food and cookers had been packed already. Even the camouflage netting was rolled up at nightfall and strapped to the side of the turret to do duty as spaced armour.

At about four o'clock on the morning of February 8th someone switched on the light and we woke up gradually to remember where we were and what we had to do. I groped for my cigarettes. Someone was already moving about in another room, pumping a cooker. Voices were muffled. Feet stumbled on the stairs. I lay back and puffed smoke at the ceiling but there was not much time to lie in bed.

Dressing hurriedly, I snapped a boot lace. I took more care in folding my blankets than ever I did in the Training Regiment, for there was not much room in the back bin in which to squeeze sixteen blankets, four ground sheets and five greatcoats. Not to mention such oddments as an aircraft recognition sheet, steering brake slings, a flue brush (use unknown) and a spare Methyl-bromide bottle.

Lurching outside with my arms full, I tripped over a wire, bumped against a gatepost and barked my shins on a derelict air louvre. It was not a good start. I groped my way across the road, hoisted my bundle on to the track guard and clambered up beside the turret. My flaps were shut tight. I felt my way to the rear, unscrewed a shovel and prised them open.

Then I put on the master switch and a faint glow from the instrument panel illuminated the front compartment. I switched on the turret lights, opened the cupola, tested the wireless, and then remembered that I had forgotten to clean the periscopes the previous day and that had to be done. As there were eight in the cupola, two for Jack and one each for the rest of us it took some time. Then on to the engine deck again to pack the rest of the blankets which Fred had brought over. That done, I swept a few odds and ends into the pannier and went over to the house to get my breakfast. The crews were taking a last look round and it seemed that a lot of men had lost their jack-knives, which had an irritating habit of disappearing but never before in such quantities. One man was hunting everywhere for his mess tins. Gradually the rooms emptied.

I finished breakfast, gathered the remnants of kit and went back to the tank. What was claimed to be the biggest artillery barrage of the war, over a thousand guns firing for five hours, was scheduled to begin at five o'clock when the leading troops crossed the start line. We were to move at six.

We hardly noticed the gunfire above the racket all the tanks were making in warming up. Jack was peering into the gearbox compartment by the light of a Hellesen lamp. Fred was adjusting his firing gear. Slim and George were fastening the trailer sheet. Then someone came hurrying down the road telling each tank to get ready to move. Moments later the engine of the tank in front roared in crescendo, the exhaust belching blue flame, and the tank lurched on to the road. We followed, Slim swinging himself up by the Seventy-five as we started to move. This was it. We were going to finish the war.

The streets were still dark. The sky was black in contrast to the flashes of exploding shells which silhouetted the trees and housetops. Infantry plodded beside us at the edge of the road. A column of Carriers was stopped at a cross-roads to let us by. A scout car made vain attempts to pass the tanks in front. An officer was standing on the pavement and shaking his fist at us.

I asked George to tell me when it was ten minutes to seven so that I could get ready to net the wireless and down in the turret I studied my list of code signs under the glimmer of a festoon light. It was warm there and I was glad that netting took a long time, as it always did out of harbour. I sorted out a packet of biscuits to go with a bar of chocolate.

Then we were out of the worst of the traffic and thundering down the main road. Held up again. Through and speeding up. "Christ - you nearly had that Jeep, Jack! See that bloody Jeep, George? Turning right here, Jack - take a wide sweep." On, and out of the town. The houses were straggling and we were turned off the road into a tank track. A sign read:

"SUN ROUTE UP"

It was getting light by then; a grey, cold, misty dawn with the smell of rain. Now we were out in a wasteland of gorse, blackberry brambles and coarse rank grass with here and there a cluster of stunted trees and bushes. On both sides of the track was dispersed a regiment of Sexton SP guns, muzzles lifted in expectation. The farthest fired, and flame and pale smoke rippled down the line. We passed near enough to hear the clang of breech blocks opening and ejecting spent cases and the shouts of the gunners.

Then our tanks were halted at the top of a rise and our bogies were submerged in grey mud through which a few belated infantry were wading. There were a few houses scattered among trees and on our right a children's playground with swings, slides and roundabouts. Jack suggested a brew but when I looked for the dixie which had been stowed on the gearbox deck it was missing.

This was a crisis. Then Fred suggested that there was a tin of biscuits on the trailer and I should dump them and use the container. I jumped down and sloshed back for it, hoping my boots were proof against the slime. I shoved a couple of packets into my pockets but the rest, to my regret, had to go into the mud. Back to the tank and I filled the tin from the water cans which were already nearly boiling, while Jack got the cooker going. Then we were moving again, with Slim holding brew can and cooker in place and burning his fingers in a good cause.

The next halt seemed to be the start line. I stood up in the turret and had a good look round, sipping the scalding tea. An immense ploughed field, filled with tanks, was intersected with paths on which Jeeps, Carriers and anti-tank guns were jumbled together. Forlorn wrecks of gliders lay everywhere, tattered and rotting skeletons. The infantry stood about, loaded with equipment. There was no talking or laughing and very little smoking. They just stood and watched us and when I imagined myself in their place I did not like the idea.

The Guards were moving and we followed, losing sight of the infantry behind the woods. The going was very sticky and the pace slow for the tanks had churned up the ground everywhere. A Flail lay almost on its side, the crew regarding their situation helplessly. In a hollow two columns converged, with consequent confusion. Heavy tanks wallowed in the mud, Honeys lurched about trying to find a way out of the tangle. We saw 14 Troop crossing our front and waved.

Then came a very steep bank. The Valentine SPs sped up the slope without effort. An AVRE, loaded with a Bailey Bridge, followed and I thought it must turn over, but it reached the top in safety and disappeared. Then it was our turn. Two of our tanks were bogged at the top and a bulldozer also stuck when it tried to pull them out. We could see the Bailey Bridge ploughing on without effort - the weight at the front was keeping the back up and helping where I had expected it to hinder. A big Guards major came stumbling past, almost knee deep in mud, and we heard him shouting to one of his tanks. Over towards the Siegfried Line there was a brew up and an Eighty-eight was thought to be responsible.

From where we stood there was a gentle slope of ploughed land, downwards for about half a mile, and then flat country, blurred and indistinct under haze and smoke, stretching as far as we could see. This flat ground was also dotted with glider wrecks, with here and there a burnt-out vehicle and ruined farm buildings. Away to our right the black mass of the Reichswald lay along the horizon.

Shells were falling in front of us. A Guards tank lay on its side blazing furiously with a broken track flung upwards like the sail of a windmill. Smoke wafted across the landscape, enveloping the burning wreck as ammunition exploded. The turret lay a dozen yards from the hull, and green, red and yellow flares gleamed spasmodically. We heard later that commander, operator and gunner had been blown out with the turret and had miraculously survived.

We moved on, past some M10s standing by a house at the foot of the slope. Their turrets had open tops and the crews had got into a ditch for cover - they would not trust to the galvanised iron weather shields that had been rigged on some of the tanks. The house was burning.

Our squadron waited in a slight depression beyond. The Germans seemed to be concentrating on the M10s and the Guards tanks sweeping across the plain. It seemed a good moment to refill the brew can and as we wished to conserve the water in the turret tank I got on to the engine deck to do so. This was silly. Every gun in the Siegfried Line seemed to be banging away at me. My hands were shaking and much more water went into the gearbox compartment than into the tin. I lost very little time in getting back to the turret and studied the battlefield through my periscope after that.

There were glider wrecks everywhere. Tattered fabric flapped in the wind. Girders and struts were warped and split, wings and tail assemblies snapped off and tangled with the parent body. A Panther tank stood beneath a hedge. It looked undamaged but the hatches were open and a still form lay beside the track. A lorry was half out of a copse, its bonnet riddled with bullet holes, the windshield shattered. A Half-track standing clear of the gliders had a great hole torn in its side. Among the gliders, but thickest about the Half-track, lay German soldiers, green and black flesh rotting and mouldering. They must have been there since the gliders landed and we guessed the airborne troops had boobytrapped them. It was all rather horrible. The tanks avoided the bodies where they could but as I watched a tank swerved, the rear gave a little curtsey in the mud and the track touched a tin helmet. What lay below the helmet just fell to pieces.

Amongst other things we had been briefed to flame the village of Kranenburg, on the Nijmegen-Kleve road and railway. We now received the order to move against this place but the going was becoming increasingly difficult. Incessant rain and, no doubt, the nearby flooding, had turned the ploughed ground into slush and we were down to the air louvres in places. It was not surprising, therefore, that in swerving to avoid some gliders we bogged down. Steve O'Neill, just returned from leave, bogged the Able tank a hundred yards further on. Not one of our tanks reached Kranenburg.

In fact, there were bogged tanks all the way from Nijmegen to the Siegfried. There were not nearly enough ARVs to serve them all and those that there were had to work in couples. So it looked as if we were in for a long wait. On the positive side, it seemed as if our area was now out of range of German guns because for some time it had been quiet. So we decided to have a look around although I had to stay close to the tank to listen for the wireless. All I found was a loading scale outside one of the gliders, which was interesting but of little value. The others roamed farther afield and I sat on the track guard and watched them prying among the gliders.

Then a piece of cloth fluttered from a crater on my left. I saw it before the others, jumped to the ground, pulled out my pistol and ran to where four dishevelled and woebegone figures trudged with a handkerchief tied to a shovel. I was so excited at having four prisoners all to myself that my hands were shaking and I doubt if the pistol would have been much use had I needed it. As it was, there was no need. Their leader, a corporal, spoke in English.

"Please put that thing away," he said. "We shall not hurt you. We are surrendered."

Perhaps he did not mean to sound condescending but if he did then he was, perhaps, unwise as he could not know what my reaction would be. In fact, I took no notice and his words only served to steady my nerves and I kept the pistol ready until the others rushed up. My share of the takings was a wristwatch, unfortunately with one of the shoulders missing but otherwise in good working order. As always on such occasions, I felt pretty mean but if I did not take it someone else would and I had more right to it than anyone except its original owner. He did not seem to care, anyway. No doubt they were all very pleased to be out of it.

Although we had four prisoners we had no means of dealing with them so we told them to walk towards Groesbeek and report to the first infantry they saw. The last we saw of them they were heading in the right direction with the white flag still much in evidence.

By the time the ARVs - ours and that of B Squadron - had got up to us it was growing dark. To make the task of extricating bogged tanks the harder, we discovered that the airborne troops had wired up a lot of hand grenades as booby traps and, obviously, my friends had been lucky not to encounter these during the afternoon. The ARVs, shunting about among the gliders, frequently exploded these unpleasant contraptions.

Our tank was dragged forward, we unhitched, moved about twenty yards and bogged again. Then the whole process was repeated and it was only at the third attempt that we reached ground that seemed to be able to take our weight. By this time it was completely dark and with darkness came rain. We huddled in the tank and waited for Steve to declare himself ready to move. The water seeped through the sheets covering the hatches and dripped on our heads and shoulders. I switched on the wireless and although it hissed and crackled and weird oriental music had infiltrated on to our frequency, I managed to contact the HQ tank commanded by Mr. Grundy who was nursemaid to our Troop. He ordered us to move over to the forest on our right where we should find a road running along the edge. Somewhere along that road we should find the Fitters' Half-track.

I passed this information to Steve, saying that we were moving off. He acknowledged this and we started. The track through the minefield had once been clearly marked with white tapes but now these were so bedraggled and trampled down that it was only just possible to distinguish them. So we reached the road more by luck than judgement.

George went off on foot to look for the Fitters and I turned my back to the driving rain and peered through the darkness for a sign of Steve. At first I could see only the dim outlines of gliders but presently there was a flash of light, such as is made by a Hellesen, which seemed to be moving in our direction. I called him up,

"Hullo Peter Three Baker, message for Peter Three Able. Is that you with the light? Peter Three Baker, Peter Three Able, over."

"Hullo Peter Three Able, yes, over."

"Then pull to your right a bit. You'll be on the minefield in a minute."

"Thanks. Where are you?"

"On the road. Keep going as you are now."

A little later a dim shape crept up on my left.

"Turn to your right now and you'll be on the road," I said.

"Is that you on my right?" he asked.

"Yes. You're OK now. Out."

Presently Steve came across to us and we told him where George had gone. He expressed the opinion that no one but George would be wandering about on a night like this, looking for something that might be miles away - and was, if Steve knew the Fitters. And why did we want them, anyway. This was a question we could not answer although we presumed it was because the Fitters generally knew where everybody was, or where they ought to be.

He also had a good story about the Guards, several of whose tanks had been bogged near his. Andy Stevens, his temporary driver, was a recent arrival in the squadron - I had known him at Montague. He had no zoot suit and Mr. Childs, our acting Troop Officer, (Sherry was in command of the other half-squadron), had lent him his suit with the lieutenants pips still attached. Andy was oldish and weather-beaten and, prior to the recovery of their tank, he had been accosted by a young second-lieutenant of the Guards who had taken him at pip-value, saluted him and suggested they jointly mount a guard. Andy, of course, had been warned by the salute, but he had the presence of mind to respond indignantly that his men were far too busy to be bothered with guards or any nonsense like that. The officer accepted this rebuff, saluted, and retired into the night.

While we were laughing over this anecdote, heavy footsteps mounted the tank. George put his head through the cupola. He was soaked to the skin and had been unable to find the Fitters. We were of the opinion that they were probably back in Nijmegen by this time and passed a few bitter remarks about them and a few more about the weather. Then Steve went back to his tank and left us to settle down for the night. Fred, George and the two in front were soon asleep but I had to call up the HQ tank every half hour in case there was an order to move. This meant that I could only sleep in snatches and I found my new watch most useful.

The night dragged on. A dim light glowed in the roof from the festoon in front of the wireless set. Water dripped through my hatch and collected in muddy pools on turret ring and floor. George was seated on his pedestal, his legs tucked up as much as possible, his head thrown back against a girder, his face haggard and very dirty. Fred was hunched upon the gunner's seat, an arm thrown over the Seventy-five, his cheek resting against the breech. I reached up a grimy hand and switched on the wireless. It whined into life and the ruby light gleamed. My ears tingled as I settled the headset in place. The code sign was changed after midnight. I grasped the microphone.

"Hullo, King Three Baker, anything for me? King Three Baker, over."

Faintly across the distance a voice whispered, "Hullo King Three Baker, no, out."

My head sank back against the wall as the wireless died and in a moment I was asleep again.

* * *

Morning could not come any too soon. Our breakfast meal was bacon, which we cooked and ate in a ruined house beside the garden gate of which we found we had parked. It was not until afterwards that we discovered the bodies of two Germans lying on the ruins of their Spandau in the back room.

These soldiers had been well armed. Apart from the Spandau the room was littered with bazookas - the primitive 'panzerfaust' - lying under the rubble and stacked against the wall. We took great care to avoid them, not knowing how much it took to set them off.

The day was clear and pleasant after so much rain. I called up on the hour and got instructions to join the other tanks on the other side of the great plain which the gliders occupied. The going was very sticky at first so that several times we narrowly escaped being bogged again. At length we got on to a fairly firm track with no impediment save old parachutes. These were a new and unexpected obstacle which tangled in our tracks and wound themselves round the hubs of the trailer wheels. Improbable as it sounds, more than once we had to descend with machetes, knives and wire cutters to liberate an immovable wheel or to prevent the track guards being torn from their mountings by the tenacious silk.

Near the spot where our track joined another - slightly firmer, and which by exercising imagination could be termed an extremely poor road - three of our tanks lay about in varying states of submergence. We made insulting gestures to the crews and then Mr. Grundy directed us to take the road to our right and go towards 'a prominent object'. George told me to say we understood but on looking around quite a few objects struck us as being prominent. There was a church, a wooded hill, a railway line and Kranenburg itself, just for a start.

We need not have worried. The road was very narrow, with deep ditches on either side filled to overflowing with ice-coated water. Upon crossing the railway line we found our advance blocked by a column of lorries. The officer in charge told us it was a Brigade HQ and could not move.

Steve turned upon the level crossing. It was pouring with rain again and I was down in the turret, a sheet over my open hatch, calling our officer and giving him the information. The tank dipped into a ploughed field to essay the turn and for some moments we forged ahead. Then I felt the tank shudder as the tracks raced and I pushed my way out of the turret to see the crew abandoning ship as she went straight down. I went knee-deep as I leapt after them. Struggling free, I turned expecting to see the mud closing over the turret. The top of the track was level with the surface of the ground and there the tank rested.

We looked at the tank and we looked around us. The road from Nijmegen to Kranenburg was already under water, the only traffic consisting of DUKWs[102] and Amphibian Jeeps,[103] and the floods were creeping towards the railway. Some Guards tanks bogged between us and the road were already lapped by water. The only sign of a habitation fit for human beings was the ruined house of the railway worker who had been in charge of the level crossing. Then from somewhere nearby came the unmistakable stutter of a Spandau and with one accord we ran for that shelter.

There was a cellar half filled with junk and a heap of rotting potatoes. There was a lean-to that formerly might have been a bicycle shed. Apart from these apartments the house was demolished, three walls and the roof having fallen in.

We found a stove among the rubble and rigged it in the shed. The roof leaked and the floor was a quagmire. While the others were salvaging chairs and a table and trying to stop the worst of the leaks in the lean-to, Fred and I took shovels and descended to the cellar. When cleaned out, the place was quite habitable but the dampness of the brick floor made bedsteads a priority requirement.

The lean-to was filled with smoke from the rusty stove. There were a couple of chairs, a plank on two boxes and an old table. Slim was nailing up a tarpaulin to do duty as a door. Outside, the Spandau chattered spasmodically. It made us nervous, especially as Jack swore

---

[102] DUKW. Amphibian six-wheeled cargo vehicle, propeller driven when swimming.

[103] Amphibian Jeeps. A development of the normal Jeep. This was the only time that I saw them.

it had taken a pot at him. But we had to have beds and Fred and I set out to find them.

It was not so difficult as we had feared. Just up the road but hidden by the trees was a row of cottages which were all in ruins but had been occupied by troops. There were bales of hay and plenty of beds and all we wanted was the frame and spring. Four men could squeeze on to two of these and George had volunteered to sleep in the lean-to.

When we reached our billet, carrying our booty, we found our number augmented. An artilleryman, whose Weasel[104] had broken down on the level crossing, was making himself at home with us. Fortunately, he elected to share the lean-to with George, and after this decision had been reached we all became very friendly and asked him to share our dinner. In the event, we fed him for the duration of our stay. I never found out what he was supposed to be doing and he did not seem worried.

In the afternoon Jack inspected the Weasel, which had clutch trouble and was of the opinion that he could repair it. This was comforting, as the floods were rising fast and now we could take to the boats if necessary. He and the driver worked all the afternoon and at teatime reported that they were making progress. By late evening Jack had got it going and just before dark he offered to give me a ride. We got on to the field and were doing fine until he did not see a crater. In trying to get out the clutch went again and then we began to think about mines and the Spandau and left it with its tail sticking in the air. But at least it would still float.

The country round about was still unsettled. All afternoon the infantry had been winkling out snipers, including one nest about a quarter of a mile from us along the railway and another right opposite Mr. Childs' tank, which was bogged further down the road. They could not find the Spandau and it continued to prey on our nerves.

[104] Weasel. A small, tracked amphibian. The nearest equivalent to the Carrier manufactured by the Americans. We did not see many of them.

George went away with Mr. Grundy in the evening to visit Kranenburg where the echelon was supposed to be harboured. He said he would try to collect our rum ration, which had accumulated as there was an issue every day it rained. So we said we would wait up for his return.

It was a black, windy night. Rain lashed against the tin roof of the lean-to and dripped on to the stove which half blinded us with its smoke but at least gave out some heat. It was impossible to read and there was nothing to do but talk and not much to talk about. A happy thought led us to open the two remaining tins of self-heating cocoa, which was delicious but only enough to make us wish for more.

George did not return. We pictured him going round the echelon yarning with all his cronies and drinking our rum. At this Fred and I went to bed. We were joined around midnight by Jack and Slim who said they'd be damned if they'd sit up for him any longer. He came back in the morning with the tale that the rum had been lost when the scout car in which he was travelling had been flooded. A very likely story and Fred told him a solicitor's clerk ought to have produced a better one than that.

But there did seem to be no roads left. Some were under water and the remainder so rutted and soft as to be impassable to wheeled traffic. In the afternoon some trucks drove along the railway from Kranenburg and the leader went up on a mine outside our house. We rushed out when we heard the explosion but there was nothing we could do. His mates had the driver on a stretcher and Jack was of the opinion that he would be all right, as he was groaning.

There was no prospect of help until the line was cleared of mines because it was obviously going to be the only link with the rear. We passed another miserable evening and night but on the following afternoon the ARVs arrived in force. Three of them - the whole regimental strength - jolted up from Groesbeek at the head of a convoy of trucks.

We broke the trailer and drew that out first. The earth was so liquid that it formed waves at each side of the trailer as it was dragged backwards towards the road. The tank was easier and we made the link without difficulty but everything was in a terrible state. Sides and front were caked with mud, the pannier doors were invisible. The decking was thick with clods stamped from our boots and hardened by the heat from the engine so that we had to chip the stuff off with a shovel and pickhead. By the time we had done this and loaded our kit the HQ tank had been recovered and joined us, while the ARVs were working to extricate that of our Troop Officer.

Without waiting for him we moved up the road for about two miles. Here was a cross-roads and a village clustered about a ruined convent, in front of which we halted. The village was in ruins also and lorries and Jeeps stood among the rubble while a party of pioneers, equipped with a bulldozer, worked to clear the cross-roads and find some sort of surface beneath the mud. The convent, which had been a German strong point, had been demolished save for a central passage with rooms opening from it. We unloaded our kit and then I responded to a call for a volunteer to walk back to meet our Troop Officer and guide him in. Why this was felt to be necessary was not explained.

It was not a pleasant walk. I was ankle, and sometimes knee deep in mud all the way, and ready at any moment to fling myself down should that Spandau become active again. I had got a new zoot suit at Nijmegen, the right size at last, and despite the rigours of the last few days it was still distressingly clean and noticeable. The sun, pale and watery, yet lit the countryside brilliantly after so many days of grey skies and driving rain, and I could see for miles across swollen ditches, waterlogged fields, ruined cottages and the derelict gliders, to the distant hills beyond which lay Nijmegen.

Despite my fears, I reached my destination without incident. The tank was recovered and standing on the road looking as if it was getting its wind back. Certainly it had been the most badly bogged of all, lying over at an angle that had made it impossible to stand on the decking. The concentrated efforts of all three ARVs had been needed to extract it.

We waited for the third flame tank to come up and then I directed them to the convent. Mr. Childs elected to drive but we arrived without any trouble. In my absence, our room had been furnished with a stove, beds, table and chairs and a wardrobe. The windows had been blocked up, the stove was glowing, two candles flickered on the mantelpiece. It looked very cosy. As I took off my zoot suit to hang it in the wardrobe, Mr. Childs came in to cadge a tin of sardines.

This officer was fresh from Sandhurst and only about a month older than myself. Perhaps Sherry had spoilt us, but we had a very poor opinion of his successor. He was generally a good-hearted and cheerful sort of chap but had petulant moods when his crew made difficulties in carrying out orders of which they did not approve. He did not inspire a lot of confidence. He was particularly partial to sardines.

We were rarely hungry enough to eat them and stowed a rapidly accumulating hoard on the trailer with other expendable goods. It seemed Mr. Childs could never get enough of them and while the Able, Baker and Charlie crews were glad to exchange sardines for M & V or stewed steak or anything else that was fit to eat, his own crew had several rows with him over his bartering. Had Sherry suddenly developed a craving for sardines he would have been welcome to the lot. With his substitute it was a different matter, one of business only. So the sardines were not forthcoming for free and Fred lectured him on the necessity of curbing the appetite and practising self-denial as an example to his Troop.

However, he came at the right time as we were going to play pontoon and both Fred and Jack were short of money. I was no use to them as my method was to put down ten cents and then twist, while Slim was only slightly more courageous. So Mr. Childs, who said he had only played once or twice before, and would have to stake large amounts to maintain his superior rank, was just the man for our two old soldiers.

The outcome was the classic one which will have been foreseen by the reader. Slim and I had much pleasure in reminding our friends of it whenever we played afterwards. Mr. Childs took the lot, about twenty guilders, of which Slim and I contributed about a couple. Jack and Fred were livid, but they had to maintain a pose of playing for the sake of the game only. Then Mr. Childs wanted to give it all back and pleaded very hard to be allowed to do so. It was lovely to watch them.

I explored the convent, which had evidently been stoutly defended. Weapons and ammo were scattered all over the place. A cardboard box stood on a windowsill in the passage and inside were six glass bottles the size and shape of an electric lamp bulb and half full of a yellow liquid. I thought at first it was prussic acid and was about to run and report it when the name, stencilled on the box, caught my attention: 'Blindenkorper', which I translated as 'blinding material'. An unpleasant weapon. Luckily, I never saw it used.

* * *

The rain had stopped when I went on guard and the next day the sun was shining, the sky was blue, the fields were green and the birds were singing. This last was unusual enough to be remarked upon - we had heard no birds for a long time.

We were to join the rest of the squadron at Frasselt and our route was at first along a track through ruined villages where dead horses and cattle were strewn about in profusion, swollen shapes with incongruously spindly legs like pins into a lump of plasticine. This track joined a very bad road running along the edge of the Reichswald.

On our left the flat land stretched away towards the first line of Dutch hills, clouded in the morning haze, monotony only relieved by the wreckage of a tank or the charred remains of a building. A German gun position occupied a quarry almost undermining the road; two field guns had their breeches blown and around them was scattered a heap of discarded uniforms, empty shell cases and rotting cardboard boxes.

On our right the black pines of the Reichswald towered over us. This was the German border, the actual boundary line being the ditch between road and hedge. Halted at a cross-roads by a convoy streaming south from Kranenburg, Fred ostentatiously crossed into the Reich to relieve himself on German soil. From the MP on duty we learned that we were through the Siegfried, that Kleve had fallen, and that our troops were fanning out north and south of the town. It was on this leg of our journey that our bedsteads fell off the trailer and the tank behind ran over them, much to the amusement of its crew and our annoyance.

Frasselt was our assembly point. It had been flamed by Sherry's half-squadron and all the tanks which had been bogged over the battlefield were being directed there. When we arrived the squadron was almost complete. We were harboured on the slopes of a scarp crowned by the forest. Below the road the fields dropped steeply down to the floods. The great expanse of water glittered in the sunshine and the red and grey roofs of Kranenburg shone in the middle of it.

We were to change our commander again. George was posted to England, to Bovington, for a tank commander's course at the AFV[105] School there. We told him that he needed it but he was highly delighted about the whole thing as it looked as if the war would be over before he rejoined us. Mr. Childs proposed that he should take George's place. It was common knowledge that his own crew wanted to get rid of him but although Slim and I were willing enough Fred and Jack refused to have anything to do with him. A Corporal Gotobed was offered as an alternative and they refused him, too. In the end we got a Sergeant Jackman who had just come up from the Delivery Squadron and to whom Fred and Jack could raise no objection as they did not know him. I cannot explain why, on this particular occasion, we should have had any say in the matter. It never happened again.

---

[105] AFV. Armoured Fighting Vehicle. The AFV School at Bovington, Dorset was, and still is, the 'home' of the Royal Armoured Corps.

I was carrying my blankets up the hill to the billet when the first jet plane[106] came over, a silver bullet glinting in the sunlight as it swooped down through the intense flak hurled by infuriated Bofors. The ditch was dry and I got into it. It was not so much the jet, for if it had a bomb there was some indication as to where it would fall, but the little bits of shrapnel slicing down through the trees respected neither friend nor foe.

The jet turned overhead with flashing wings and streaked for German territory. The flak thundered behind it, a deep grumble which gradually died to sporadic outbursts, then silence. A Spitfire that had been circling low out of harm's way drifted lazily westwards. Then another jet hummed overhead and the flak started again - this one was too high for it but the gunners let fly just the same.

Our cellar had a damp concrete floor and the whole Troop had to sleep there. Several people were wrenching up the floorboards in the rooms above to use as beds as the early birds had grabbed all the doors. Mr. Childs was billeted with us and that evening he decided that he ought to have a nickname, possibly to show that his Troop liked him. He asked us to suggest one. Someone asked him what he had been called at school and apparently it had been 'Spike', goodness knows why. Anyway, and equally without reason, we already had one, Captain Shearman. Someone suggested 'Nipper', which fitted very well and it was adopted despite his objections. As Fred said, he could have no choice when it was a matter of calling him names and at least it was one he could tell his mother.

I picked up an MP directing lamp on the corner by our billet thinking, since it had a red shutter, that it would make an admirable rear light for the trailer. I was always picking up things that might possibly be of use to us and shoving them on the trailer. Most of them never got used. Every time we had a clear out it was the same; the offending article would be held up, I would own up to it and it would be slung. Then we would be straight for a day or two and then the junk would begin to pile up again.

---

[106] German jets. This, of course, was the famous Me262, the first jet to go into operational service.

We moved in the morning and it was a cheerful occasion for we were going through the Siegfried Line but the dragon's teeth[107] were drawn. In fact, I saw none. If there were formal fortifications they were well hidden. The country lane curved between pine-crowned hillocks and then straightened out to cross a deep antitank ditch which was supported by wide breastworks. Beside the gap stood a great notice board:

"SIEGFRIED LINE, BREACHED 8.2.45"

and a washing line had been erected to display an impressive assortment of ladies' underwear.

Beyond the ditch the fields were criss-crossed with trenches. Bunkers were dug into the mounds at the side of the road. A field gun stood in a cottage garden, an Eighty-eight peered from a dugout nearby. Under the trees stood anti-aircraft guns, Eighty-eights and Seventy-fives. That was all there was to the Siegfried Line and we were not very impressed.

Just beyond this defended area we pulled off the road for a brew and Sherry, who had been bringing up the rear, moved to overtake. As his tank rolled past the halted column he turned to face us, his chest swelled, a gloved forefinger made to brush the waxed tips of a fiery moustache. His lips moved, "My tanks! My boys!" It was more life-like than the real Major Duffy.

At length we reached the village of Donsbruggen, on the Nijmegen-Kleve road. At least, Steve O'Neill said it was Donsbruggen and he was in a better position to know than me; I said it was Nutterden. No one was certain if we should stay there but it seemed a good chance to cook dinner. Some crews filled sacks with potatoes from a nearby clamp while Jack and I inspected a German bunker at the far end of the field. Fred and Slim went round the houses with a large box, collecting plates, cups and saucers.

---

[107] Dragon's teeth. Ranks of 4-sided pyramidal concrete blocks, about a yard high, constructed as obstacles to tanks. Some of these relics of the war are still to be seen in England, e.g. at Brenzett.

So the afternoon dragged away without incident until a Church of Scotland canteen drew up at the cross-roads. Of all the canteens that served - or were photographed while serving - the Western Front, only those operated by the Church of Scotland gained our respect. Occasionally we saw the Salvation Army, still more rarely the YMCA. NAAFI vans were always just going to get supplies or returning sold out. Only the Church of Scotland appeared frequently, opened up and served speedily, and did not seem too worried if we had not enough money to pay for all our purchases.

Towards evening we had a definite assurance that we were stopping the night and we proceeded to bag billets and procure beds. This was easy as the village was a large one, straggling along the main road, and most of the houses were unoccupied and not too badly damaged. The floor of our room was carpeted so bedsteads were not a priority requirement.

Although five men cooked, ate, slept, washed and loafed about in one room it was astonishing how cosy and comfortable that room could be made. It says something for barrack room training. At Donsbruggen we became very fastidious, laying a cloth for meals, eating from the best china we could find and refraining from serving direct from the saucepan. We organised everything so well that we decided to invite Sherry to a late dinner on the second night. There was now an officers' mess for such times as the officers could use it, but Sherry escaped to his Troop whenever he could as the food and cooking there was far superior.

I had the day clear to concentrate on the occasion. There was a huge modern range, I had plenty of wood and plenty of coal and plenty of saucepans. We had just been issued with an A pack, so there were steak and kidney puddings. There was also a mixed fruit pudding so I had to compose a sauce for it. I had got a sack of potatoes, the gardens yielded turnips and leeks, the houses onions. For a fish course I was forced to use sardines but we had plenty of cheese and biscuits to finish off. The cooking was the least of my worries as I wanted a clean cloth, dishes and plates that matched, and a good supply of cutlery. I found them in a big house a mile down the road and they were much admired but did not travel well. I was hard at it all day and the dinner was a success. I was pleased with myself and it was enough reward to hear Jack pointing out to Slim (who had been responsible the previous day) that this was how it should be done.

We spent a good deal of time clustered round the PW cage behind the MP post at the cross-roads. Here the prisoners were searched, losing most of their belongings in the process. The barbed wire was lined with envious spectators and there were loud complaints at the way the MPs were making money while others did the dirty work. We learned for the first time that many German prisoners were now wearing two pairs of trousers and concealing their possessions in the pockets of the pair underneath.

One thing worthy of remark was the enormous number of contraceptives carried by each German soldier. My own experience had shown me that every pocket yielded these useful articles and here in the cage there was a pile a yard high in the centre and they were scattered thickly over the grass.

If the prisoners excited our greed they were useful as well. Harry Garrity had four bogies to change and obtained four Germans to help him. We saw him seated on a jerrican encouraging his labouring charges. Others were clearing out houses, fetching beds and other furniture, unloading petrol lorries, and in all cases working with a will.

During the time we had been bogged in the vicinity of Kranenburg Steve O'Neill had been in Kleve. His had been the only tank to flame in the town and there he had remained until ordered to rejoin us at Donsbruggen. On the way back his tank had picked up a section of tramline that had torn the teeth from part of the sprocket. A new - or rather, reconditioned - tank was ready for him and I helped him move his kit. It was a rush, as we were to leave Donsbruggen at ten o'clock that night.

The few roads that were passable were in a very bad condition. It was as if the Germans had lost interest in their country when they got close to the frontier and could not be bothered to keep it in good order. Never designed to cope with such a volume of traffic, the congestion had to be seen to be believed. Columns of trucks, nose to tail, stretched for miles, unable to move because one of their number had broken down. It was as well the Luftwaffe was no longer in evidence.

A line of our ponderous vehicles, needing the whole of the road, would have created an impossible situation. So again all armour was directed to move at night when the traffic was not so thick; and, of course, without lights in the interests of security. To most of the tanks this last order made little difference as the headlights had been knocked off or shot away long ago, but even a flicker of light at intervals in the column would have been some help. And our best weapon for dealing with oncoming Jeeps and DUKWs, the spotlight, was denied us.

To add to our discomfort on the four-mile run to Kleve, it commenced to rain as we moved off. Soon sleet lashed into eyes already smarting from grit and aggravated the weals inflicted on our faces by stinging branches and twigs. We journeyed a hundred yards and then halted while 14 Troop got out of their field. They took a long time. The rest of the run was like that - move for a few hundred yards, then wait for half an hour. All the time the rain came down in torrents. We had sheets over the hatches but still the water trickled through.

At ten o'clock we left Donsbruggen. It was four o'clock in the morning when we halted and someone said that we were in the outskirts of Kleve. That was good enough. We dragged the sheets more securely over the hatches and made ourselves as comfortable as possible inside the tank - which meant using your beret or a rolled up shirt to keep your head off the cold and damp metal of the turret wall. Uncomfortable as it was, we did not keep awake for long.

CHAPTER 15

GOCH

When I woke it was morning and the rain had stopped. Three old men wearing clogs and shabby overcoats came shuffling along the grey street, stopping every now and again to salvage a cigarette butt. I stood up in the turret to get a better look at the first German civilians I had seen and they looked frightened and touched their hats to me. It was embarrassing. Good God, I thought, are these the Herrenvolk?

Then there was a shout from the end of the street. Tea up! The column came to life very quickly. I do not know how it came about that the Canadians should be providing tea, the proverbial 'char and wads', but there was a great urn at the back of a truck, steaming mugs, and a sergeant handing out bully beef sandwiches. It had never happened before and we surmised that they had got the wrong street. But never mind, life flowed back into chilled bones and everyone laughed and talked and offered cigarettes, the discomforts of the night forgotten. We even mustered the energy to cook breakfast before the order came to move, which it did at eight o'clock.

The infantry were now attacking Goch which, like Kleve, was supposed to be a bastion intended to delay our advance from the Siegfried Line to the Rhine, and we headed in that direction to join our echelon in the little town of Pfalzdorf. We were harboured next to a farmhouse on the outskirts which was still occupied by its owners. The civilians were scared stiff of us at first. The officers were billeted in this farmhouse and they said that whenever they met a German in a passage he shrank back against the wall and made them feel awkward. We did not know how to behave and, I suppose, behaved rather badly, even though the Germans had brought it upon themselves. After all, they had made countless civilians of other nations suffer and now it was their turn, albeit in a small and unthinking way.

Shag had found a Schmeisser[108] submachine gun in a foxhole at Frasselt and I had swapped a German compass for it. It was a beautiful weapon, the blued steel and polished hand grips as different from our rubbishy Stens as chalk from cheese. The farm had lots of poultry wandering about and we regarded these as the legitimate spoils of war.

I killed several chickens, perfecting my aim, the idea being to get them through the head if possible. I then went for the geese. Others were using pistols and Stens and in a very short time there was only one goose left and I was stalking it. The farmer, who had been watching the slaughter, now plucked up the courage to make a bid for his last bird and sprang between me and my prey, driving it towards the barn. I cut across at an angle to intercept, whereupon he changed direction and headed for the house. The goose won the race by a long neck to the farmer, who slammed the door in my face. That evening we heard the BBC news saying that 'every British soldier in Germany has a chicken on the stove in his billet tonight.' For once, propaganda was near the mark. We had so many that we could not be bothered to pluck them but just skinned them and fried the best bits.

In the morning the whole squadron moved up to flame a wood near Bucholt, east of Goch. We did not know we were going to do this, merely being told that we were going forward on call. Apart from our Crocodiles there was no lack of armour: a battalion of Guards Churchills, a regiment of Kangaroos, with Valentines, Bailey Bridges and other oddments. A regiment of Kangaroos comprised about fifty tanks, the Guards another fifty, and our own contingent brought the total to well over a hundred. All to harry the edge of a wood.

In contrast to previous exhaustive briefings we had a glance at a map, another at an aerial photograph, and received a mere outline of the plan before moving to the Forming Up Point. This was below a bare ridge beyond which lay the wood. The tanks were tightly packed

[108] Schmeisser. 9 mm. sub-machine gun with a folding metal butt, originally designed for German paratroops. A really beautiful weapon.

and the ground was a morass. Mr. Childs bogged his tank in a gateway, took over Steve's, and bogged that. So that two tanks were disabled at the start and when the time came to pressure up the number was swelled. Two trailers, including our own, developed leaks and we were ordered to stay behind.

It was a dull, misty morning. The tanks, silhouetted on the skyline before vanishing over the ridge, resembled a herd of prehistoric monsters halting here and there to browse. But even in our hollow the mortar bombs fell close enough to make us keep our hatches closed. Jeeps and Carriers scurried along the narrow road behind us. Beneath the road bank lay two dead Germans, their grey uniforms blending with the withered grass.

On the air we heard that the Guards were bombarding the wood, while our people were investigating a cluster of farm buildings believed to be sheltering snipers. The Guards had a code word, 'Jumbo', which they kept using and which we did not understand. I thought at first it was the Kangaroos and when they said 'Jumbo now' it meant they were dropping their infantry, but then I found we were not on net to the Kangaroos and had no further solution to offer.

The wireless traffic relating to the Crocodiles consisted mainly of altercations between Mr. Carroll, who commanded, and his various tank commanders. The officer was impatient to get on but his HQ tank outpaced the heavier flame tanks.

"Get a bloody move on," came over the air at frequent intervals.

At last one exasperated sergeant replied, "For Christ's sake mind your own business and leave me to get on with mine!" This appealed to the rest of the squadron and violent arguments raged between Mr. Carroll and his subordinates, usually ending with his passionate order to "Cut it out!"

He shared with Major Duffy the habit of addressing remarks to his driver over the A-Set and then doing his nut when the driver, who of course could not hear, took no notice of the order.

"Hurry up, Love Two, out," he would say. "Slow down, driver. Driver slow down! Slow down! Slow down you bloody fool!." And anonymous advice came immediately:

"Get off the A-Set!"
"Get on the I/c!"
"You bloody fool!"

We listened to all this, occasionally taking part in the 'get off the A-Set' business to relieve the monotony. Apart from the mortars there seemed to be no opposition and the Kangaroos swept in and deposited their infantry on the edge of the wood, whereupon the Guards took over and 'shot them in'. Our tanks inspected the farm, found it harmless, and returned.

Back we went across the bare fields to Pfalzdorf. Again the roads had proved unequal to their task and every tank made its own track across the meadow land so that the fields were scarred with enormous ruts, deepening towards a central track that had degenerated into a channel of liquid mud. In the middle of one field a dead German lay on his back, pallid face lifted towards the sky, a white tin hat strapped tightly and incongruously to his head. Geoff Kirk, co-driver, seated on the back bin of his HQ tank, was plucking a chicken and throwing the feathers into the exhaust stream. Clouds of feathers danced above us, settling only to be blown upwards by the following tank, settling again, drifting sluggishly in the wind.

* * *

During that night the infantry reached the outskirts of Goch town and when we moved up again in the grey of early morning it was with the expectation of being used to see them through the streets. We halted on the scarp above Goch, lined up facing a narrow road as if on parade. Goch lay away to our right, beyond the woods. On our left the fields stretched unbroken by hedge or ditch until in the centre of the horizon lay a burnt out Sherman, heeled over like a ship under press of sail. From a copse at our end of the fields peeped the muzzle of a Seventy-five. Carriers and Jeeps trickled along the muddy track towards Goch. Ambulances jolted in the opposite direction. A troop of light tanks sped by, rolling and lurching wildly in the potholes.

My wireless set had drifted off net and I was trying vainly to adjust it on such sporadic transmissions as 'roger, out' and 'wilco, out'.

Then 12 Troop Officer informed us that he was taking us into Goch to support his own Troop, which had mislaid a tank somewhere.

This officer, Mr. Dunkley, was notorious in the squadron for his pessimism. When briefing his Troop it was his habit to indulge in the blackest speculation.

"If we can get across this minefield, Dad," he would say - Harry Garrity was his driver and Mr. Dunkley always referred to him as 'Dad' - "I dare say there'll be other patches that aren't marked, and even if there aren't I don't see how those Eighty-eights can possibly miss us, do you? And if they do I expect these woods will be full of bazookas - and then there's this minefield here. I can't see how the Flails are going to get up to that. It's a very dodgy do, altogether. I don't like the look of it at all." He used to scare his Troop until they got used to him.

On this occasion, fortunately, he merely briefed his tank commanders and left them to put us in the picture. Sergeant Jackman merely said that we were going into Goch to clear a nest of snipers out of a church and left it at that.

"Are you on net yet, Smudger?" he asked as he settled himself in the turret and adjusted his headset.

"No," I answered. "I'm waiting for someone to send a long message."

"Well, look jilo! Dunkley's moving. OK, Jack!"

The Troop corporal, Jock Robb, was leading, followed by Mr. Dunkley, then by us. We dipped over the edge of the scarp and descended towards the town. The road was lined with trees and scattered houses. As I watched the Troop tank negotiating a bad crater there was a sharp explosion and black smoke swept across the road. Sergeant Jackman dropped his hatches with a bang and we grinned at each other before turning to our periscopes.

I was back on net now and heard Jock Robb being directed to turn to the right and then left and we followed along a new suburban road towards a cluster of red brick houses. Sergeant Jackman thought there was supposed to be an Eighty-eight about here somewhere and Jack immediately brought his wings up to within a yard of the trailer of the Troop tank. The mortars were dropping steadily and once I saw a tracer fly across the front of the Troop. It looked suspiciously like an AP and our sergeant, who evidently saw it also, told Jack to speed up.

The houses were not far away and we reached them safely. In the narrow street Jock was halted by a deep crater and had to find an alternative route. All drivers had the same idea when halted in action; that is, to close right up behind the tank in front and thus protect themselves from enemies on either bow. This made it a job for Jock to reverse but eventually we got sorted out and he and our officer turned the corner. Our tank gave a convulsive leap backwards and stood still. We could hear furious cursing in the front and the clang of metal on metal. The tank was stuck in reverse and Jack was clouting the gear lever with a spanner.

I heard no more as I had to go over to the A-Set to answer Mr. Dunkley.

"Hullo, Jig Two Baker," came the faint voice, amid hissing and crackling and an ear-splitting whistle. "What are you doing? Jig Two Baker, over."

"I am stuck in reverse gear," I answered.

"Say again."

"I say again I am stuck in reverse gear."

"Say again."

"I say again - I - am - stuck - in - reverse - gear."

"You say you are stuck in reverse gear?"

"Yes."

"Roger. Report my signals."

"Strength two."

"Roger, out."

By this time Jack had hammered the lever into second and we swung round the corner. For one awful moment I stared down the barrel of a Seventy-five. Someone gasped and I realised it was not manned. Thank God for that!

A minute or two later we debouched into a square and swung towards a church on the far side. Presumably Mr. Dunkley had given the order to flame, for a jet sped from Jock's tank, shot between the iron railings and cascaded against the wall. There was no opposition and both tanks plastered the building with their Flame Guns so that it was soon well alight. We stood clear and swung the Seventy-five to and fro in case a target offered. The infantry lounged in doorways smoking, hands in pockets and watching with interest. It did not take long to make sure no snipers could live in the church and we then withdrew to join up with the rest of the squadron and learn that Goch was now in British hands. This being so, the divisions which had converged on the town had to be sorted out, regrouped, and directed against a new objective. We were released, to return to Pfalzdorf until our services were required again.

The flaming of the church had amused us; we were coming out; I was netted to the AEF programme. So it was in merry mood that we bowled along the road at the rear of the column, singing and waving to German girls who were cautiously emerging from the farmhouses. Even when we turned to the right when we knew that our way was to the left it made no difference. The officer would take the can back if he lost us, so who cared.

However, Mr. Carroll must have realised his mistake soon afterwards. We halted. The tanks at the head of the column ploughed into a field on the left, turned in a wide sweep and crashed through the fence back on to the road behind us. They made heavy going, their bogies digging deep into the green turf. Then we saw the reason for this sudden change of direction. At the side of the road a notice, evidently home-made, proclaimed:

"DANGER! JERRY AHEAD!"

below a swastika. Now Mr. Carroll's mistake ceased to amuse.

We dipped into the gateway. The field looked very soft but Sergeant Jackman had had no experience of handling Churchills in sticky ground and he ordered Jack to pull left. Jack, who ought to have known better, obeyed. Down went the rear of the tank, the tracks churned furiously and Jack switched off the engine. The same old story.

I stood up in my hatch and something whistled through the air that could have been a bullet. I ducked down hastily. The other tanks were going away in a hurry. I tried without success to get back on to the squadron net, swearing all the time at the others for wanting music for the ride home. We knew the ARV was off the road for an engine change and we could only hope that one of the HQ tanks would be sent to drag us out.

So we sat in the tank and I ate a bar of chocolate. The sun was setting and mist lay thick along the ground. Fifty yards away stood a low, grey stone farmhouse, a plume of smoke ascending from the tallest chimney stack. The tank was cold and cramped and we discussed making for the farmhouse. If there was a sniper about it was probably getting too dark for him but, to be on the safe side, we waited for the gloom to descend and then ran for it. We reached the house safely. It was occupied by the crew of a 17-pounder anti-tank gun and what remained of an infantry section. The latter had only just arrived and constituted the advanced post of their forward company. The gun crew had been there for some time and it was they who had erected the notice after having seen several Jeeps go down the road and not return.

The 43rd Wessex Division, to which the infantry belonged, seemed to have taken heavy punishment in the advance from Nijmegen. This particular company had suffered severely in Kleve, where a German SP had crept behind their lines and done great execution before escaping in the consequent confusion. So the company sector was manned very thinly and they were much more pleased to see us than we were to see them. Although it was now dark we loaded the Seventy-five and the Besa and traversed to cover the road. Also, we could not very well refuse to help out with the guard which even we could believe was necessary.

Having done all we could in respect of the military situation, Fred and I searched the house by candlelight. I found a set of knives and forks, what appeared to have been a wedding present, in a cupboard.

In a wardrobe stood an immense pipe with a china bowl holding at least an ounce and a stem a yard long. Tucking this under my arm I followed Fred to the pantry, which was well stocked with bottled fruit, vegetables and jam. Obviously, we had to make room on the tank for all that.

Fred secured the pantry door carefully and we returned to the front room, where the previous friendship with the infantry was being disturbed. Their company commander had arrived and seemed to be in a temper over something. In a corner a wireless operator was trying to establish communication and I went over to offer expert advice but lost interest when I found there were no knobs to twiddle.

There had been a quarrel between the infantry major and Sergeant Jackman. The major had said that since we were staying in the house we must help with its defence. Sergeant Jackman had said that while we were quite willing to do so at night, in the daytime our first duty was to our tank, and as soon as we got it clear we should be off. The major then ordered us to remain at the farm until he gave us permission to leave. Sergeant Jackman retorted that he already had his orders - to rejoin the squadron as soon as possible. So no wonder the major was upset - the free and easy atmosphere of the tank corps never went down very well with officers of other arms.

The artillerymen did not seem to be very disturbed by the lack of supporting troops. They had taken the best room and all the best furniture, they had a stove, a wireless set and a pack of cards and were quite happy. I never saw their gun - they never seemed to go anywhere near it.

When we tossed up for guards I got first 'stag', going on at ten o'clock with one of the infantry. I wore my zoot suit, my pistol, and carried my Schmeisser. He had all his equipment - tin hat, small pack, water bottle, rifle and bayonet - which could hardly be regarded as suitable for night work.

The silence was almost uncanny. There was not even the rumble of distant gunfire which would have been normal and comfortable. Compared with the infantryman, who had only just come out from

England, I was a veteran of warfare, but he was completely at ease while I was jumpy as a cat. I was not used to silence, to a situation calling for the use of ears and not eyes, to the knowledge that if anything happened I should not know what to do. I was tremendously relieved when the grandfather clock in the hall chimed midnight and I roused Sergeant Jackman.

It was about nine o'clock when I awoke, to find the sergeant the only one of the crew out of bed. He explained that the regiment's Technical Adjutant had been up and promised to send help as soon as possible. In the meantime we were to try and dig the tank out and he was looking for shovels.

As we went out to the tank a long line of people topped the rise that hid the chimneys of Goch. A soldier came first, bearing a large Red Cross flag. Behind him filed German civilians, all carrying bundles, all looking very miserable. We stood watching this procession until they disappeared in the direction of Pfalzdorf, and then commenced digging. It looked hopeless. The rear of the tank had sunk down to a level with the bottom of the air louvres.

Then the first mortar came over. Smoke mushroomed a couple of fields away. Another dropped closer and we huddled in the lee of the tank and hoped for a lull. A shrill whine filled the air, a Moaning Minnie. Down they came, six almost simultaneously; and then another six, another and another. In the next field the earth was flung about amid a maelstrom of whirling smoke and splintering flame.

We dug for ten minutes. We were sweating and swearing and stopped to listen after every movement. The mortars came again. We decided we had had enough and Sergeant Jackman told Jack to start up to see if we had done any good.

Jack climbed into his seat, the starter whirred, the engine roared. Smoke billowed a hundred yards away.

"Get down!" yelled someone, and we flung ourselves into the ruts. That lot was the nearest we had had and as soon as we could we pelted for the house. It seemed as if the Germans had heard the engine, which was not a comforting thought if we were going to need the ARV to get the tank out.

Anyway, it was decided to wait for help and as we were now free the infantry corporal asked Slim and I to go into the attic with a pair of binoculars and observe where the mortars were falling and what areas seemed to receive particular attention.

I fetched two jars of pears from the pantry and joined Slim, who was kneeling on the floor and peering cautiously over the windowsill. I found a large frying pan in a corner and placed it by the door where it would not be forgotten. Then we got down to business. I took the binoculars and tried to find a position where the sun would not flash on the lenses, a precaution I had read about. Slim took the compass and found north, which seemed to be all he knew about its use.

From the attic we had a very good view of the countryside. Our road ran straight until joined by another, when it curved away behind the grey stone wall which surrounded a farmhouse and attendant buildings about a mile away. Then it disappeared into the woods. As I watched a man popped up from a gateway and ran alongside the wall. I distinguished rifle, pack and tin hat. British. A Jeep passed our house and sped up the road, halted, turned, and came belting back while mortars crashed down. Slim went downstairs to tell the infantry the road was still under observation. He returned with the corporal, who stayed with us and tried to see whence the mortars came. In this he was unsuccessful, but said he was glad to know about the road.

Then we heard the angry mutter of flak, grumbling in the distance, swelling in crescendo as a jet plane sped overhead, glinting silver in the sunlight, a pale trail of smoke in its wake. Another jet, appearing from the direction of the German lines, whirled on a wing tip and dropped in a screaming power dive to weave away at treetop level. The first made a wide circle and then shot straight up through the heart of the crackling flak and, miraculously unscathed, disappeared in the clouds.

We sat in the sun for another hour until, faint in the distance, we heard the unmistakable rattle of Churchill tracks. I ran to the other window. Breasting the slope, two HQ tanks rocked in the potholes and from the turret of the leader the commander pointed. A Jeep jolted behind.

I yelled for a relief, we passed them on the stairs and joined our crew mates. Sergeant Jackman went to the Jeep to see the Tech. Adj. while the rest of us tried to put the wind up the HQ crews who did not believe that mortars would be a problem.

They had less than a minute to wait. The Germans had evidently heard the noise of their arrival and the first mortar fell as we were hitching the towropes. To add to the confusion, the jets reappeared and the whine of their engines, the violent crepitation of flak, the screech and thud of the mortars, the clanking of tank tracks and the roar of tank engines, the hoarse commands and warnings, all combined in an inferno of sound amid which we dug and strained with logs as our tank inched its way towards the road. Our rescuers then cast off and made away, leaving us to pack our kit, including our share of the bottled fruit and vegetables, and to follow at leisure.

As the rumble of their tracks died so the whine and crack of the mortars ceased and the last jet was only a speck in the darkening eastern sky. When we drove away, we left mortars bursting once more in the fields behind and it was with relief that I saw the farmhouse drop out of sight. So to Pfalzdorf, where I received the order to transfer to Steve O'Neill's tank in the morning.

CHAPTER 16

WEEZE

The half-squadron comprising 13 and 14 Troops and two HQ tanks was billeted in the loft of the barn behind the farmhouse. A large mound of hay was piled against one wall and we made our beds on this, while in a cleared space by the trapdoor stood two hurricane lanterns, their dim light being supplemented by several cookers. The arrangements could hardly be described as meeting recommended fire precautions, especially as many of us smoked heavily, but they were the best we could do.

There had been a fuss about the guard. Captain Shearman had been complaining that he had been searching for half an hour without seeing anyone and although the two men who had been on guard at the time stoutly maintained that they had been doing their duty it was certain that henceforth we should be subject to stricter supervision.

Also, there had been complaints to the crews of a battery of Five-fives sited in the field opposite. Our people contended that the guns attracted the attentions of a number of jet planes which had swept low overhead, ignoring attempts to shoot them down with pistols, Bren Guns and Stens. The Artillery said they did not and, anyway, what if they had. On reflection, the Artillery had a job to do and we were wrong to complain but it did not seem like that at the time. The Five-fives were firing as I got into bed, the barn shaking at every salvo.

Overhead droned an aeroplane. It seemed to circle and then came the crash of bombs - a stick that started far away and leapt nearer in giant strides. For a moment everyone was still. Then out went the lamps and we piled down the ladder in the darkness; my fingers came under someone's boots, something hit me in the face. Bare legs sank in the filthy farmyard. I saw Steve run by with his shirt tails streaming. There was the clang of hatches closing, a mighty roar as the bomber swept low overhead and away. A few moments silence. Then the Five-fives opened up again.

In the morning we shared out the fruit and jam and I carried my portion with the remainder of my kit to Steve's tank, T.173174/H, where I spent several busy hours stowing it and cleaning out the turret. Turret cleanliness was one of my fads and it was heartbreaking work in wet weather. We had a lot of spare kit and, owing to the abundance of fresh food, a large surplus of compo rations. Stowage was generally considered as a task for the operator and I had attained some skill, having had George always ready to sling any of my loot that he could see. Every nook and cranny in the driving and fighting compartments was utilised. Tins of M & V, steak and kidney and bully beef were beneath the turret floor, thermos flasks were secured in place between the air cleaners and the carbon dioxide bottles, plates were jammed between the wireless set and the turret roof, biscuits stacked neatly behind the bins beneath. I carried the entire spare compo pack in the turret, distributed among different spaces which had been designed to hold something else. A small library was stowed beneath the smoke bomb box; in addition to 'Teach Yourself Dutch', I had had 'Vanity Fair' and 'The Pickwick Papers' sent out to me, had read them both half-a-dozen times and still carried them - tattered, dog-eared, soaked and bleached, ready to pass an hour when nothing else would serve. Stowage was a continual compromise between fighting efficiency, safety and comfort.

Ted and Len came back from leave on the morning of the day we were to move. The majority of 13 Troop had been due for leave in January and February as it was the D-Day Troop and now the tank crews were almost back to normal. Sherry again had the Troop tank (Sandgate), Reg Webb the Able (Sandling), Steve the Baker (Sandwich) and Sergeant Jackman the Charlie (Sidcup). My own leave was so far distant as to be completely out of sight.

The condition of the roads was by no means improved so that although we were ready at dinnertime no one expected to move until after dark. So it turned out. At nightfall we were lined up on the road by Pfalzdorf railway station, waiting for the Fitters, whose Half-track had broken down just outside the harbour. A thin drizzle had started. Steve, who needed to wear glasses at night, found his vision restricted and told me to take command. We sat down in the turret, tried to keep dry, and listened to Mr. Carroll calling the Fitters and, occasionally, the Fitters answering.

There seemed to have been little point in waiting for darkness as we only stayed on the road for about half a mile. Then we drove across country, twisting and turning so as to make me lose all sense of direction. However, at least there were no tricky manoeuvres to perform as all we had to do was follow the tank in front and my proficiency in command was not tested.

I have never seen a more desolate prospect than the place where we stopped, in a field where the tanks drew in close together as if huddling up for warmth and company. The dominant shade was grey. The thin, eddying drizzle blanketed everything. The fields, wet and soggy, seemed to stretch for miles in each direction with here and there a tree, stark against the monotonous background, rearing from the darker line of a hedgerow. So we were surprised when Reggie Webb came amongst the tanks saying he would lead us to our billet.

Although we had not been able to make it out in the wet murk, this was a cow shed attached, in the fashion customary on the continent, to a farmhouse that was still occupied by its owners. The cow shed also contained its legitimate occupants and we had to make do with the passage in the middle and the odd empty stall.

There were bundles of straw on the loft over the stalls and we used these to block holes in the walls and for our beds, lying two by two along the aisle. In the morning Len swore he had been woken in the middle of the night by a cow licking his face. He had also had his face scratched by a cat - certainly he showed a weal on his cheek. For this reason, he said, he had felt safer awake and on guard and had decided to let Ted, Jinx and me sleep. We three had all had a good night.

It was an early reveille again with all the usual fumbling and stumbling. It had stopped raining but the morning was dark, cold and windy. Word had gone round that we were on call to the attack on Weeze and soon came the expected order to pressure up. Len and Steve messed about with the trailer, which groaned and hissed as usual, and then came spattering and splashing and the noise of Len swearing. Fuel was spewing from joints in the link and Steve went to fetch the Fitters.

We blew down and broke the link, working feverishly in the hope of being repaired in time to move out with the others, but although breakfast was forgotten in the rush it was all to no avail. The Fitters rummaged about in their Half-track and then announced that they would have to go back to Pfalzdorf to get a new seal. Five minutes later the Squadron moved out and vanished over the skyline without us.

There was nothing to be done for the tank until the Fitters returned. We ate breakfast as dawn broke over the roofs and church spires of Weeze which we could see in the distance. The pale sky was sullied by the smoke clouds hanging over the town. Typhoons appeared and we draped the aircraft recognition sheet - a brilliant magenta rectangle - over the trailer.

My headset, hanging from the turret to be within easy reach, hissed and crackled. I passed several unimportant messages between our Troops and the Armoured Command Vehicle, a Half-track. This latter was a new acquisition as our CO was now supposed to be too valuable to be risked in a tank. As the day wore on I became the accepted 'rear link' - the wireless link between Squadron and ACV when these stations are too far apart to hear each other - and varied this duty by stalking chickens with Ted, he with Sten, self with Schmeisser.

Jerome K. Jerome maintains that the really expert marksman is he who can claim to have hit a cat. I would say that a moving chicken is an equally elusive target, especially if the hunter is armed with an automatic weapon designed for close work and needs to hit the chicken in the head. This German family were more active than their compatriots at Pfalzdorf and got most of their stock under cover before we could get going, but I picked off one straggler and took it back to the tank in triumph.

I did not know much about chickens and neither did the others. An inquest upon the remains returned the verdict that death by misadventure had occurred only just in time to forestall death from natural causes; in fact, the corpse seemed to be going mouldy. So we buried it with honours and Steve made an affecting speech at the graveside.

When it grew dark, as our tanks had not returned and there was no news from them, we marched up to the farmhouse, went in at the front door, and looked for the cow shed. I tried two doors while the family, seated round the table, watched us in silence. When I found the right one they all started up at once.

"Nay, nay, nay!" they all babbled. "Hier kommen! Hier kommen!"

I think they believed we were after their cows, having failed to get the chickens. At any rate, they showed us into another room at the side of the house where there were mattresses on the floor and a stove in the corner and which had evidently been used by the officers the night before.

We selected our positions, put our blankets in place and arranged that Jinx should stand guard with my Schmeisser while the rest of us brought food and cooking utensils from the tank. Just as we were loading ourselves along came Jinx, having taken no notice of our instructions and without my gun. I have said before that it was no use swearing at Jinx but at least it relieved our feelings. However, it did not relieve us of worry. Civilian attitudes were an unknown factor. There were several men in the house and now they had a sub-machine gun if they were silly enough to think of using it. In the end Steve and I crept up to the house with our pistols ready while the others stood to the tank. The family were still seated peaceably round the table and my gun leaned against the wall where I had left it.

The Fitters had come up with the seal and the news that our half-squadron had been forced to accept a night action. We learned later that the infantry commander led them to the wrong wood and that in flaming it we had killed some of our own men. However, while this was happening, we had a cheerful evening with plenty of food and a sing-song. The Fitters were always good company for their roving commission meant they had all the news and all the funny stories. We did not venture to fraternise with the Germans and felt it necessary to have a guard, just in case. Ted and I were on in the middle of the night but there was no need to actually get out of bed so we took it in turns to keep awake.

In the morning the Fitters repaired the trailer link and led us in to where the Squadron was harboured in the shadow of a large camouflaged gasometer in Goch. All the tanks were badly in need of maintenance and, indeed, our Able crew had been forced to take over the old tank which Steve had discarded as unserviceable at Donsbruggen.

Goch was so ruined and so crowded with troops that it was very difficult to find an empty cellar, at a time when cellars were the only accommodation sought. Most of them were large and comfortable, were fitted with a stove, and seemed designed for just such events as had taken place above ground. They were always well supplied with coal bricks, which we broke before burning as it was rumoured that some contained sticks of dynamite. In every house there were abundant stocks of bottled fruit and vegetables; so far from starvation, the German civilians seemed to us to have been wallowing in luxury.

Len puzzled me. He violently denounced everything German and would express wonder on seeing me eat a jar of pears straight from the pantry shelf. But a leg of pork cut from a German pig, cooked in a German oven heated by German coal, served up with German potatoes, beans, peas and leeks, and eaten from German plates with the aid of German cutlery, he could and would polish off with relish. I had never lived so well as during those early days in Germany and had no such scruples. Ted was an excellent cook, mainly because of his patience. There was a rumour that German foods had been poisoned but we considered it an adequate precaution to use only bottles and jars that had obviously never been opened.

Someone had found a box of German money but, unfortunately, it was all the inflation currency of 1923 and worthless. The notes were blown all over the rubble and I picked up two for a hundred million marks each, which I considered was a big enough sum to be kept as a souvenir.

At length a cellar was procured about half a mile from the tank and while Len and Jinx started clearing out the rubbish Ted and I foraged for furniture and provisions. Toppling a spring bed from a window into a bomb crater did it little good as regards appearance but left its essentials unimpaired. Dragging jars of pickled onions and gherkins over rough ground in a sack meant a high breakage rate but there were plenty more. We also found a pile of gramophone records in one room but half the house had fallen down and presumably the gramophone was on that side.

There was an operator's briefing at two o'clock, to get a week's code signs and the Unicode and Slidex which took a long time to write down, and when I returned to the cellar I found it clean, snug and fully furnished. A fire crackled in the stove, a kettle sang, Jinx sat watching it and Len was getting the mugs out. In fact, tea was all we had time for, after all that effort, because Steve came in with the news that we were to move at four o'clock.

We were furious about this, especially as we were only going across to the other side of Goch. There was hurried packing. Such of the bottled food as we decided to retain was packed in a basket for carriage to the tank, where it was stowed in the pannier since we were not going into action. The bedsteads went on to the trailer, this time lashed securely.

It was a bumpy and unpleasant ride in the half light with the red brick dust stinging our faces and dangling wires plucking at our clothing. Much of the time we were gingerly feeling our way between lines of parked trucks and tanks, avoiding bomb craters once marked with white tape and threading piled banks of rubble marked every few yards with:

"DANGER! SCHU MINES IN WRECKAGE!"

Our new harbour was on the very outskirts of Goch, on the German side. One side of the road was lined with battered, windowless houses and on the other was a cratered field where we could park the tanks. No sooner had we stopped than people came round warning us not to enter the alleys between the houses as these were reported to be strewn with Schu mines and at first glance it seemed we were not to enter the houses either, for all such doors as remained, and where there were no doors the walls, were marked:

"RESERVED C COY"

of some infantry battalion. These were soon rubbed out where necessary and since possession is nine points of the law we moved in.

What a contrast to the neat cellar we had just left. A heap of potatoes lay in one corner and in their midst was a German hand grenade. A pile of dirty clothing was mingled with fragments of brick and plaster. There were rusty garden implements, a wrecked pram, a broken bed, and a torn mattress with the stuffing littering the floor. In another corner were lumps of coal, a rag doll with one leg missing, a broken rifle, a respirator case and a German uniform cap.

We cleared all this out except the hand grenade, which we left among the potatoes as no one understood how it worked. Sergeant Jackman joined us as his billet was too small for five. The guns were still banging away. Presumably they knew what they were firing at and they did not keep me awake.

All the next day we stood by ready to move. Early in the morning the infantry occupied our cellars, giving us the choice of clearing such of the rooms above ground as were habitable or of living by the tanks. Fortunately, the weather was fine and, anyway, we were sick of clearing out rubbish, so we stuck to the tanks. There was quite a lot of oiling and greasing that needed doing and it was rumoured that we were to move again. This was confirmed but was delayed again and again. Even when we were told that we were moving at midnight, although it was a likely hour we refrained from stowing our kit until the last moment. Then it was a rush.

In contrast to our run of the previous evening, although we covered much the same ground it was top speed all the way, through the town and out towards the scarp which loomed against the sky illuminated by the flashes of the guns. We topped the scarp and turned into a large open field of soft turf. We were too tired to go to the trouble of unsheeting the trailer and finding and pitching a bivvy so, although it was February, Steve and I elected to sleep on the engine deck and leave the turret for Jinx.

Sleeping on the engine decking was an emergency measure ordinarily only attempted in summer and then only if conditions made it impossible to sleep under the tank or pitch a bivvy. On these occasions, with perhaps the prospect of moving at dawn, driver and co-driver slept in the front, the gunner curled up in the turret, and commander and operator shared the space between the exhaust stacks. Traversing the turret to three o'clock gave most room but even then the space was nowhere near long enough. The exhaust housing served as a pillow and the projection in the centre for the hatch supports was the dividing line between the 'beds'.

There was nothing difficult about making the beds, unless it was windy or raining. Nor in undressing. The trouble came in trying to find a position in which to sleep. In any case my knees had to be hunched up and very soon I found that the heat from the engine was searing my hip bone. I turned over and rested my knees on the top of the exhaust. Steve swore at me for kicking him and said I was taking more than my share of room. He turned over and wedged himself in behind me. Then my other hip began to ache. Much to his annoyance, I had to disturb Steve again and get him to turn back. Just as I was getting off he woke me for the same reason. However, at length the engine cooled and we were both able to settle down for what was left of the night.

CHAPTER 17

KERVENHEIM

Steve woke me and it was still dark. There was dew on my blankets and a cold wind made us shiver. We dressed as quickly as possible, sheltering in the lee of the tank. In the front the cooker was already going. Tea came first, then breakfast and then we would wash if there was time. If water was short the inner man, sensibly, always took precedence over the outer. However, it seemed that an early move was not contemplated so we drank our tea, ate our breakfast, and reluctantly got out the washing materials.

We were on call to the Guards Tank Brigade so Steve said we had all better shave. There was a rumour that the Guards had it in for us. Captain Shearman was supposed to have refused a job in which they wanted us to go down a forest track and flame positions five hundred yards from it. As for getting out afterwards, that was our worry. The Guards had had nine tanks bazookaed in the wood and our officer would have nothing to do with the job, on this occasion having the right to take that attitude. Word went round the Squadron that the Guards were really mad with us and would land us in a mess if they could - and they had a reputation for being good at this.

However, no one was greatly worried and we spent the day trying to make rockets from 25-pounder charges. They were not a great success. We tried a number of different designs over which there was a good deal of argument but when we lit the blue touch paper and retired immediately in the approved manner it was always an inglorious fizzle. It passed the time.

It was still too much trouble to erect the bivvy and Ted and I, this time, slept under a sheet beside the tank. In the morning came the awaited order to move. Having failed to hold Goch, the Germans were putting up a strong resistance around Kervenheim, a small town a few miles to the south-east. Our task was to flame troops of the 3rd British Division into the town.

Although reveille was put forward we did not move out as early as had been planned. A scout car from HQ Squadron brought the RSM for a visit. His polished brasses and gleaming boots were incongruous against such a background as we afforded.

Anyway, strangely human for an RSM, he went to every tank, wished us luck, collected the letters we had written and stayed to watch us start.

The day was sunny and our route lay mainly through shaded woodland paths along the side of the scarp. There were a number of civilians living in the woods beside carts piled with furniture, standing in groups to watch us go by, a dismal ragged collection. The men raised their hats, the women smiled nervously. They embarrassed me - it was not pleasant to watch them crawling, even though they were Germans. Valentines of the 3rd British also stood under the trees.

We lost a tank at a very nasty right hand bend, where the road had been filled with loose bricks in an attempt to provide some sort of surface. The tanks dipped down into an enormous rut. Tracks clawed wildly and slowly, with infinite exertion, each tank dragged its way out. Sergeant Ellis came last and stuck.

We crossed the Goch - Üdem railway. The crossing keeper's hut was pitted with bullet holes and a gap had been torn in the roof. A little farther brought us to where an AVRE had ploughed its way through the forest, sinking deeper and deeper until well and truly bogged. It lay in the middle of the track, the muzzle of the petard lifted towards the sky. We squirmed past and onwards.

Presently we were out of the woods and into a ploughed field, hugging a hedge along a beaten track. Across a ditch into a meadow. Then another ploughed field. We were halfway across when there was the hiss of boiling water and the turret filled with steam. On rejoining the Squadron three days previously our left hand mud plough had broken loose and, dragged up in the track, had torn off the rear wing and a long section of the track guard. Our left hand air louvre cover, designed to cope with such an eventuality, had been ripped off by a low bough long before. Now mud had overflowed from the track, blocked the louvre, and caused the near side cooling bank to overheat. Nothing could be done then save to scrape away as much mud as possible and wait for the temperature to drop to normal. As the rest of the Squadron passed we saw Sergeant Jackman's tank clouded in steam and he halted just ahead of us.

When we caught up our tanks were harboured in a space, part garden and part orchard, behind a burnt-out farmhouse. A dead horse lay by our off front wing, half buried in the mud. Some infantry in a German dugout were trying to coax a few chickens within their reach. A thin, misty drizzle was falling and some of the crews had spread sheets over their trailer links and were huddled beneath. The majority, however, preferred the security of their tanks as an AP shot had been heard to whistle overhead just before our arrival. Ambulances and Jeeps moved sluggishly along the Üdem - Weeze road on our left. Towards Kervenheim a pall of smoke hung in the damp air. Shells whined overhead and all around the guns were banging away.

Dinner was out of the question since the order to move might come at any moment. We sat and read, wrote letters and dozed, ate chocolate and boiled sweets, and listened to the wireless. There was a lot of traffic between the Squadron and one of the scout cars, which appeared to be lost and a long way away.

At about midday we crossed the road and headed along a muddy track towards Kervenheim. We were back in the woods again, which were full of vehicles. A Guards tank lay knocked out and sunk deep in the mud on a corner. A large Red Cross banner was displayed before a house half hidden among the trees.

Then with a fork in the road and a cluster of buildings came the end of the woods and we were out in open country, driving along a narrow road with low hedges. The fields to either side were pockmarked with mortar craters and a thin haze of smoke drifted sluggishly down upon us. There were no more 'soft' vehicles to be seen and such infantry as were visible were well down in their holes. With the crump of bursting mortars we also judged it time to close down, as did Mr. Carroll, who was in command. He called up 11 Troop Officer, "I wouldn't sit up there if I were you." Mr. Bottomley looked all around as if waking from a deep sleep and then sank into his turret.

Ted reported that the temperature was rising and then Jinx, who was 'creeping' as usual, complained that the turret would not traverse. Peering cautiously over the side, Steve discovered that mud was again blocking the air louvre and had piled up on what remained of the track guards so as to jam the turret. Although Steve was prepared to take the tank into action with the turret jammed, provided we could still flame, the overheating of the engine was a serious defect that could leave us a sitting duck if we had to stop to cool down.

The FUP[109] was a green and soggy field bordered on three sides by woods and on the fourth by the road. Directly we arrived Steve called the Fitters over but they had hardly started their inspection when the mortar bombs began to fall. Steve leapt from the engine deck to the turret, tearing his trousers and barking his shin, while the Fitters bolted for their Half-track. Chris Pye, the Fitter sergeant, said he could not work under such conditions and secured an order for us to go back to the previous harbour in company with Sergeant Jackman. Three other tanks were left behind in the FUP with trailers U/s and the two HQ tanks, with Mr. Bottomley's flame tank, moved out to attack Kervenheim.

We had reached the fork and passed into the comparative safety of the country behind when we were met by a scout car, coming up the road at a furious rate. It halted in the middle of the road and as we swerved into the field to pass the officer passenger jumped to the ground, shaking his fist and signalling us to stop. We complied, wondering at such vehemence. He was a perfect specimen and I called Jinx up to have a look at Colonel Blimp.

[109] FUP. Forming Up Point. Another name for 'Start Line'.

Sergeant Jackman descended to meet this officer, who was standing by the car firing remarks into a microphone. We watched him shouting and gesticulating until Sergeant Jackman, impassive as ever, returned to his tank and drew it off the road. Steve jumped down, waved Ted in behind him, and conferred with the Sergeant. The scout car bounced away. Presently a sprucely attired officer came walking up the road and Steve and Sergeant Jackman went away with him.

A quarter of an hour passed in speculation. The Colonel - from his complexion he could not be less than a Colonel - was out of sight. Steve was the first of the two tank commanders to return. He looked concerned and our questions were anxious. He said that we were to stay put, as both tank crews were under close arrest for 'misbehaviour' - in other words, for desertion.

We were first amused and then very angry. The whole charge was so obviously ridiculous that it seemed impossible that even the Guards could have made such a mistake. We were out of action - as were the majority of our tanks by now - and had our orders to retire, so what was all the fuss about? Then someone mentioned the rumour that the Guards were gunning for us, and that while the charge was farcical no doubt the Guards were slinging mud in the hope that some of it would stick.

I went back to the wireless in time to hear what might almost have been a sequel. Our flame tank had been knocked out. Mr. Carroll had picked up the crew and was calling the ACV for instructions. A battalion of Guards tanks stood in a field outside Kervenheim, and their commander wanted our two HQ tanks to go in on their own. He had a 'stoppage'. What sort of stoppage? Mr. Carroll was not informed but the Guards would follow as soon as this defect was rectified. Then I could no longer hear the ACV, but it appeared that Mr. Carroll was going to attack without support. The wireless was silent for a bit. Unfortunately, we were not on net to the Guards, for I should have liked to have known more about a stoppage that could immobilise a whole battalion.

There were a few disconnected phrases from the tanks and then suddenly another voice, that of Jack Washington, Mr. Carroll's operator, cried hysterically, "My Sunray is hit - seriously wounded - dead... hit very bad!" Then silence again. I shouted to the other tank. Nothing more came from the wireless. Everyone got very indignant about the 'stoppage'.

"It's like misbehaviour," said Jinx. "It's a polite name for desertion."

At this moment - and probably fortunately, for we were getting worked up - a Very light shot up from a wood away on our left. There were explosions and the crackle of rifle fire, and smoke billowed into the still air. We all got into the tanks, reloaded the guns and traversed to cover the wood. I looked on the Defence Overprint and saw that the area was marked 'probably fortified.'

Presently we got news. Two members of the crew of the knocked out flame tank walked down the road and stopped to talk to us. They were in a bit of a state - pale and jumpy and spotted with blood. Mr. Bottomley and his gunner, Bob Taylor, had been taken into a Field Dressing Station, but neither was seriously hurt. Their tank had been knocked out by a bazooka and they had all sheltered under the trailer until Mr. Carroll had picked them up. There had then been ten men in the HQ tank when Mr. Carroll was killed - they believed by the same bazooka. Jack Washington, it appeared, had done a very good job in turning the tank and getting out of further danger. However, they obviously wanted to get away and Len flagged a Jeep to give them a lift back to the echelon.

An hour later a column of tanks came down the road. First came a flame tank, then Mr. Callingham's Mark V. Then its consort with the cupola blown off, Bob Cheney in the driving seat chain-smoking cigars and Geoff Kirk seated on the wing giving him directions. Two more flame tanks followed.

They were all very surprised to see us. Sergeant Jackman told Mr. Callingham the position and he went away to see the Guards adjutant and got our condition changed to one of open arrest. This allowed us to move.

Everyone was furious with the Guards. There was a lot of wild talk about doing something - such as getting a courts martial which, with the evidence we could bring, would clear us triumphantly and ventilate the subject to the embarrassment of the Guards. Steve, however, counselled letting the matter drop if possible. The officers would stick together whatever the facts; the Guards Colonel was undoubtedly wrong and might have acted spitefully, but he need only say he was mistaken and we should be left with the reputation of trouble-makers. No good ever came of appealing to one officer against another.

Steve had been in the army five years so his opinion carried weight. The affair blew over, and if we were ever officially released from open arrest no one bothered to tell us about it.

It was dark before we could get back on to the road and reach the Squadron, and the wind was getting up. I had a wireless watch to do in the 14 Troop Tank and the rest of the crew were on guard. A Carrier had caught fire at the edge of the wood, throwing a flickering light over the waves of mud and our cluster of tanks. It burnt well and at another time would have been a beautiful sight as the different coloured flares exploded. At first there were men running about beside it, presumably trying to put the fire out, but after a bit they let it be and the light was of great assistance to the Fitters working on our tank.

An artillery barrage was going down to distract the attention of the Germans and my head ached dreadfully. I went back to the turret of my tank when the watch was over and I could hardly keep my eyes open. We had extended hospitality to one of the Fitters, another Bob Taylor, who did not seem to fancy sleeping in his Half-track and, in a space where there was no real room for three to sleep, four was a crowd.

Then Bob Cheney wanted help to lift Mr. Carroll from the track guards to the ground. He sounded all in.

"It's all right," he said. "I've got him out of the turret and his head is covered up. I just want a hand getting him to the ground, that's all."

I felt I had had enough already and pretended to be asleep. Steve and Ted went in the end, but not very willingly.

Despite the fact that I was so sleepy I had little rest that night and most other people were in the same state. Everyone in the tank was twisting and turning about and swearing all the time. My head was throbbing and I ached in every joint. I sat on the ammunition bin and leaned against the Seventy-five but even the metal felt hot.

In the morning everyone still felt bad. The dead man lay on a stretcher in front of his tank and although he was covered with a blanket his feet and one gloved hand were visible and it was nasty to see him there.

Of the tanks only ours was reported fit for action. Of the men, not one was really fit. We had come all the way from Nijmegen without a break, in the expectation of being in action at any moment. Although my tank had not fired a shot the necessity had never been far away and the opportunity at times would have been a great relief. I was feeling the strain, so people like Bob Cheney must have been very near the breaking point. There was a rumour that we might be released for a rest and everyone hoped it was true.

There was a lot of traffic on the road, particularly staff cars with stars all over them. The Guards were harboured on the opposite side of the field and had all got out their best battledress with belts and gaiters. This only increased our contempt for them as being nothing but a bunch of bullshitters!

Later in the morning, some infantry brought back a number of German children, boys of about fourteen and presumably members of the Hitler Youth. They pointed out one of them as having fired the bazooka which brewed up our flame tank and killed Mr. Carroll, although how they knew this they did not say. The boys all seemed very pleased with themselves and the infantry called them cocky little buggers. They suggested we go into the woods and shoot them as they were escorted to Üdem. Mr. Carroll had not been greatly liked but he was dead and there was a feeling that somebody ought to pay for it. None of us, however, would have been prepared to take up the infantry offer and soon the boys were marched away and we were glad to see them go.

I do not know when and where Mr. Carroll was buried, although Yossel Franklin was making the cross when the Major came up to the Squadron. That job was, probably, indicative of how we were feeling. So it was probably a relief to him to be able to give us good news. We were released and going back to Goch.

CHAPTER 18.

XANTEN

We started back after dinner. The prospect of a rest had dispelled the gloom, on my tank at least, and we were cheerful and talkative. As far as Üdem we kept to the road through the battered woods. Here in the ditches lay overturned Carriers, burnt out cars and trucks, a German SP gun on its side, ammunition cases, empty boxes and tins, splintered wood and metal everywhere.

The skies were grey. Flurries of snow and sleet lashed at us, whipping inside the hoods of our zoot suits. Üdem was crowded with tanks, some wrecked, some whole, and from here we struck across country to join the Goch - Calcar road. The Germans had fought hard to hold Üdem, which had been strongly protected by a vast anti-tank ditch and numerous devices to hinder the infantry such as great steel spikes set in the ground at six inch intervals. The fields were littered with barbed wire and most of the tanks picked up great hanks, tangled in the tracks, and trailed it behind them.

Sleet and snow swept across the open country unhindered and we took turns to thaw out on the engine deck. Some light Honey tanks raced us, bouncing and rolling over the ploughed land, heeling over like yachts as they turned away. Shell craters and foxholes scarred the fields, which were littered with bits of German uniforms and equipment. Here a tin hat lay beside a broken rifle and a stained tunic. Or a Spandau, lying on its side, the ground about it strewn with ammunition cases. A filthy greatcoat, torn up the back to reveal the white lining, with a grey balaclava and a woollen glove beside it. Now and again we passed a rough mound with a rifle butt stuck upright at the head, or two sticks tacked together to form a rough cross. We ploughed steadily on, across green meadows and scrubby wasteland, until at last we sighted the line of pylons marking the road and, as darkness fell, followed them into ruined Goch.

We had a cosy evening. In the street above the rain was pelting the water in the potholes but below ground all was snug and warm. The stove glowed, the flame of the hurricane lantern burned without a flicker. We sat on our beds in our vests, mugs to hand, pronging pickled gherkins from a tall glass jar and listening to Steve talk, which was something he did very well. Ted bent over the frying pan, in which sizzled a mound of chipped potatoes. On the table, waiting, a plate of spam steamed beside a pile of fried bread and several jars of peaches and pears.

In the morning the mutter of the cooker woke me and I was surprised to find that it was nearly eleven o'clock. Only Ted was up, slicing sausages for breakfast. I could not remember when I had had such a lie-in and felt better for it. No one was bothering us and it did look as if we were going to get a rest.

In fact, there was a lot of work to do on the tanks to get them back into shape but it was all done at a leisurely pace, without fuss, and we had four days with plenty of time to eat and sleep. Only on one occasion did we go anywhere, to a bathhouse at Kessel. I disliked the look of the place from the moment I saw the oily yellow smoke curling sluggishly from the tin chimney and although I undressed and washed myself a bit it did not count as a bath.

Ted and I searched the nearest houses while waiting for the party to assemble for the return journey. He picked up a broken tank cooker that he thought he could repair, or at least exchange for a new one. I contented myself with some packets of 'peppermint tea' as souvenirs. It certainly smelt of peppermint but we never ventured to find out if it tasted of tea.

The Squadron was together at Goch. The scout car crews were there and even Paddy had come up with the rear echelon, which came in for a good deal of chaff as usual. HQ Troop had their share. Shag Taylor - now gunner on a Mark VI - had remarked that in future their

Ninety-fives would be used to fire tins of concentrated soup up to the rear echelon and this bon mot was a great success.

Paddy met us as we arrived back from the bath expedition and we sang 'Our Sergeant-Major's Got The MBE', which decoration had just been awarded him. Of course, he claimed he did not know the reason for it. We certainly did not.

No one had taken much interest in the progress of the war but it seemed that the left bank of the Rhine was nearly clear. We were at six hours notice to move, then two, then one. Then we were definitely going to move at four o'clock. Everyone packed. The move was postponed until five.

Jinx was going on leave and was removing his kit from the tank with his usual infuriating lethargy. Another gunner, Stan Sutton, was waiting to take his place and we urged Jinx 'to get a bloody move on we ain't got all bleeding night' but it was not the slightest use.

We were to move out in Troops at intervals of a quarter of an hour. Our destination was a cluster of houses just on the outskirts of Xanten, to relieve a squadron of the Fife & Forfar Yeomanry[110], the 'Knife & Forkers'. There was some grousing about this but Steve explained that they had just done an action, an unwelcome night action, executed with conspicuous skill and gallantry - against no opposition whatsoever! We were in support of 2 Canadian Corps, which had taken over from 30 Corps.

The Canadians were engaged in clearing the 'Wesel Pocket', the last ground on the west bank of the Rhine in German hands. At Wesel the Rhine describes a wide curve and it was the object of the Canadians to dash across the ground within this loop and capture two bridges intact.

We moved out behind time and although it was fast growing dark Sherry led at full speed. Trees and houses flashed by, dim shapes

[110] Fife & Forfar Yeomanry. This was the second Crocodile regiment, which came under the command of 31st Armoured Brigade in Oct. 1944. The third regiment, joining in Feb. 1945, was the 7th. RTR.

looming up and vanishing into the night. There was the usual danger from low branches and wires that kept us on the alert and the usual dust and grit flung up in our faces. There was little traffic on the road but the fields were filled with motionless shadows showing no gleam of light.

Calcar: skeleton roofs and walls fretted against the night sky. A jolt and a bounce over the level crossing and we were on the road to Xanten. Trees made a gloomy tunnel, with here and there a dimly illuminated sign piercing the blackness. A Bailey Bridge lay over a crater, red and green lamps at each end, the iron railing gleaming as we eased our way across with inches to spare. Then speeding up, with a clash of gears and a tremendous jolt we were clear. Ted was complaining that his gear change rods were sticking but there was no time to stop and look at them.

A fork in the road and houses. The leading tank dipped into a field and we could see the outlines of the others. "Close right up!" someone was shouting and we surged up behind, swaying in the ruts made by our predecessors. Almost before we had halted an agitated officer was fluttering around us giving orders.

"Don't show any lights - this place is under observation. Keep to the right of the tanks as this area has been shelled and we're expecting more. Not a glimmer of light, for God's sake! No cookers must be lighted, even inside the tanks. Periscopes must be shuttered. We may have to go into action tonight. The Fife & Forfars should have stood by until morning but they've gone back already. Who's that smoking over there? Put that bloody fag out - put it out!"

Len, Ted and Stan opted to sleep in the tank after that but Steve and I decided to sleep in one of a group of houses that had been secured by 13 Troop. Sorting out the blankets from the back bin was difficult without a light, especially as Ted claimed five and I could not find the last one. By the time we reached the house there was only one room left. The window was already sheeted so I could light a candle. In one corner stood a bed, in another a chest of drawers - drawers and contents being thrown about the floor. The doors of a wardrobe hung drunkenly. A broken chair, a sound chair, and a table heaped with old clothes, bricks, plaster and scraps of paper, completed the furnishing.

We made down our beds, Steve appropriating the strategic position next to the wall. Then from the darkness outside came the wailing cry, "Petrol up! Come and get yer petrol!"

I pretended not to hear and unlaced my boots but Steve was not going to let me get away with that. By the time we got to the tank Ted had calculated that we needed a dozen jerricans, and the spare hands on the back of the truck flung them into the mud, whence I swung them on to the track guard with a crash. Ted opened the cans with a pick and Stan held the Hellesen with his finger over the bulb to let a tiny point of light strike the filler. Steve whipped out the filters so as to be able to pour more quickly; a good deal of petrol found its way into the hull that night. Acrid fumes rose from splashes on the exhaust.

Then back to bed and since I was still in bed when I woke in the morning I presume I did not kick much. Steve said a few shells had come over in the night but nothing to worry about.

We were up early, ready to move, but no order came. All morning Carriers, tanks and guns were rolling back along the road from Xanten. The pocket had been cleared, although not quickly enough to save the bridges. Now the German big guns across the Rhine were pounding the area and it was being evacuated. Away to our left dense clouds drifted across the level fields from smoke dischargers near the river bank. Just visible above were the hills on the German side.

It seemed a pity to have come all that way in such a hurry and then not do anything, so it was decided to test our guns by firing a few rounds of HE across the Rhine. Some of the tanks took a bearing from a Bofors battery in order to be sure of dropping their shells somewhere near Wesel. We aimed at a church on the skyline and then put on maximum elevation.

Ours was a new gun which we had never fired before and we found that it did not run out fast enough to eject the empty case. We blamed Jinx for this, as his maintenance was usually slack, but later investigation showed him to be guiltless and the gun to be at fault.

Cleaning the barrel took some time. Then we breakfasted. Afterwards, in looking round a nearby house, I found an ornamental beer mug with a pewter cover, a stein - something I had long coveted. After we had proved that this held a pint there was nothing to do but watch the traffic, which was mostly trucks and therefore uninteresting. We were told that we were only waiting for a break to slip in and join the procession. Our work was finished until the time came to cross the Rhine.

CHAPTER 19

INTERLUDE

The opportunity to move came just after dinner. I felt sick after bottled blackcurrants brought from Goch, but apart from this it was an uneventful run back to Marienbaum on the Xanten-Calcar road.

Here the tanks were harboured in the field behind the billets except for HQ Troop, who were parked in the garden beside their house. My crew took over a roomy outhouse already containing a pot-bellied stove and I found a length of stovepipe unguarded outside the HQ Troop billet. The problem of beds was solved by breaking into a garage, the loft of which had been used for storing new furniture and where there were a lot of spring mattresses. I also found a pair of German jackboots which fitted me.

One member of the Squadron lately come up from the Delivery Squadron had been a butcher in civvy life and while we were getting our beds he was cutting up a pig in our garden. From across the fields came the squeals of another. Presently it came in sight, on a wheelbarrow, its snout digging more furrows in a ploughed field.

We lived very well at Marienbaum. Our compos always ran the same brand for about a fortnight and just then we were receiving the coveted A packs, containing steak-and-kidney pudding and tinned fruit. Ted had the opportunity to show just how good a cook he was.

There was the prospect of a long rest before us while the armies were regrouped for the crossing of the Rhine. No one worried much about that part, for it was bound to come in its own good time and meanwhile we would take things easy. I hoped we would be returning to Holland but Major Duffy had been overheard to say that he thought we had seen the last of friendly countries. He said he did not want to go back to Bergeijk, anyway, as he had never liked the place. We thought he had had a girlfriend there but evidently, like so many latrinograms, there had been no truth in that.

Someone found a bazooka lying beside the railway line and Sherry said it would be good fun to set it off. Half the Squadron assembled at a safe distance - even Reg Webb, who was of a serious nature and ordinarily took no part in that sort of thing. A handcart was found, the bazooka lashed to a wheel and the wheel banked with earth. Sherry tied a long wire to the trigger and he and his assistants squeezed into a foxhole about fifty yards away. He tugged and nothing happened. He tugged again and then gave a mighty wrench. The cart spun round and faced us. We all ducked. Nothing happened, but they did not know whether or not the trigger had been pulled so no one would go near the thing.

News came after four days; the whole regiment was to assemble in the forest between Weeze and Üdem, one of the offshoots of the Reichswald and Hochwald that cover the plain between the border and the Rhine. Apart from the somewhat unfortunate visit of our Colonel at Bergeijk and the more pleasant sight of the RSM before Kervenheim, I had no experience of a regimental HQ. My companions, however, viewed proximity to RHQ with annoyance, informing me that we could expect a shower of petty restrictions. RHQs always make good use of the word 'will' - men will march to meals, guards will wear Number Two BD,[111] courses will be undertaken by all squadrons, first parade on tanks will be carried out, and so on.

I was reminded that when we were in action, most of the time RHQ did not know where we were and when they did they held no communication with us. We drew our own rations, fuel and ammunition direct, and since both Recce and Ack-Ack Troops had

[111] Number 2 BD. We were issued with two sets of battle dress, No. 1 being our 'best serge' for special parades (e.g. General Simpson), walking out etc., our 'best suit', in fact. No. 2 was the working set for when we had to be 'properly dressed', such as the formal guards in the Weeze forest. Normally, we wore denims and all sorts of odds and ends, including the comfortable leather jerkins, for working on the tanks. During the winter we managed to acquire spare items of battle dress, through 'lost in action' claims, to wear under our zoot suits.

been broken up long before there seemed no reason for RHQ to exist. From what was said it appeared that RHQ were about to seize the opportunity to justify their existence by trying to turn us into proper soldiers. If that meant that the really important task, the maintenance of the tanks, had to take a pace to the rear, that was too bad. It would seem more essential that our webbing be clean than that the tanks be battleworthy.

The Squadron left Marienbaum at five o'clock in the morning, the noise of our tracks echoing in the dark streets as we ground round the corners and out along the twisting road into the forest. My crew had hoped to escape this early reveille. Ted had reported the trouble with his gear selector rods which we had experienced going up to Xanten and it was hoped that we would be left behind until the Fitters had corrected the fault. However, as we were preparing for bed, Chris Pye put his head through the window with the bad news that the work was done and we could go with the rest.

The twin spires of Üdem church towered above the trees in the distance, red brick glinting in the rays of the pale dawn. Choking alkaline dust rose in swirls. We climbed the side of a hill where real live cattle grazed unconcerned and dipped into the valley beyond where a rusting Panther nestled beside a thatched cottage.

Üdem. The cross-roads and the ruined church, of which only the spires remained, watching over a wilderness of windowless walls of roofless houses. A burnt-out Sherman stood by the level crossing, suspension sunk deep into earth that had been soft when the tank met its end. Engineers were working on the railway, ripping up the twisted metals and re-laying the sleepers to make way for a new track.

In the woods beyond the same cars, the same Carriers, the SP gun still in the ditch. The litter of soggy cardboard and paper, tins and boxes, still choked the watercourses. A rutted field and a blackened farmhouse and, on the opposite side of the road, four graves with one cross that we thought we recognised. An AVRE, bogged down and abandoned, stood beneath the trees where the Carrier had burnt a little while before. Then we were in the forest again and the leading tank lurched off the road to follow an arrow with the number 993 and C Squadron's blue circle.

The track twisted among the trees. Low branches forced us into the turret and to close the hatches, until hazel and stunted birch gave way to tall pines. A violent turn to the left and there was Paddy waving us from the road with his silver knobbed stick. That stick was a bad sign.

We nursed the tank carefully in among the pines, watching the mud shields. The tank behind charged straight in and lost both; the trees went down all right but the wings were buckled beyond repair. I was puzzled about this later when I found the tank had been driven by Jack, who was usually so fussy about his wings. Perhaps he was having an off day.

Paddy warned everyone against straying too far into the forest as parts were heavily mined. Also, he advised us to make ourselves as comfortable as possible as in all probability we should be staying some time. The pine trees offered a way of helping our comfort. Each crew unearthed the necessary tools and all day long the forest echoed to the thud of axes, the squeak of saws, the long drawn out cry of 'timber!' in the approved manner followed by the tearing crash of the falling tree. Then hacking and rapid sawing to lop the branches and finally the thump of hammers on soft wood as corner posts were driven into the ground. By mid-afternoon four log cabins stood in the Troop area. We had managed to bring our stove from Marienbaum and all the rest of the Troop had managed to get something similar. The stovepipe ran out of the wall as the roof of the cabin was made from tank sheets over pine rafters.

"Now," I remarked, as I rigged electric light and wireless loudspeaker running from the tank, "now if only they leave us alone we can be very comfortable here."

"They won't leave us alone," was the general opinion.

The general opinion was correct. Orders appeared the next day.

To begin with breakfast. This and all other meals were to be in a central cookhouse half a mile away on the Weeze-Üdem road. This meant a march and the vexation of providing mess orderlies, while of course we would have preferred to remain on compo so that we could please ourselves what we ate and when. Fortunately, we had enough buckshee rations to have fried bully beef or spam with chips for supper most nights and we managed to replenish our stock of tea whenever a member of the crew went on mess orderly for a day.

First parade at nine o'clock, with inspection by Troop Officer or Troop Sergeant. Then maintenance parade on the tank. There was not time to start a big job. Ted would sit looking at the engine with a spanner in his hand. I would net to the BBC and arrange the headsets so that everyone could hear. The CO was sure to be prowling round the Squadron ready to pounce on anyone found smoking 'within five yards of a WD vehicle', so if we wanted to smoke it was necessary to get inside the turret and close down. Steve's principal employment was to keep an eye open and tell us when to look busy.

After maintenance came the NAAFI break - half a mug of tepid tea from the cookhouse.

Then PT. No one liked the idea of this. In the Training Regiment I had to make the best of it. Since being on active service I had only been caught once, back at Bretteville. Fortunately, here it was under 'Troop arrangement', which meant that we doubled until out of sight, as if starting for a cross-country run, fell out and smoked for half an hour, and then doubled back.

After that we were at 'Troop Officer's Disposal' for the rest of the day. At first we had our gun to change, which meant removing the back bin, unscrewing the hatch in the turret wall which was placed there for this purpose, removing the wireless set and taking the gun to pieces before drawing out the barrel. Then we had to fit the new gun and replace everything. The whole operation took two days and very glad we were when it was done.

Many of the tanks had to have names and signs painted on them and ours was one. There had to be 'Sandwich' in pale blue on each air louvre; blue circles containing a white 13B on a black centre on the turret; the yellow triangle and black and white bull's head of 79th

Armoured Division and the green diabolo of 31 Armoured Brigade, the number 'T.173174/H' in white on each side; the weight classification on the front; and indication of positions of infantry phone and infantry first aid kit.

Dinner, back to work, tea. Then, for the unlucky, guard mounting. Equipment had to be scrubbed, ready for this. A guard tent was erected near the cookhouse - a cold, dreary, cheerless place. While the guard in itself was nothing, having to sleep away from the crew, being cut off for one night from the happy comradeship of the cabin, was not to my liking. There always had to be one man outside the Squadron Office, so it was impossible to spend the guard in the billet as had been customary previously. However, while at this post one evening I got chatting with the squadron clerk and learned that my leave date was April 23rd. That was something to know.

For those not on guard there was a considerable variety of entertainment. The AVRE attracted our attention at first but it had been thoroughly plundered and there was nothing worth the taking. At the other end of the wood on the main road was a house that had been a German strong point and was more interesting. Often, leaving one man to keep the stove alight and fry the chips, the rest of us would creep away into the forest, treading warily and keeping to well-defined paths for fear of wooden box and Schu mines. Our destination was 'the dead 'uns'. On a mound among some fallen trees three German soldiers had attempted to stay the advance of a column of tanks, identified as Churchills from the ruts they left. The area was littered with papers, books, photographs and equipment, presumably the property of the dead men. Under the tree trunk felled to cover their foxhole the three corpses were muffled in blankets, save for their feet which protruded clad in thick white socks. Steve removed the blankets once but hastily replaced them - the faces were going mouldy. We did not disturb them after that.

What we wanted were the three rifles which, with a couple of abandoned Lee-Enfields, were used for shooting practice. The woods were full of ammunition and we could blaze away until our ears were singing. Then, after stuffing the rifles under the tree trunk for the next-comers, back to supper.

Or we would go hunting. Shag and I would climb a rotten home-made ladder to a keeper's tower perched in the tree tops and there we would sit and wait for rabbits or deer that were supposed to be in the forest. Disappointed, avoiding the bodies under the fallen tree, we would hurry back in the twilight to warmth and company.

Or we would stay in to read or write letters. Or merely to chat and drink tea before a roasting stove while music came intermittently from the loudspeaker and we soon ceased to notice the undercurrent of popping from the auxiliary charger out in the tank. Until came the periodic stoppage and it was necessary to go out and start it again.

One night a truck caught fire on the road near RHQ and that was a pretty sight. No one knew how it had happened and as the petrol tank was blazing merrily it did not last long but we were pleased with the entertainment. Not so pleasing was the mass migration of frogs from one side of the road to the other that happened to coincide with the passage of several convoys.

On the debit side, there were nearly always brasses to be polished, and sometimes all the loot had to be hidden away in the bushes in readiness for some brigadier or general who would descend upon the regiment spreading confusion before him and leaving criticism and despondency in his wake. Still, photographs of our crew taken at the time and which not only got developed but of which we actually received the prints, showed us all looking very cheerful. Despite the petty annoyances, the break must have done us good.

CHAPTER 20

THE RHINE CROSSING

'Operation Plunder' - the assault across the Rhine and subsequent drive across Germany - had the strategic intention of joining up with the Russians (who timed an offensive to coincide with ours) and so cutting what was left of the German Army in two. The Germans were supposed to be short of weapons, ammo and fuel. As for their men, it was believed that only the SS and armoured units retained much spirit; the infantry divisions were reputed to be very much shaken and their losses being made up by the untried Volksturm.[112]

The assault technique was to be similar to that used on D-Day. Our infantry would be ferried across in Buffaloes, which were amphibious cargo and personnel carriers propelled by their tracks on both land and water. Such supporting armour as would be immediately necessary would be provided by DDs. These were Sherman gun tanks fitted with a canvas framework which could be inflated by gas to turn them into boats. Motive power was then transferred to a propeller - hence the name DD,[113] or Duplex Drive. Eight Class 50/60 rafts were being built by the Assault RE squadrons and these would be used to ferry Kangaroos with supporting Crocodiles, AVREs and Flails. These would suffice until bridges were constructed.

The target date was March 23/24. The crossings were to be between Rees and Rheinburg, the US 9th Army on the right, the British 2nd Army on the left. The 2nd would capture Wesel to allow the 9th to commence bridging operations, would build its own bridges

[112] Volksturm. The German equivalent to our Home Guard.

[113] DD. See description in text. The DD had been specially designed for D-Day where it was very successful. Units equipped with the DD were the Staffordshire Yeomanry and the 44th. RTR.

at Xanten and Rees, and would allow 2 Canadian Corps to pass through to capture Emmerich and build another bridge there. The 18 Airborne Corps, comprising 6th British and 17th US Airborne Divisions, would be dropped north of Wesel to assist in taking the town.

The 1st Canadian Army was to take no part in the assault, its task being to hold the banks of the Rhine and Maas from Emmerich to the sea and so protect the left flank, the existing bridgehead at Nijmegen and the port of Antwerp. The Air Forces would attack communications, draw German fighters from the Rhine area by diversionary attacks, damage the aerodromes from which German jet planes operated and shoot up targets in the battle area.

2nd Army had its 12 Corps on the right and 30 Corps on the left. 12 Corps assault was to be by 15th Scottish Division and 1 Commando Brigade, which would be carried in Buffaloes of the 11th RTR, East Riding Yeomanry and 77 Assault Squadron, RE. Other units of 79th Armoured Division included Crocodiles of 7th RTR (newcomers to 31 Armoured Brigade from the training ground at Dunkirk), Kangaroos of A and C Squadrons, 49 APC Regiment, Flails of the Westminster Dragoons, AVREs of 82 Assault Squadron, RE and Canal Defence Lights of half of B Squadron, 49 APC Regiment.

30 Corps attack was to be by the 51st Highland Division, carried in Buffaloes of 4th RTR and the Northamptonshire Yeomanry. 79th Armoured Division units in support comprised Crocodiles of C Squadron, 141 RAC, Flails of B Squadron, 22nd Dragoons, AVREs of 26 Assault Squadron, RE, and the other half of B Squadron, 49 APC Regiment, which provided Canal Defence Lights to give 'movement and direction light' to Buffalo crossings and protect them from drifting mines or sabotage swimmers.

The DD tanks concerned in the operation had been removed from our division, 44th RTR coming under 12 Corps and the Staffordshire Yeomanry under 8 Independent Armoured Brigade in 30 Corps.

Once the bridgehead was established the plan was for 12 Corps to use 53rd Welsh Division and 7th Armoured Division to expand to the east while 30 Corps used 43rd Wessex and 3rd Canadian Divisions to capture Emmerich and the high ground to the north of that town.

* * *

The only flaw in our departure from the Weeze forest was the necessity of abandoning our log cabins to the mercy of the elements, or to the bands of homeless wanderers living in carts or dugouts in the woods.

"ASHES TO ASHES, DUST TO DUST:
YOUR DUST WILL TURN US TO ASHES."

Thus the signs lining the roads to the Rhine, but all to no avail. Our tanks at full speed moved only at a snail's pace but great swirls of yellow, clinging dust rolled in the sunshine. Throats and mouths muffled in scarves, eyes goggled, we peered anxiously to pierce the flickering veil which hid the tank in front.

There was not a breath of air and the exhaust fumes were trapped in the dust. The sun blazed, the sky was blue. Bundles of silver paper dropped by passing aircraft fluttered down; we did not know their purpose at that time. The dried out countryside lay dead beneath this unseasonal heat haze. Sweat trickled down our caked cheeks, the scarves clung to our jaws and throats and made us itch. The dust filtered into the turret and settled everywhere. It lay deep on the floor and ledges, clung to the oil-coated guns and swirled into the air filters. It ran down inside our shirts to rub the skin beneath our belts, crept under the edges of our goggles and brought tears to aching eyes. The water in the turret tank was tepid and tainted with rust, the surface thick with dust particles. The rustle of the wireless set was a constant irritant. From the driving seat a croaking voice informed us that he could see 'bugger all and would we guide him'. We were doing our best.

Through Üdem, Keppeln, Calcar and along the Kleve road; just beyond the village of Moyland, we turned off and it was a great relief to get into a shaded and relatively cool lane. One of the HQ tanks had been polished with oil in the Weeze forest and we could now see how dust had stuck to the outside and converted the smartest tank in the Squadron to being one of the dirtiest. This was pleasing.

A Churchill tank stood on the verge of the road, hatches open, two neat holes piercing the air louvre. A little further and two Honeys were heeled over in the middle of a field, suspension caught in earth set as hard as cement. For half a mile the fields held two-wheeled carts converted into dummy Five-fives, poles making the barrel and distinctive vertical recoil cylinders. Beyond these, the fields were filled with vehicles and tents and the sun gleamed on the white bodies of sun-bathing soldiers who glanced up incuriously as we passed. At a corner, propped against a burnt-out Sherman, a great sign proclaimed

"MOYLAND CONCENTRATION AREA."

We swung left along a track with dust deeper than that on the road.

Our harbour was set among pines round a mound at the south-eastern end of Moyland Wood. The ground was full of foxholes and dugouts, all roofed neatly with logs and lined with straw, tarpaulins and blankets. Our Troop drew just off the road along an avenue bearing the name 'Beringen Straat' - a name that brought back memories. All the 'streets' had names tacked to the trees: Wilhelmstrasse, Adolf Hitler Strasse, Friedrichstrasse, Dr. Goebbels Strasse, Rue Neuve, Rue Royale, Boulevarde Adolphe Max, and so on. In a field on the other side of the road were two marquees, one a canteen, the other a mobile cinema.

Our tanks lined the road, save for 13 Troop in 'Beringen Straat' and HQ Troop in a grove at the top of the rise. North of the rise were a large number of 17-pounder Shermans. On the opposite side of the road were the DD Shermans of the Staffs Yeomanry.

Great importance was attached to camouflage, but after we had stretched our nets between the trees and piled branches and brushwood along the sides of the tank, especially over those telltale trailer wheels, we had little to do. For want of something better we cleaned the tank, removing all the dust although a mile on the road would put it back. The trailer was unloaded and all our furniture dumped after a warning that we should have no opportunity to erect our stove or use our table and chairs once we had crossed the Rhine. However, that evening the 17-pounders moved out, perhaps intending that their echelon should pick up all the kit they left behind. We laid hands on sheets, bivvies, water and oil cans, and anything else that promised to be of use and the trailer was soon piled as high as ever. As long as we stacked it so that our Seventy-five could fire over it, no one bothered.

Len was always doing something energetic and he brought back a rope, tied it to a tree, and tried to swing like Tarzan across a ravine. He was unsuccessful and then Jinx had to try. He climbed the tree, could not get down, and shouted. We stood at the bottom and jeered. In the end, Len had to go up to the rescue.

Len was always having to get his brother out of some difficulty, although Jinx was the elder by several years. He had come back to us in the Weeze forest, although for some time it was uncertain if he would. Reg Webb detested him and while we did not go so far as this we did prefer Stan Sutton as our gunner. But to exclude Jinx would hurt Len, who was universally liked and probably worked harder than any other man in the Troop.

The weather was perfect and we had the time to make the most of the sun. In the evening we had the choice of seeing 'Going My Way' or 'Winter Time', which were the only two films available. We appreciated that marquee cinema - it seemed we were being shown a deserved consideration. I went once and our form collapsed, so we sat in the dust for the remainder of the show but this did not detract from my enjoyment of the film.

Len slept in the driving compartment, Ted and Jinx were in a dugout on the edge of Len's ravine, and Steve and I slept in the open beneath the trailer link. The Luftwaffe was unusually active at night. The second night, Steve and I were lying in bed, staring up at the stars and talking in whispers. Then in the distance there was the drone of engines and the steady beat of flak. As it grew louder so we edged further under the tank, rolling in our blankets as best we could. Then with a roar a great black shape swooped across the sky, machine guns rattling viciously. Probably the pilot had seen people coming out of the cinema tent but, so far as I know, no one was hit.

Despite such alarms I enjoyed it all. Even the guards were pleasant. Steve only did them in emergencies, such as when I had a wireless watch, or Ted had had a long drive, or something like that. Len and I were partners at this time and would trail about the wood or up and down the starlit road, ankle deep in dust, smoking and talking in whispers, watching the searchlights dim against the bright sky and gently curving tracer falling over the Rhine valley.

During the hours of daylight the loudspeakers hanging from the trees were always chattering, usually quite unintelligibly, but on the afternoon of the third day they blared forth with unaccustomed strength.

"Hallo! Hallo! Hallo! Will the commander of the Crocodiles report to the command tent and all troops get ready to move immediately!"

There was a tremendous flap, of course. We heaved the stove and its sack of coal from the trailer, stowed blankets, cooker and food, and tore down all the camouflage. Then it was declared that only 14 Troop had to move, to follow up the first wave that was going over that night.

The DDs were already swinging out of their harbour, raising clouds of dust, jolting on to the road and away over the hill. The restful atmosphere was gone. Everywhere was the bustle of preparation, shouted commands, the whine of straining engines. I got quite a kick to watch the armour sweeping purposefully up the hill, tank after tank nose to tail and rendered even more imposing by the dust clouds, and to think that the whole world was watching what we were doing.

That afternoon the German bank was bombed and shelled and the first infantry were due to land at 2100 hours under a barrage of 1700 guns. In the morning we saw troop-carrying planes on the way back and all sorts of rumours flashed round the Squadron. We had linked up with the Airborne already. No, we had not - it was another

Arnhem and they had been cut to pieces. The DDs had been out of luck and had suffered terrible casualties - and then it was reported that they had got ashore without opposition. Nothing was known about 14 Troop, but the 79th Armoured Division had been mentioned on the News.

In point of fact the airborne landings proceeded smoothly, the bridges over the River Ijssel being captured intact and the link-up with the ground forces being made without trouble. As for the Staffs Yeomanry, for whom we were mainly concerned as we knew their vulnerability while swimming, C Squadron lost six ashore and three in the water and landed eight, while A and B Squadrons only lost two tanks each through shelling before they were launched. Everything went like clockwork.

We moved in the afternoon with one of the HQ tanks detached to lead the way. It was uncertain when 11 and 12 Troops would start. Down the hill and on to the Rhine plain; bare, rolling country, the track winding between grassy mounds, occasionally striking a stretch of gravel road in a tiny hamlet. At first we made for Wissel but soon turned right and across country to Hönnopel. Beyond was 'Waterloo' track junction and here we turned towards the river, making for 'Tilbury' ferry. The other, 'Gravesend', was not working so well. We crossed a road, lurched through a gap in the hedge, and saw before us the embankment bordering the Rhine.

Huddled under this embankment, scores of tanks were awaiting their turn. The most were Shermans of 8 Armoured Brigade with their attendant Honeys, but there was a sprinkling of Valentine SP guns and Scissors Bridges, Sherman and Centaur-dozers[114] and a few Buffaloes. Beside a hedge, painted grey, was one of the CDL[115]

---

[114] Centaur-dozer. The Centaur was the tank from which the Cromwell was developed and was not used as a tank in action. I had trained on it as preparation for the Cromwell. Minus turret and fitted with a bulldozer blade, it was replacing the earlier armoured bulldozers.

[115] Canal Defence Lights. This was a carbon arc light mounted (with a machine gun) in the turret of an old Grant tank. The turret also carried a dummy 37 mm. gun. The tank retained its 75 mm. in a sponson on the right-hand side. Its use was as described in the text.

tanks, a Grant with a dummy gun in the upper turret which housed the light. It was the first we had seen.

We halted behind some Shermans of the Sherwood Rangers bearing the fox's head of 8 Armoured Brigade, dismounted, and scrambled up the bank to get our first view of the river. It lay about a hundred yards away, the ground dropping gently to the water's edge where the bank was liberally reinforced with rubble. With pictures of the Rhine castles and the Lorelei in my mind's eye the actuality was a disappointment to me. Except for the current - that was frightening, for the water raced and boiled furiously, swung by breakers jutting at an angle into the river. On the far side everything was dimmed by smoke.

The raft, carrying a Sherman and an assortment of Jeeps, was in midstream, carried seawards by the whip of the current. An AVRE with a steel hawser attached formed an anchor, while beside it the winch let the other hawser dip gently into the water. Engineers in boats stood ready to help the raft home against the improvised jetty. A canteen dispensed tea to the waiting crews while one member of its staff loaded an urn and a box of buns into the Buffalo that was to take him across. A Sherman, followed by a Valentine Scissors Bridge, crested the embankment and taxied gingerly down to the loading point.

Farther along, Buffaloes manned by the Engineers sidled down to the river, tracks threshing up spray as they laboured towards the far bank. Shells fired by German guns on the flank were plunging down below the ferry, throwing up great gouts of water and making the Buffaloes swerve in their course. The light was failing fast. Tracer arched against the darkening sky and a CDL cut a broad beam in the drifting smoke.

Although we had - or were reputed to have - absolute priority, yet we had to wait while other tanks were shifted out of our way. This took a long time and it was quite dark when Reg's tank jolted on to the jetty while we waited at the top of the embankment. The HQ tank, having no trailer, had already gone with a Sherman, and the ferry lay apparently motionless in midstream on its return journey.

As it neared the shore we saw it to be crowded with men. Some were passengers but the majority were tin-hatted REs with boathooks and sounding poles. Reg was loaded and we sidled down to take his place on the stage. The water lapped against the piles. The winch motor hummed steadily, and presently the ferry loomed out of the darkness and grounded gently before us.

While in the Weeze forest, our drivers had been taken to Nijmegen to practise loading on rafts at one of the Wings set up there for experimental and training purposes. It was the ordinary Bailey Bridge on pontoons - two narrow trackways and an alarming expanse of water between them. The officer stood at the far end and waved us forward, the pontoons lurched as they took our weight. It was simple. Before we knew it, we were loaded, the winch hummed again, and the strip of water between the raft and the bank grew wider.

We were afraid German aircraft might be about and kept inside the tank but the batteries of Bofors on either bank kept good guard. Occasionally a shell splashed into the water downstream but otherwise the only sounds were the muffled voices of the Engineers, the steady throb of our idling engine, and the slap of waves against the pontoons.

Gradually the northern bank grew more distinct and I could see a deep cutting, a gravelled staging, a knot of men. With a slight jar the raft checked and ropes were twisted round bollards. Our engine roared in relief, the tank surged forward, and twelve minutes after leaving the south bank we laboured up the slope to join our Troop waiting at the top of the north shore.

* * *

Rees had held out longer than was expected but fell at last and now our troops were pushing a salient northwards in the direction of Ijsselburg. Rees lay approximately in the base of a triangle of captured territory and we were to harbour there in readiness for any call.

On leaving the ferry we turned right along a tank track. The sky was bright with artificial moonlight. Columns of German prisoners trudged along the road which ran parallel to the track. Others, bandaged, were riding in Jeeps. Ambulances hurried between the Dressing Stations and the nine-ton bridge which was already laid over the Rhine.

The track swerved to avoid a mined Honey, neatly fenced with white tape. A soldier was making half a dozen prisoners double down the road and was evidently swearing at them. A Jeep lay under a hedge, twisted and torn above a shallow crater. The river embankment was pitted with foxholes where our men had dug in directly they landed. We passed the light bridge, a thin black strip upon the silver water, with masses of vehicles waiting to cross.

On our left Canadian Carpets - mass salvoes of rockets - and shells were bursting on the German positions at the side of the salient. We passed through a ruined cluster of houses, the street black after the brilliance of the open country. Then along a reasonably good road into what Steve said was Rees. At our briefing we had been told that it was our intention to utterly destroy every town and village that resisted our advance, and that the Germans had been told about this. We had certainly started well, for Rees was a shambles. But I was very sleepy and only took a brief look at the square in which we halted before making myself as comfortable as I could in the turret.

The next I knew, Steve had opened my hatch and was shouting at me to get up. It was daylight. To prove that I was awake I lit a cigarette and presently climbed outside. I was glad of my zoot suit, for the turret had been comparatively warm.

Our tanks stood on one side of a triangular patch of earth with a few tufts of grass remaining. On the other sides ran the main Rees-Ijsselburg road and the fork to Esserden. Beside us, amid the rubble of two houses, stood a pair of SPs and a Valentine HQ tank mounting a 6-pounder. The infantry occupied the houses about the square save for one large building where a Red Cross flag drooped from a first floor window. In a street leading off the square DUKWs were unloading RASC stores and convoys of heavy lorries bearing red signs 'AMMO' and 'POL' were streaming up the main road.

Almost immediately on showing myself I was asked to do an hours wireless watch on the HQ tank. I disliked wireless watches intensely, for it was only rarely that I had the slightest idea of the identity of the other stations and this occasion was no exception. Someone called what I thought was my code sign. I answered. There was dead silence from then on and I worried if the other end thought I was German Intelligence. The whole exercise was futile.

My breakfast was ready by the time I was relieved. The rest of the crew had finished and were washing at the front of the tank. I decided to let my beard go another day or so but all the others looked so clean that I had to wash at least. Not that it made so much difference, as Steve and Ted had used the water before my turn came.

We were on call to the Sherwood Rangers, the regiment which had been the first to enter Germany. Parts of the Squadron had worked with them before and had always found them reasonable in their requests and ready to give plenty of fire support. So we had confidence they would never ask us to do anything in which they would not accompany us and this was a good feeling, after our recent experience of co-operation with the Guards. Indeed, in contrast to that shower, all the Yeomanry regiments enjoyed a high reputation.

The rest of the morning was spent in exploring houses in the neighbourhood, inspecting the Valentines, and examining German arms and equipment discarded on the pavements. An anti-tank ditch was discovered, intended to cut both roads before they reached the fork but commenced too late.

We moved at about four o'clock, just after the arrival of the echelon. From Rees the main road runs due north to Ijsselburg and this was the centre line of the salient. An unfinished Autobahn, cutting the road just north of Empel, was being defended by the Germans and we were to help the infantry across this obstacle. This struggle was later to be dramatised in the newspapers as 'The Battle of the Autobahn'.

We had hardly got started when press of traffic forced us to enter a field and wait. The ground seemed firm but as we turned the tracks bit through the turf, sank deep, and water brimmed the ruts immediately. We had to make a very wide sweep, turning gradually to face the gate, to avoid being bogged.

I had to attend to the wireless but the rest of the crew found a tobacco pipe factory and brought back a sack of brown sugar, presumably intended for sweetening the pipes. This was a welcome addition to our stores.

Empel. A Canadian Carpet had been laid down upon the village, which had suffered accordingly. The network of trenches on the perimeter was littered with dead Germans, some huddled in the dugouts, others in the open. One 'blond giant' lay on his back beneath a shattered tree and Fred Bass, again gunner on the Troop tank, secured an undamaged watch.

A and C Squadrons of the Sherwood Rangers already occupied a field beside the road and bordered by the trenches, but as we squeezed in beside them we saw they were making ready to move. Which they did soon afterwards, their place being taken by some AVREs. We circled the field to get as near as possible to the trenches as shelling was expected. It was getting dark and dew already glistened on the short grass, while a thick mist hung over the waters of a lake at the bottom of the field. Above the mist stood the spires and turrets of a mansion set amid a grove of pine trees. The last rays of the sun lit up the tarnished brickwork and gaping windows. An owl hooted. It was like a Gothic novel.

Then the peace of evening was shattered by the crackling of machine guns. We had seen an MG battalion in position as we came up and now it was in action, firing over our heads. It was the first time we had been so close to such a unit and we discussed the range of machine guns as best we could in such a racket. Steve summed up.
"If machine guns can reach the Germans, then shells can reach us."

So we voted against a bivvy and Steve and I volunteered to sleep under the tank. On such occasions I wished I was a driver or a

Flame-gunner, who could always make themselves reasonably comfortable in the front of a Churchill.

Sleeping beneath the tank was better than trying to do so in the turret - once you were in bed. If the ground was hard it was nearly as safe. If it was soft no one in their right minds would take the risk of the tank settling down. That horror was always present even when I was working underneath with the tank on a firm road or hard standing and I knew there was no chance of the bogies giving way, or anything like that. Strangely enough, this fear never prevented me from sleeping.

There is only about eighteen inches clearance under the belly of a Churchill and the pipe to the Flame Gun reduces this still further. Naturally, as junior member of the crew, that was the side I got. So laying a sheet, making the bed and then undressing and getting into it, required some skill in contortion. Especially when two of you were trying to do it at the same time.

The Able crew called Steve and I just before midnight. We lit cigarettes to prove that we were awake and lay talking for a bit. Dressing under the tank was even more complicated than undressing but presently we built up the energy to achieve it.

Everything was peaceful. It was brilliantly moonlit but the mist had crept up from the lake into our field. The dew lay heavily on the ground and dripped from the tank. The owl still hooted. Faintly in the distance we heard a peculiar moaning sound, rising and falling.

"What the hell is that?" I wondered.
"God knows. It's on the road, I should think. Let's go and have a look."

We strolled to the end of the field and leaned on the fence. The road glistened black. The eerie noise grew louder. Then a man came out of the fog. Behind him the bagpipes blared and then died as the piper saw he was nearing a village and men asleep. The infantry slouched by in single file, boots padding in the soft verge.

Steve said he liked the sound of bagpipes, they stirred his blood. I said that they reminded me of cats on the roof and that one tune was just like another. We argued about it and then he called me a bloody fool and moved back towards our tanks.

"Look!" he said.

I looked. The AVREs stood along the far side of the field, their outlines dimmed by the mist. In the moonlight we saw a dark figure emerge from the bulk of the farthest vehicle, hurry to the second, bend under the nose for a moment, hurry on to the third and repeat the action.

"Come on!" said Steve. "We'll nab him."

We ran up past our tanks, past the RE scout car from which we heard the hum of a wireless. Our quarry came nearer. I cocked my Schmeisser. Steve had his pistol out.

"Shall I challenge him?" I whispered.

"Wait until he gets right close, then. Stand back in the shadow."

"Halt or I fire!" I cried, and my order had its effect.

"Friend!" replied the unknown. "It's all right."

"Come here, then."

We peered at the dim face and he was peering at us. Then Steve said:

"Oh, it's OK. Didn't know it was you, sir."

"Who are you? The Crocodile people?"

"Yessir."

"Oh! I'm just going round to my men. I ought to have told you."

"That's all right, sir. Thought we'd better have a look at you, that's all."

"Yes, of course. Thanks very much. Goodnight." He turned away.

"Shows we were on the job, anyway," said Steve.

"Good thing we were up," I said. "Very likely he was checking on us as well."

"Could be. Look here, it's long past time. Shall we do the stag for Len and Jinx and let 'em sleep?"

"Might as well. It's nice out."

All the next day we stayed at Empel and most of the following day. There were wireless watches all the time, both on the HQ tank where one set was netted to the Sherwoods and on the troop tanks which were in touch with 'Startline Dan'. This was our new name for our Major, given since he got his ACV. At this time he was back at Rees. Because of this I had very little leisure to look around and got only a tin box full of ammo for my gun, a wallet from one of the dead Germans, a shaving mirror from the wreck of a searchlight in one corner of our field and the ribbon of an Iron Cross from among the rubbish scattered round the graves in another corner. We were shelled once but they fell in the orchard where they did us no harm.

We moved on the evening of the second day along the road towards Ijsselburg. The town had been captured, after the crossing of the Autobahn, without our assistance being necessary, but there was talk of a possible night action around Leink, a tiny hamlet between Ijsselburg and the Dutch town of Dinxperlo.

It was dark by the time we reached the Autobahn, about three miles north of Empel, and the high embankment was the only interesting feature in the sombre countryside. A DD, burnt out, stood with its nose protruding from beside a house. The muzzle of an anti-tank gun, now overturned, was perhaps five yards from the wreck. A German SP gun stood in the shadow of a battered flyover bridge. Its fellow lay in the ditch a few yards along the road, half buried in brushwood. The road itself was heavily cratered with the largest holes hurriedly filled with rubble. The avenue of trees was shattered and gapped in many places; branches dangled across the road and crashed against our hull and turret. The Able tank was leading and the operator, Chung Murray, kept up a flow of warnings for which we were all very grateful.

Ijsselburg. Narrow, winding streets, overflowing with rubble and packed with vehicles. The only lights the hurricane lanterns suspended above Military Police signs. The corners were sharp and sudden and the tanks backed and crashed into walls as they explored a way round. We hit a lorry, then crossed a Bailey Bridge, sparks shooting from the air louvre as it grazed the railing. Then we were out of the town under brilliant artificial moonlight. A mortar thudded in a field close by.

"Close down!" yelled Steve.

I had already done so and was answering Chung, who had sent the same warning. Through my periscope it was impossible to distinguish all the twistings and turnings of the road. The mortars exploded frequently and it was with misgivings that I emerged from my hatch to see the tank through a gateway of a field wherein a mass of Shermans was parked.

We stayed closed down. I found some biscuits behind the wireless and Ted handed up the chocolate. Steve had gone off to see Mr. Guthrie, the officer, and we expected him to return and brief us for action. Instead, he heard that the Sherwood's Squadron Leader had refused to risk his tanks at night and would not allow us to go in without his support. So we were to get as much sleep as possible and see what the morning brought.

The night passed - uneventful save that Jinx would drop his cigarette ends on my clean turret floor and I made a fuss about it. The morning was bright and sunny and the Sherwoods were outside their tanks so we judged it safe to emerge also, and cooked breakfast. We all washed and there was still no interruption so we put a brew on. If we were to move it would be then. But we drank it in peace.

Later the news went round that the Sherwood recce tanks had advanced into Holland and were reporting no opposition, so it was safe for the Guards Armoured Division to pass through and exploit the situation. The Sherwoods spoke too soon, however, for there was some resistance and one of their Honeys was cut off and shouted for help. A troop of Shermans moved out to the rescue and a little while after the Honey came back, smoking, the operator killed by a bazooka. The Sherwoods gathered round looking worried.

Mr. Guthrie then confirmed the rumour that we had broken through the German 7th Army and were advancing into Holland without much trouble. The war, he said, was nearly over, for only the Volksturm and the Werewolves[116] were left.

* * *

We parted from the Sherwood Rangers that evening, moving back south of Ijsselburg to join 11 Troop, who occupied a farm lying some distance from the road. In moving back we expected to get a rest but were welcomed by the news that a dark wood that stretched along the skyline was occupied still by SS troops. Furthermore, it was expected that the Highland Division would attack us at any moment.

The farmhouse contained its original occupants and the previous evening a drunken soldier had attempted to rape the daughter of the house. According to the civilians, he had been carrying on in this way ever since Ijsselburg had fallen. His unit was not known and the man had made his escape threatening to return with his comrades and a Bren Gun. So 11 Troop, in preserving themselves, found that they were defending their enemies against their friends.

It was a difficult position and we in 13 Troop who had taken no part in the original fracas rather resented being dragged into it. However, 11 Troop had made up their minds and we had no choice but to stand by them. The more readily as the Highlanders, if they were drunk enough to return, would make no distinctions. Guards were doubled and, for a change, were done conscientiously. It was a lovely night, there was no trouble, and as we moved out in the morning no doubt the situation adjusted itself.

The Squadron was gathering itself together at Bienen, on the way back to the Rhine. The older men were pleased about this but some of us younger ones felt that since the war was nearly over it would be nice to be in at the death. We were not the only tanks moving back and we drew on to the road just in time to get ahead of the Shermans of the 13/18th Hussars, who were also travelling towards Bienen. No

[116] Werewolves. The German resistance movement which was, in fact, only a propaganda scare as it failed to materialise. At the time, however, the propaganda stories were sufficient to make us very wary.

doubt to their great annoyance, as their speed was at least twice that of ours.

We passed under the Autobahn and then turned off to the right along a minor road. The broken mud plough which had been responsible for the loss of our rear wing and track guard around Goch had also damaged the sprocket teeth. Now, grinding round a heavily rutted corner, the track slipped to one side. Very carefully, we nursed the tank into a nearby field, which we were lucky to reach safely, and dismounted to inspect the damage.

The strain on the track had bent or snapped some of the pins. The track had to be broken before it could be replaced in position and new pins fitted, but a heavier sledge borrowed from the 'Three and Eights', who had harboured nearby, was not a sufficient weapon.

There had been orders not to net to the BBC, which I had obeyed. Steve and I fixed the map reference as 084582, where there was the requisite fork, sharp turn and cluster of buildings marked as Junkermannshof. Then I called up the Squadron and asked for the ARV with its oxyacetylene plant.

It was a long wait. There was a bitterly cold wind and we huddled in the lee of the tank before a huge bonfire. I rigged the loudspeaker to provide music as the rest of the crew insisted that there was no sense in remaining on net. It was not until the early afternoon that the ARV arrived but then it made short work of the buckled track. An hour later we were entering Bienen.

The Squadron was sharing a field by the main road with a knocked out DD. We erected a large bivvy by the side of the tank and I fitted electric light and the loudspeaker. The only snag to this arrangement was that someone always had to get out of bed to put off the master switch and this usually fell to my lot. We would argue about it until someone said, "Oh, leave the damn thing! It won't matter for one night." The others would agree and then I knew I had to get up. If the batteries got flat we should have to ask for a tow to start up and mine would be the blame. Steve said, on this and any similar occasion, that the experience would mould me, give me character, and prevent me from falling into lazy ways. He said that I was the baby of the tank and he felt responsible for my upbringing. "You'll bless me one day," he always ended.

After tea, Ted and I strolled round the village and found an SP gun with its nose driven into a dunghill. Another stood further down the street but had a large hole in the armour and the interior was a shambles. There was not much room inside, for the Seventy-five was very bulky; the driving seat, in particular, was very cramped. The inside walls were painted red, which was very dingy compared with the aluminium or white of our tanks. Altogether, they seemed a shoddy weapon, but then the chassis was that of a Mark III, which the Germans had at the beginning of the war.

The narrow lanes were littered with German weapons and equipment - rifles, Spandaus and bazookas - and vehicles - cars, carts, trailers, a field kitchen. On one corner a boot lay in the middle of the road. I gave it a kick and there was a foot inside it!

The circuit of the village made, we struck the main road again and chased two tame rabbits across a garden and into a house where they were cornered beneath a bed. The larger of the two raised a weal across the back of my hand but we carried them home in triumph. Then there were arguments as to whether they were buck and doe and, if so, what ought to be done about it. I was worried as to whether or not my hand had been poisoned by the scratch. Steve said that rabbits were riddled with venereal disease. In the end we let them go.

In the morning news went round that we were returning to the Weeze forest for another period of waiting. I was disappointed. Steve said that we boys did not savour life as he did and, for his part, he would be content to scrub equipment in a back area all day and every day until the war was over.

When we got going we soon came to Emmerich. The town was ruined, dead. I did not see a whole house and three-quarters at least were just heaped rubble. The streets were reduced to narrow, potholed lanes bulldozed between banks of brick and shattered concrete.

"Keep a lookout for a stove," remarked Ted. "We shall need one again."

Going through Emmerich, a slow and tiresome procession, Len descended and entered various ruins but to no avail. We crossed the Rhine by the new pontoon bridge. On reaching Calcar we found it crowded with Buffaloes and Cromwells, but there we saw a stove lying before a front door. Steve and I both shouted at once and Ted stopped with a jerk. Len and Jinx raced across, picked up the stove, and heaved it on to the front as Ted started forward. He had to drive at full speed to overtake our convoy, with Len clinging to the Seventy-five and keeping the stove half on the hatches with his foot and expecting to be flung into the road at every bounce. Jinx struggled to get the stove placed more securely but was of little use, with Len swearing at him all the time. There was a lot of traffic and both Steve and I had our hands full. However, they got it fixed at last and Len clambered to safety.

When we passed the turning of the road to Üdem which led on to the Weeze forest, I was struck with the idea that perhaps we were not going there at all but to another front in Holland. As the twin towers of Üdem church dropped below the trees, my hopes rose.

We entered Goch, bumping over the level crossing where stood two abandoned SPs and, in a crater, a little vehicle with tracks only about six feet long, almost a model tank, which I guessed to be a wireless controlled device for carrying explosives into enemy lines. I had heard of these but never seen one before.

Len picked up a stovepipe in Goch and then we turned south along the road to Weeze and Geldern. My hopes faded - we were simply going the long way round. We bypassed Weeze, turned towards Üdem, and with darkness were back in our log cabins where all was as if we had never left them.

CHAPTER 21

ARNHEM WEST

Another fortnight in the Weeze forest. More parades and polished boots and regular shaves and so-called PT. More excursions to the 'dead 'uns' who still retained their rifles. More explorations in the woods with Shag, who was as mad as ever and had taken to wearing a sheath knife in his gaiter, for some reason. We had a parade for the Colonel, and for church. General Hobart, who commanded the 79th Armoured Division, paid us a visit and made a speech, the usual things. We assumed that our idleness was decided by someone high up to give the newcomers, the Fife & Forfars and the 7th RTR, a chance to earn a living.

We improved the log cabins, trimming up all the ends. I offered to dig a garden and plant primroses but it was felt this was going too far. We were on 'fresh rations' - that is, compo spoilt by the cooks - but every night we cooked a chip supper. Squirrels played in the trees above our cabin and once a deer blundered into the camp area, giving us all the idea of doing a bit of deer stalking, although we never saw another. The weather was beautiful and in the evenings we could sit in the open and enjoy the stillness, the blue wood smoke rising in the calm air, the purple sunsets seen through the pine trees, the faint haze clinging damply about the bushes.

During the daytime we were busy conforming to the well-known abridged form of King's Regulations which runs:

If it moves, salute it.
If it doesn't move, pick it up.
If you can't pick it up, paint it.

There were always rumours, but after a while they came more frequently. We were going back across the Rhine. We were going to Holland, to the Zuider Zee. We were going to Dunkirk. We were going back to England and then to the Far East. We were going down to help the Americans. Or to help the French. There was a separate batch dealing with demobilisation.

At last orders to move did come, although we other ranks had no idea of the destination. We got out on to the road, no one smoking, operators all looking to the rear because the Squadron office had to be passed and the Major would be watching.

Along the well-remembered road to Üdem under the avenue of trees. Through Üdem and on to the Calcar road, a crashed Typhoon the landmark in the middle of the cross-roads. The Buffaloes were still harboured in Calcar. The road to the Rhine and Emmerich, a broad main highway lined with the usual trees. Fields were cratered. There was an overturned Buffalo with the tracks wrenched off and the bottom stove in; another on a corner almost torn in two.

A large notice at the verge:

"TRAFFIC CONTROL POST. ALL CONVOYS REPORT HERE."

This stood at the end of the Rhine bridge and the tanks stopped in a gravelled space where there was another instruction:

"WARNING! ALL TANKS KEEP 80 YARDS DISTANCE"

Then the MP at the bridgehead waved us across.

I did not get a chance to take another look at the river. There were only six inches between my air louvre and the railing and I concentrated on that gap, as did Steve on his side. "Just a touch left - just a touch OK... just a touch right... bit more OK... left a bit... left a bit... left a bit OK... OK as you are..." and so on until we surged up the bank on to the road again. Our DR pointed along the street, shouted "Follow Ruby Up", and I waved acknowledgement.

It was dark before we were out of the maze of tangled tracks through the rubble that were the streets of Emmerich. Out along the main road. A village. A cross-roads. A man ran out from the pavement and shouted.

"No!" I bellowed.

"What was that?" asked Steve.

"Bloke wanted to know if we were the last tank."

"What for?"

"Dunno."

Jinx, seated on the back bin, started to talk. Steve, intent on the twisting road, shut him up abruptly. Jinx sulked and I stuck two fingers up at him.

The speed of the convoy increased. Len took over from Ted and he had a habit of straying to the wrong side of the road despite constant correction. We rushed under a railway bridge, the tracks echoing thunderously. The road curved gradually to the left and over a Bailey Bridge, a river gleaming below. Then it followed the base of a steep hill. A church on the summit was silhouetted against the sky. It looked good. I later discovered the place to be named Hoch Elten and, passing in daylight, saw the hillside scarred, the woods shattered, the church a ruined shell.

Soon after, we turned off the road along a moorland track. The column, as was usual on a long road run, had split into several sections according to the top speed of particular tanks and we were the last tank in our section, with the DR following us. Ted, who was again driving, complained that the reflection of the motorcycle head lamp prevented him from seeing either the tank in front or the sides of the road. We waved, we flashed the Hellesen, but with no result.

"Get the spotlight out!" snarled Steve. "We'll show the bastard!"

I fumbled in the piasipa bin beneath the commander's pedestal, where it was stowed. A terrific lurch threw me across the turret and I grabbed my mike and demanded to know what the hell was happening. The roll had been caused by a ditch we had crossed to enter our harbour, and the spotlight was no longer necessary.

As far as we could see there were no houses for miles around. Only rolling heathland, the frontier 'heide', with a dark mass of woods in the distance. The ground was sandy, sparsely covered with coarse grass and heather. Len and I stumbled down the track to investigate a rumour that tea was waiting in the cook's wagon, while the rest of the crew pitched the bivvy. Steve shouted an ultimatum after us - no tea, no bed.

We got tea, although apparently it was for the echelon only. Q. Grace was by the truck and we always maintained that if he had to give anything to anybody he looked upon it as a personal injury, but we had filled our mugs before he saw us at the urn and escaped into the darkness.

It was past midnight before the beds were made and although we were cramped in the bivvy the ground was soft, we slept well, and reveille came too early. Another move was expected and at daylight we began to pick up our trailers, which stood on the opposite side of the track where the trucks had dropped them the previous night. This job was completed by eleven o'clock and we moved back down towards the road, past the wood where the echelon had parked, to a spot scattered with young pine trees.

We had seen the odd civilian and now they appeared in force, clamouring to barter and declaring loudly that they were Dutch. We inspected their identity cards - not that they told us much - and a brisk trade began; salmon and sardines for eggs and guilders. The harbour was a hive of activity and a babble of tongues - rapid Dutch, halting English, swearing, adamant refusals, scornful laughs, the clang of tins thrown back into boxes, a renewed chorus of Dutch. Then there was a furious uproar at one end of the column.

"Get those bloody people away from here - get 'em out! You there! Get those bloody people away!"

"Look out - Dan's on the warpath!" flashed round the Squadron.

"Officier! Officier!" we said as we pushed the Dutch through the bushes. "Niet meer kopen! Ga weg you silly buggers! Officier niet goed! Nix in the winkel! Alles kaput!"

We got them all out of sight before the Major got to our end and when he had gone Mr. Callingham came round to see it did not start again. We were busy turning the Dutch away all morning - they said all English soldiers sold food and could not understand why we would not.

The day passed without further excitement save when our petrol fire got out of hand and we had to rally the whole Troop to stamp out the blazing heather. The following morning the news came that we were to move into Arnhem, which had fallen to the 49th Division, the 'Nijmegen Home Guard', two days before.

It was a glorious day and the populations of the little Dutch towns turned out to make our ride a triumphal progress reminiscent of the Channel Ports. The roads were broad and smooth, the trees bursting into leaf, the fields to either side of the high embankment fresh and green in the spring sunlight. At one point a field of red tulips made a striking contrast among the damp meadows. The houses were neat and clean with scrubbed bricks and polished tiling. Here and there a stork's nest perched on a scaffolding built against a chimney. Fat cattle in the fields. Orchards. Girls waving from bedroom windows and garden gates. The town of Zevenaar with spotless streets, glistening houses, and gilded church with a green steeple.

Not a window cracked in Zevenaar but in the next village, Westervoort, what a contrast. Trees shattered, roofs without tiles, walls scarred and pitted, windows gaping and gardens trampled. A sign declared,

"DANGER! THIS AREA IS HEAVILY BOOBYTRAPPED AND MINED!"

We halted in the road but no one left the tanks.

The railway bridge over the road was still standing but was expected to fall at any moment. Dislodged bricks kept falling into the road with mortar dust trailing behind. The vibration caused by a squadron of tanks meant a grave risk of collapse and we were ordered to go under singly, in first gear with the engine ticking over, and closed down. Len, for some reason, wanted to stay outside but Steve would not allow that. In the event, we all passed under safely.

A pontoon bridge lay across the Ijssel beside the ruins of its predecessor. On the far bank we halted to collect the Squadron and saw Arnhem ahead, grey roofs glittering in the sunlight. The broad white road was lined with model factories and housing estates, all in different stages of demolition. Arnhem was dead. There was a big notice:

"THIS IS HOLLAND. THESE PEOPLE ARE YOUR ALLIES.
DO NOT LOOT!"

It did not look as if there was anything worth the taking, anyway.

We drew into the side of a wide avenue and cooked a belated dinner before linking up the trailer which, as usual, had been dropped to enable us to cross the lower weight bridges. Also as usual, no one knew what was going to happen - whether we were going to stay there, if billets were reserved or had to be found, if there was a job for us or not.

So the afternoon was passed in drinking tea and sunbathing. A long column of Canadian Shermans rolled past down the hill, raising an immense cloud of dust, and we had to move into the shade on the other side of the tank until it had settled. We had tea and then Jinx began to complain of a festering finger. I advised him to go sick at once, before we had to move, but such action was too definite for Jinx.

We continued to wait. The sun went down and the evening was cool. Steve had been to see our billet and reported that a lot of cleaning would be necessary before we could occupy it. The other Troops were already settled in and we could see the glow of their cookers reflected in the windows. Reg Webb came round to tell us that our Troop was going to move, but when or where he did not know.

The evening was very still. The traffic was hushed, only the faint murmur of tank engines in the distance; there was no sound of gunfire. Suddenly a nightingale trilled from the grove behind the palings against which we were leaning. I had not heard bird songs for a long time - I did not count the owl at Empel which had been in keeping with its surroundings and the jays in the Weeze forest did not count as songsters. A burst of music from a tank along the road seemed wrong after that.

When I got the order to net to a group of Shermans a few streets away, and a move was fixed provisionally for nine o'clock, Jinx decided he must go sick. Steve was furious and everyone else very angry - especially Reg Webb who had never had any use for Jinx. We threw out his kit with little ceremony but even then Frank Harvey from the spare tank had no time to transfer all his belongings. I stowed his blankets as we moved off down the hill.

The delay in picking up Frank had left us far behind the Troop and a fork road appeared.

"Which way did they go?" asked Steve.

"Left, I think."

We swung left, ducking under dangling wires.

"There's a rear light ahead," I said, congratulating myself.

"I see it. Speed up, Ted."

We cut in front of a parked lorry. The light ahead vanished and we strained our eyes to make out the turning.

"That's it," said Steve.

"No, it's not," I disagreed. "It's the next one."

"Are you sure?"

"Yes."

"I hope you are, then. Turn right here, Ted."

We ground into the side street, crushing the kerbstones and knocking down an MP sign.

"Left here!"

Ted saw a Jeep just in time and I grabbed my hatch as we rocked to a halt.

"OK - you missed the bugger! Carry on left."

We found ourselves in a road running round a green square. On the opposite side a church spire pierced the night sky. Beside us gaped the windows and doors of shattered houses. Our tanks had drawn in beside the green and their exhausts flashed as the engines coughed out. A Hellesen waved at us.

Sergeant Webb had gone off in Captain Shearman's scout car to be briefed, he being acting Troop Officer and he had promised to collect any of Frank's kit that had been left behind. In the meanwhile we spread a tarpaulin on the grass and made our beds down.

Our briefing took place in a dingy room smelling of rotten food. A fragment of curtain flapped at the partially shuttered window. The floor was strewn with bricks, plaster and pieces of broken furniture. There was a weak table from which dirty plates and bottles had been swept. Three or four maps had been laid out and a Hellesen played feebly upon them. Reg balanced on a chair which was diffy a leg and read from his notebook. Steve and Harry Grossman (who had been shifted from the ARV to command the Baker tank as we had been elevated to Able) took down what they deemed important on scraps of paper. The rest of us craned to see the table.

The map was Arnhem West and we had to clear the north bank of the Lower Rhine as far as Wageningen. There were two columns, each containing a Troop of Crocodiles and a Troop of Flails. The latter were acting as gun tanks and we came under their command. 14 Troop and a Troop of the Lothians were the northern column, north of the Utrechtsche Weg. We, also with the Lothians, were to take the southern route through Oosterbeek and Renkum. We were in support of a battalion of the Ox and Bucks, and in the morning a force from the Essex Regiment would cross the river and take Renkum.

The side roads and forest lanes were to be cleared by a separate 'Guy Force' in Carriers and Jeeps. Little opposition was expected as it was understood that only Dutch SS were in the area.

While all this was going on, a column of Canadian armour was to pass through Ede and exploit to the north.

Reveille was at 0500, check call at 0600, move off at 0630. Everything seemed very vague. Fred Bass asked a few questions but Reg did not know the answers. He said that now we had as much information as he. No one had any good ideas but Steve and Len were still talking when I fell asleep.

* * *

A bitterly cold morning.

"The trouble is," says Steve, "the trouble is they're in a rut. They've got the attack to start at such and such an hour, so they must have reveille two hours before. It's always the same. Reveille 0630, breakfast 0730, first parade 0830. OK, if we had to wash and shave and make our beds and sweep the barrack room. But I'm not going to wash and shave and if I don't, I know you won't, Smudger. So getting up at this ungodly hour is just plain stupid."

I lie on my back and look up at the sky and agree with him. Steve sits up and hunts for his socks.

"You awake, Smudger?"
"No."
"Three seconds and I'll whip the blankets off you!"

I turn over and my blankets go and I light a cigarette and start to look for my socks, which are somewhere in the bottom of the bed. Steve calls Ted, who has been sleeping in the driving seat. He lights the cooker and I edge shivering along the track guards to find the mugs. I pack the blankets and then sit and listen to the whine of the wireless set and yawn. Frank has found some plates in a nearby house - we are always short of plates - and Ted is cooking breakfast while Len tidies in a room for the meal by throwing the rubbish out of the window.

Netting finished, I bolt down my breakfast, which has had time to get cold. The others finish packing.

It is getting light. The engine purrs. Steve and Frank warm their hands in the exhaust streams. I get a piece of cotton waste and rub soot from the dixie over the conspicuous yellow triangles of the 79th Armoured Division between the driver's vision block and the Flame Gun and on the offside rear wing. The first is a known aiming point for German anti-tank gunners. Then the same treatment for the squadron circles on the turret.

The infantry go by in Carriers, de-bus at the corner of the square, and slouch away out of sight. Someone shouts, "Get ready to move!"

The Flails appear and we round the square to halt behind them. More Flails overtake, followed by 14 Troop. 'Guy Force' - merely infantry in Carriers - moves ahead, followed by a Sherman command tank. Then our Flails, chattering among themselves, and we string out behind.

A blackboard on its easel stands in the middle of the road with

"START LINE"

chalked upon it. This looks absurd. Another notice:

"WATCH YOUR UNIT SIGNS"

which precedes the allocation of parking places. All very neat.

The Canadian armoured column - new, clean Shermans - moves off. Our Flails are talking about a Jeep to lead our column and I retail this to Steve, who says that 'Jeep' must be a code word as whoever heard of tanks being led into action by a Jeep. Then a Jeep with a very high wireless mast passes us and halts in front of the Flails.

Frank is asleep with his head on the power-traverse gearbox. Steve is complaining of a headache and I busy myself with the radio, trying to eliminate crackling and whistles. The sun is very hot and I take off my jacket but retain my jerkin over my shirt. Frank sleeps on when I load the Bombthrower and the Seventy-five.

The Flails move. Ted wakes up and we jolt forward. The suburbs of Arnhem are left behind. Below us, between gaps in matting camouflage which lines the road, we can see the river and the flat meadows beyond. The main road drops gently through flowering woodland where pretty little cottages are dotted among the trees. A Flail commander relays the eight o'clock news over the air; we have destroyed over 300 German aircraft and all the officers are very bucked about it and are talking about it being the end of the war.

The leading Flail beats a way round a road-block. A black and yellow sign,

"OOSTERBEEK"

heralds the village. The houses are scattered at first and I search the windows, the gardens, the woodland in the background, for any signs of hostility. None. The place is deserted. Steve puts his head outside the turret. The hatches open on the tank in front.

The Flails remark on the absence of opposition and one suggests that we pick up the infantry and push ahead as fast as we can. We halt. The infantry come swarming back to meet us, laughing. All hatches are open now; the infantry sit on the wings, on the turret, some even want to ride on the trailer.

The Flails talk of pushing right into the woods and no one thinks of fighting any more. We drop over the edge of the scarp and speed down the lane towards the Rhine. The tank lurches and sways in the ruts. I watch in case the infantry risk being swept off by branches or fall when we hit a pothole. There is one man stretched out on the wing, with no hold, and I expect to see him go at any moment.

Another roadblock gives us a breather and a chance to make bully beef sandwiches. This amuses the infantry, who say that the front of the tank looks like a bleeding grocer's shop. They want to know if this is our usual style of living. One of them then gets hold of my microphone and speaks to puzzle Ted, who is complaining of boredom. Cramped in his seat, seeing nothing save the rutted track and the tank ahead, he may well complain. No one else is working.

On down the lane to Doorwerth. This woodland area is the spot selected for the ill-fated paratroop landing of the previous autumn. Red, green and white parachutes hang from branches, trail along the ground, or have been rolled up and stuffed into the ditches. The once white containers are stained by time and scarred by bullets. Some are still fastened, others burst open and scattering mines, mortar bombs and anti-tank ammo among the brambles.

Burnt-out Jeeps lie beneath budding trees and are overturned in flower gardens, rusting and bullet-riddled. A tattered Red Cross flag droops from the window of a roofless house. An antitank gun stands amid a pile of rubble at a corner. Nearby, in the ditch, is a solitary grave with two twigs split to form a miniature cross and an alloy moulding reading:

"UNKNOWN BRITISH SOLDIER"

Scattered among the woods are blackened ruins of houses surrounded by mines, cast off hand grenades and twisted weapons. On one corner stands a paratroop success, an old French tank, a Char B[117], the puny turret blown off, the hull covered with the red rust that follows fire. Its fellow lies half buried in a field of turnips nearby. A German steel helmet caps a grave in the ditch.

We career through the woods, only stopping occasionally to investigate little clusters of houses. The whole countryside is still, the atmosphere heavily brooding with a sense of desolation, abandonment and decay.

There is a halt by the river at Doorwerth to brew tea. The infantry do the same but their cubes of tea-sugar-milk mixture are so inferior to our fresh brew that we share our dixie. Then off again towards Heelsum. It is just a joyride now and I remove my boots and don a

[117] Char B. The French heavy tank, mounting a 47 mm. gun in the turret and a 75 mm. in the front of the hull. Although it was supposed to have given a good account of itself in 1940, by 1945 it was quite outclassed and, probably, the Germans were using it only as a mobile pillbox or roadblock.

pair of slippers picked up in Goch. Len cuts sandwiches in his pannier, careless about blocking his means of escape.

A factory on the outskirts of Heelsum. The infantry from the leading tank explore, are satisfied, and wave us on. Down the hill and round the corner. Reg Webb's trailer begins to leak and leaves a trail of flame fuel in the middle of the road. Over a flimsy bridge and up the hill beyond. An Eighty-eight stands deserted in the corner of a field on our right.

We near the main road to Wageningen and hear the northern column on the air as it converges on the same point. A Flail has gone up on a Teller mine and it seems that two of the crew are dead. The Germans have linked three mines together, the third having the detonator so that the other two would explode under the belly of the tank. We are sober for a bit and then good spirits return. There are seven tanks ahead of us, not to mention the Jeep..

From Heelsum down towards the Rhine again, to Renkum. Then back into the woods.

"WAGENINGEN 1 KM"

on a milestone. 'Guy Force' and the northern column have already rendezvoused and throng the main road. We sidle past and drop our infantry. Steve complains of a splitting headache and sickness and goes to sleep in the co-drivers seat while I turn the tank. Back along the road by which we have come, leaving the infantry to enter and occupy Wageningen.

The Essex have crossed the Rhine at Renkum as planned, but such roads as are not mined are impassable to Jeeps and lorries and we are to ferry the troops into Wageningen. We try to work out the cost per man, reckoning petrol at half a crown per gallon.

We are tired and dirty and do not relish the idea of acting as troop transports. Nor do our officers and the plan is abandoned as suddenly as it was proposed. The infantrymen are used to being mucked about and make no objection when we leave them sitting on the bank at the roadside.

Back towards Arnhem. Fill up with petrol and change gas bottles by the side of the main road. Then north to Heelsum and westward to a little scattered village that seems to have no name. I pore over the map and decide it must be No. 1 in t'Bosch.

A dim figure in the half-light waves us into a narrow lane leading to a large white house which is to be our billet. I bend both wings backing the tank into position and have to hammer them back into something like normal shape before Steve will let me come in to supper.

* * *

Nol in t'Bosch was just a jumble of houses among the woods. We all spent a good deal of time looking them over. Not that there was much of value in them but so many empty houses were a temptation. It was too hot to work on the tanks anyway, or so we said.

One house had been used by the Germans as a clothing and equipment store and we spent many hours sorting through the masses of clothing, bales of packs and boxes of ammo, lamps, batteries, coils of wire, Wehrpasses and Soldbuchs, and all the rest of a quartermaster's paraphernalia.

Mines were a nuisance. There were occasional British mine markers but our experience of airborne troops led us to believe that a lot would not be charted. On top of this it was by no means certain that the woods were uninhabited. The intense silence and oppressive heat was all around us and I, for one, had always a feeling of being watched. Of course, woods always do give that feeling, but one afternoon Chung and I returned from a wander to see a platoon of infantry just setting out in search of reported Germans. We did not roam so far after that.

When we were in the Squadron area the only work done was to brew tea - the dixies boiled all day. We did not fancy hot food so even our store of sardines was depleted and it was fortunate that we had secured such a large stock of bottled fruit. The compo packs were not designed to take account of changes in the weather.

CHAPTER 21

FINALE

With the Germans in full retreat, rumour had it that we were going to stay in Arnhem until the end of the war, which seemed only a matter of days. We were not particularly surprised, however, when the order to break trailers came one evening just as we were getting ready for bed. No one knew where we were going or how much time we had, so there was frantic dressing and packing to the sound of tanks being started outside.

Ted started our tank, I held the spotlight, Len got ready with a sledgehammer and Steve gave instructions to Ted over the infantry phone. Although not installed for this purpose, we found this instrument very useful for making and breaking the trailer link as it was often necessary to rock the tank back and forward to ease the connecting pins. I never heard of it being used for its true purpose - but then I doubt if the infantry had been told that we had such things.

On this occasion the trailer was on its best behaviour and gave no trouble. Having broken the link, we edged the tank into line with the others, smoked and waited for news. It was a long wait and, having packed the tank, there was nothing to do but smoke and doze on the engine deck until long after midnight.

Still without knowing our destination, we rattled into Arnhem at top speed just as it was getting light. Although the sentries standing in doorways, muffled in greatcoats and scarves, looked cold and miserable, we were all in the best of spirits with everyone singing over the I/c. We had been getting bored with No. 1 in t'Bosch and it was good to get moving again.

From Arnhem we turned north towards Zutphen, waking the sleepy little villages with our clanking tracks and spitting engines. Obviously, we were rushing to the front, wherever that was, and the Dutch came running into their gardens or waved from bedroom windows to give us encouragement. That, and the noise and bustle of our passage, was all good for our morale but this took a downturn a few miles south of Zutphen when a thin drizzle gradually intensified into heavy rain. Steve and I struggled into our zoot suits and stuffed a tank sheet round the hatches but the scenery was now dismal as the grey clouds settled across the flat countryside.

We stopped in Warnsveld, a suburb of Zutphen, to load on to transporters. Having loaded, we found we could not move as the roads up to the German border were jammed with traffic and no one knew when we would be able to move. It was not long before we were surrounded by Dutch civilians, all clamouring to buy. There was quite a lot of pushing and struggling and I felt well out of it on the decking, sorting out the buckshee food that we were never likely to eat, while the rest of the crew held the crowd back and conducted the sales.

Each tank had its own crowd, all waving money and shouting "Tommy! Tommy! Tommy!" to attract attention. All, that is, except the prettier girls, who were able to stand back, smile, and get tins thrown to them. The Fitters, of course, did the best trade. In their position between the tank crews and the echelon and with their ability to do favours, they generally managed to get the best of anything that was going.

The turmoil ended in the usual way with the shout of "Offizier! Offizier!" along the line. At this we cried "Winkel kaput!" closed all the bins and hid inside the tank to share out. Not a bad morning's work.

That was all we saw of Zutphen. As a town with a lot of history, I ought to have taken more interest in it but I found that being in the army was not conducive to academic interests. We moved off towards the German border, at first sitting outside to enjoy taking the salute. However, the weather did not improve and I tried to keep warm in the co-drivers seat, kicking my feet against the glacis plate to try to get some warmth into them. This annoyed Ted, who was muffled in blankets in the driving seat and had managed to get to sleep until I woke him. Then I had to get out to make a bully beef sandwich for Jinx, who was travelling with us, as no one else knew where the bread was. Reading was impossible as I could not see without opening the hatch and creating a bitterly cold draught.

Also, our comfort was not improved by the behaviour of our transporter driver. Quite early on the tank hit a tree and the whole vehicle lurched in a sickening manner before regaining the road. It was a Canadian transporter unit and maybe the driver was used to wider open spaces than Holland. He certainly seemed to be in a hurry, swinging round corners with horn blaring and utter disregard for anything else that might be on the road. At high speed we passed through Lochum, Goor, Hengelo, Oldenzaal and Denekamp until in the afternoon we were relieved to draw into the side of the road to unload. We were then a few kilometres short of the German frontier and were to proceed under our own power.

The red and white striped poles of the frontier post were still there. There was also a big notice:

"YOU ARE NOW IN GERMANY!
BEHAVE LIKE CONQUERORS!"

We were not sure how British conquerors were supposed to behave - no one has given us any instructions about this. We halted in Nordhorn to brew tea and collect the Squadron together. The town had escaped with little damage. Steve was of the view that this was a pity as the more the country was knocked about the less likely the Germans would be to start another war and with this we were in general agreement.

From Nordhorn we followed Route 213 through Altendorf and Sudlöhne to Lingen. Lingen lay on the Dortmund-Ems Canal, had been bombed by the RAF, flamed by our A Squadron, and reduced to rubble. It satisfied Steve's view of the fitness of things. I was interested to see two very old French tanks standing by the bridge over the canal, probably as roadblocks as I could not imagine they would have been much use in a fight.

We turned north along Route 70 to Meppen. There was a cold, blustering wind with rain and sleet and darkness falling rapidly. The water of the canal was grey and dirty. The marshland on our left was soggy and desolate, dotted with gently heaving lakes fringed with acres of rushes. A thin film of mud coated the road and our faces until periodically swept clean by the chill rain.

Ted was getting worried about petrol. Reggie Webb's tank had already run dry and we had passed him stopped on the verge. Then, before we knew it, we were crossing a bridge never constructed to take our weight. It rocked and swayed and we had some bad moments. The tanks behind, wisely, decided to make a detour and we had to slow down for some time to enable them to catch up. We still did not know where we were going and the whole situation was becoming increasingly unreal. The war was so obviously almost over. Every village seemed to have camps for Displaced Persons and ex-Prisoners of War. The roads were lined with plodding figures in every variety of uniform, carrying bundles or pushing loaded bicycles. They were all walking away from Germany and most waved cheerfully as we passed.

As the grey light turned to wet darkness, our tanks pulled off the road into a sticky ploughed field. Tired, dirty and hungry, we filled up with petrol and oil and put up our bivvy in the lee. We never did learn anything about the operation that had been the cause of our haste, only that Crocodiles had not been asked for at all. The requirement had been for Kangaroos which made sense, when we came to think about it, at this stage of the war.

In any case, I had more important things to think about. In the morning I was to leave for England and nine days at home.

* * *

It was a long ride in the back of a truck down to the transit camp at Nijmegen. I was very tired. My only companion was the Dutch officer who had been attached to the regiment as interpreter and who was being demobbed. Also, I was disappointed as our stores had run out of the American shirts with collars and ties, which until now had been issued to every man as he went on leave.

The Transit Camp was dreary as are all such units. I had a bath and got a shirt with a collar but they had run out of khaki ties and I had not the nerve to try a Canadian accent and get a black one, as some of my companions did. It seemed very important to get a collar and tie.

The march to the train was a long one and my kit was very heavy as apart from the more valuable and useful articles I had acquired, I also had my Schmeisser in bits and a good supply of magazines and ammo for it. At this time no one was being prevented from taking such things home. The train had wooden seats and crawled across Holland, Belgium and Northern France, stopping for no apparent reason for lengthy periods. The river bridges were particularly dodgy as most of them had been hastily repaired and were without such comforts as side barriers. As the train inched its way across you could look out of the window straight down into the river. At Lille we got a cup of tea in the middle of the night and there was another Transit Camp at Calais with the same long march to the boat. It was late afternoon but the sun was shining when I threw my large pack over the garden fence and went indoors.

* * *

The journey back was miserable. The final acts of the German surrender were being performed and there were all sorts of rumours of two-day extensions in celebration. The Transit Camps were even more gloomy because of this, because if the rumours were true we had, of course, missed out, and that made going back even worse. So far as I could see I was the only member of the Buffs at Nijmegen and I felt even more lost than when I had landed in Normandy. I did not think it likely a truck would come specially to pick me up, even if anyone remembered that I was there, so I decided to hitch-hike in the last known direction of the Squadron.

For a start, I got a lift in a 79th Armoured Division truck to Division HQ at Enschede. The HQ was to move in the morning, could not give me transport and had no idea of the location of my squadron. So in the morning I went with some trucks being transferred to 30 Armoured Brigade HQ, at Hengelo. The 141 was in 31 Armoured Brigade but I thought the Flails were likely to know our position as they had worked with us so often. I was wrong. They did not even know the location of their own units, let alone any others. However, they gave me dinner, haversack rations, a pile of maps, advised me to make for the Oldenburg area, and wished me luck. The Flails were a nice lot.

I got a lift to Nordhorn by Canadian truck and thence by Jeep and tank transporter to Haselünne. From there another lift to Loningen, where I was lucky enough to find a Canadian bound for the Bremen area. He took me through Cloppenburg and Wildeshausen, looking for his own unit, before he decided to try Oldenburg. Then, on the main road, I saw our sign pointing down a lane. He dropped me and drove off. The lane petered out after a hundred yards. Our sign must have been an old one, so I returned to the main road and started to walk. It was dark and cold and very eerie under the trees and I began to think I had been rather foolish. I was unarmed. No one knew how the Germans were going to react to defeat but there had been a lot of talk about Werewolves. In fact, this idea of a German resistance movement never got off the ground but the idea of it worried us for quite a while - and this was a good time for me to worry. Luckily, an Artillery Matador stopped and took me several miles and then the last lap into Oldenburg was done on the pillion of a DR.

There were lots of troops in the town. Most of those I asked had seen Crocodiles but their directions only led me to Valentines and Shermans. I tried a Canadian MP post but they had lost their own HQ and had never heard of the 141. So midnight found me wandering in the streets, continually startled by sinister black figures painted on walls and boarded shop windows with the sibilant injunction:

"PSST! DER FEIND HÖRT MIT!"

I found these more unnerving than anything else in the entire trip.

Sergeant Scurfield, I am sure, was out for no good purpose, but when I saw him his motives did not concern me at all. I greeted him like an old friend. He was returning to the Squadron, which was just around the corner.

So on the night of May 6, I arrived back 'home' and on every side the army was preparing for peace. Canadians of the Toronto Scottish were parading for drill every morning with scrubbed belts and polished brasses. German prisoners streamed in by the thousands without guards, driving their own trucks and singing 'Tipperary'. Oldenburg, it was said, had surrendered by telephone. It was also said that the representative of Woolworths had beaten our troops into Hamburg to make sure their store was OK and that the population had turned out to cheer us when we did march in. It was all crazy and there was a sudden feeling of emptiness and pointlessness about everything we were now doing. But my war was over.

APPENDIX

Map 1 *Le Havre - Area*

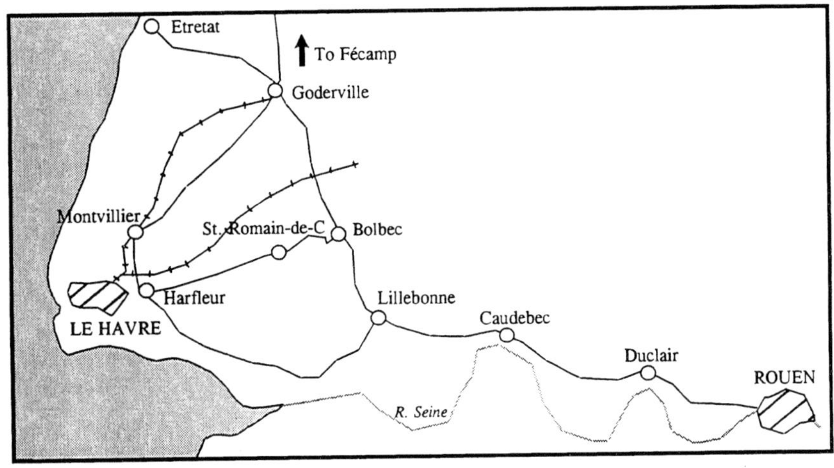

Map 2 *Le Havre - Assault Plan*

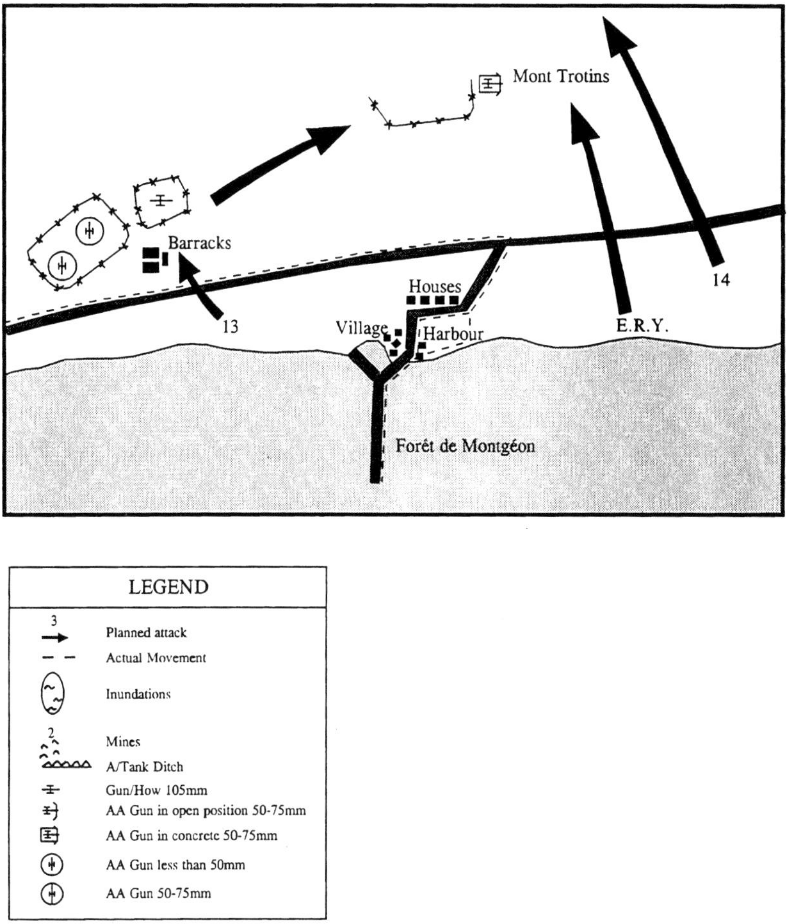

Mont Trotins
Barracks
13
Houses
Village
Harbour
E.R.Y.
14
Forêt de Montgéon

LEGEND

3 →	Planned attack
– –	Actual Movement
	Inundations
2	Mines
	A/Tank Ditch
	Gun/How 105mm
	AA Gun in open position 50-75mm
	AA Gun in concrete 50-75mm
	AA Gun less than 50mm
	AA Gun 50-75mm

Map 3 *Le Havre - Troop Movement*

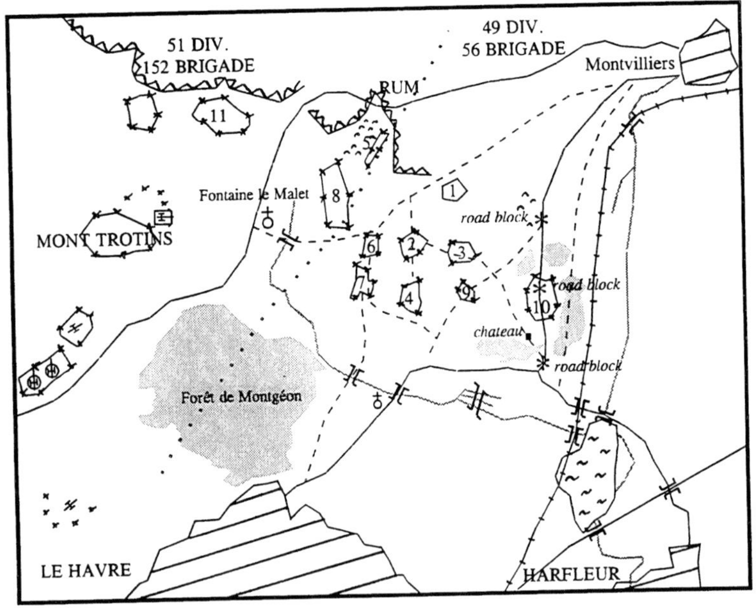

Map 4 *Boulogne - Area*

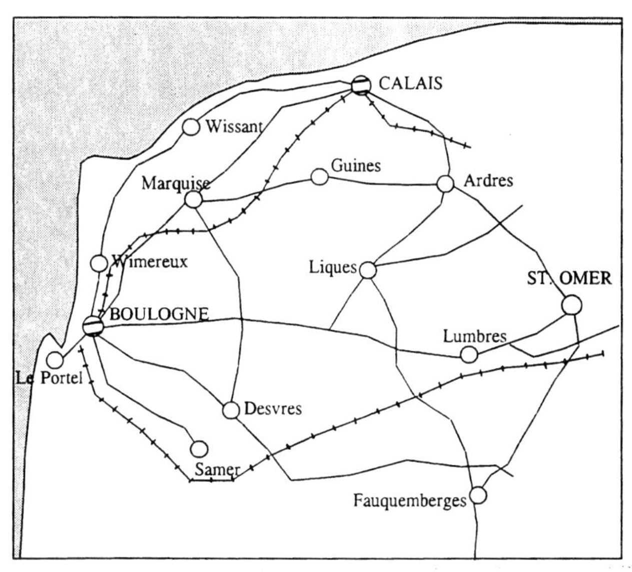

Map 5 *Boulogne - Town*

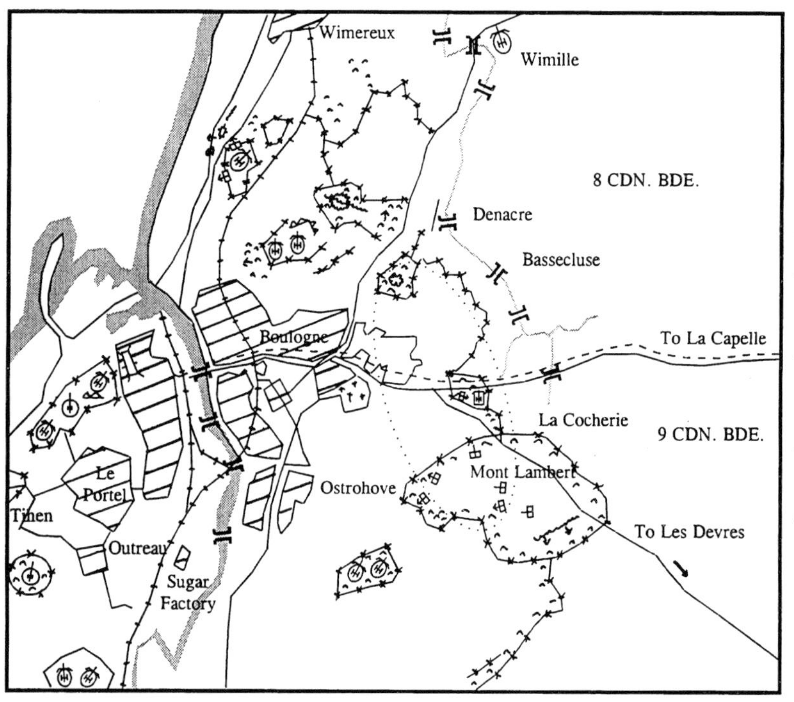

Map 6 *Calais - Noires Mottes*

LEGEND

- Infantry gun casement
- Wire
- Inundations
- Mines
- MG or Weapon pit
- A/Tank Ditch
- Trenches
- Mobile Gun/How up to 105mm
- Mobile Gun/How
- AA Gun less than 50mm in open position
- AA Gun less than 50mm
- Concrete shelter

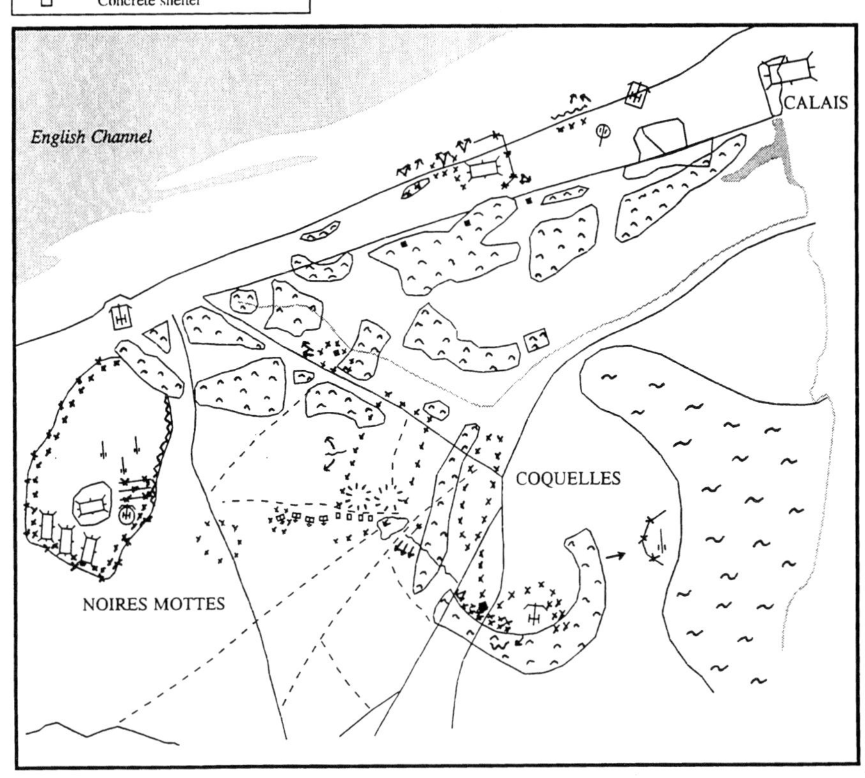

Map 7 *S'Hertogenbosch - Area*

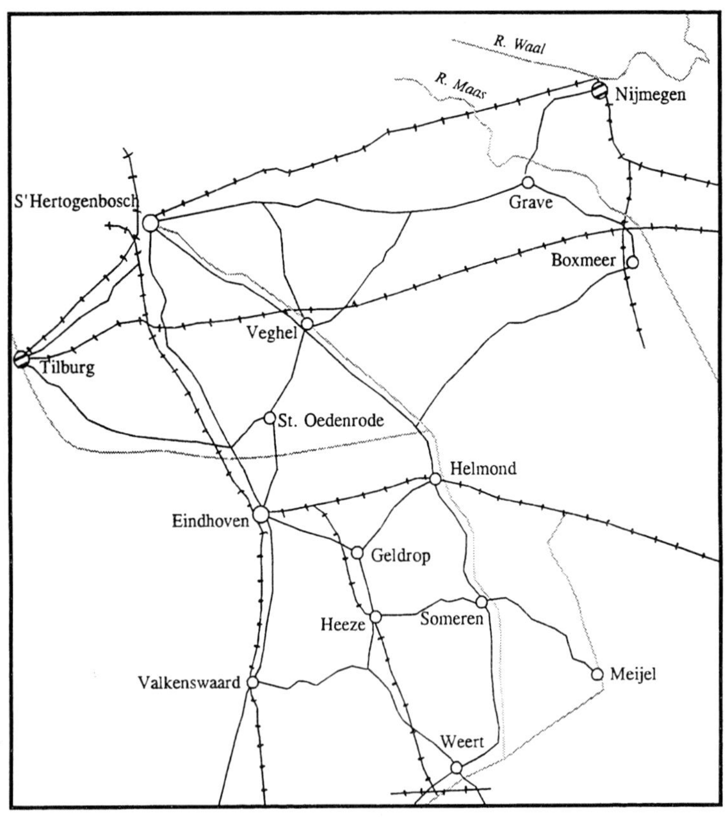

Map 8 *S'Hertogenbosch - Town*

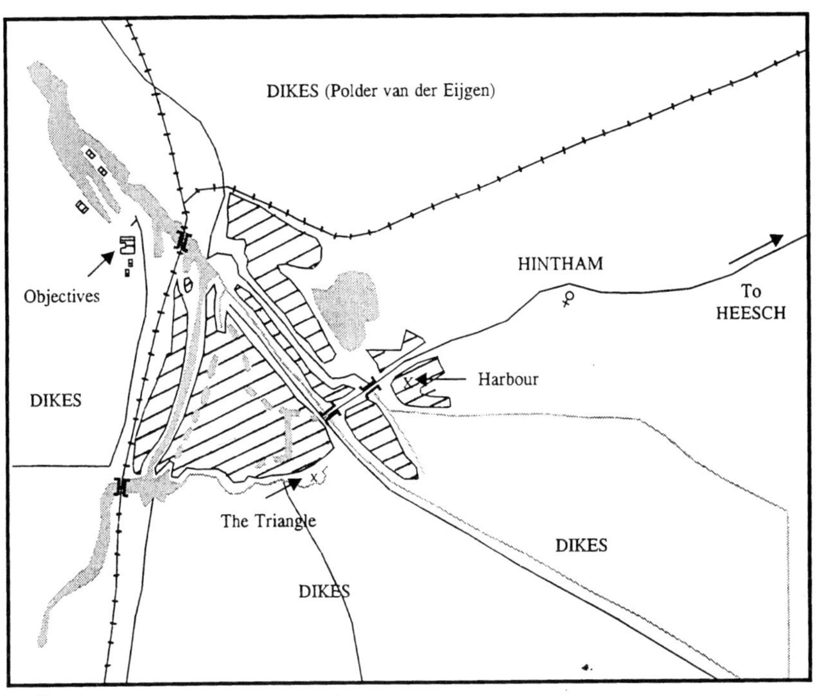

Map 9 *Meijel*

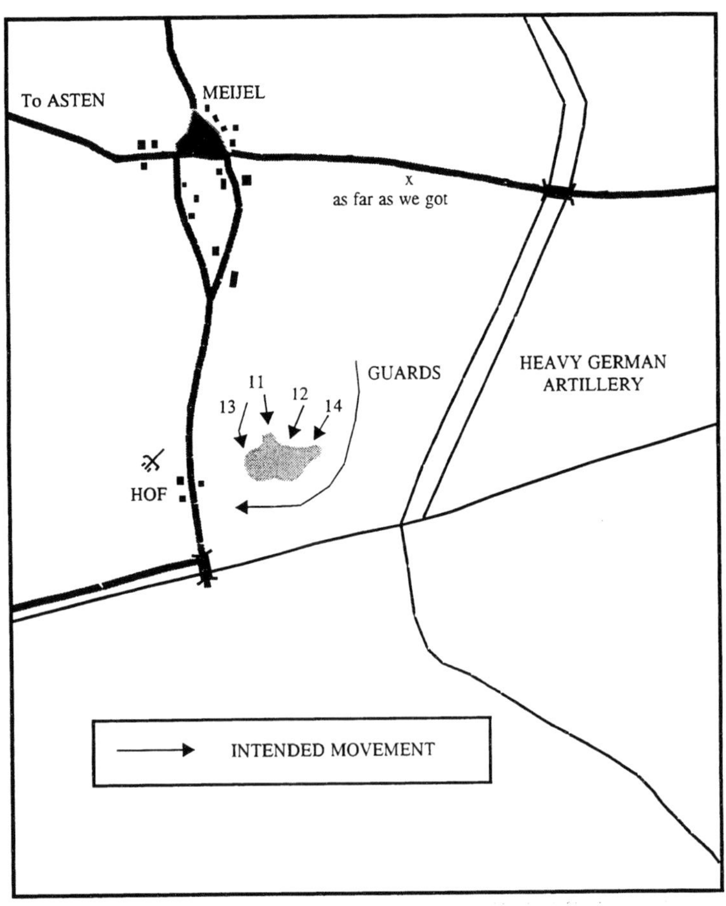
To ASTEN
MEIJEL
x
as far as we got
GUARDS
HEAVY GERMAN
ARTILLERY
11
12
13
14
HOF
INTENDED MOVEMENT

Map 10 *Operations between the rivers Maas and Roer*

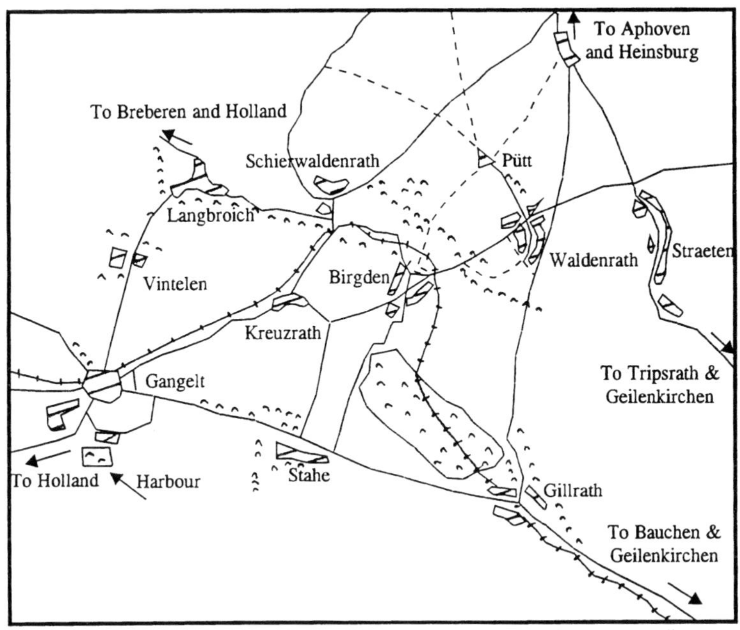

Map 11 *From Nijmegen to the Rhine*

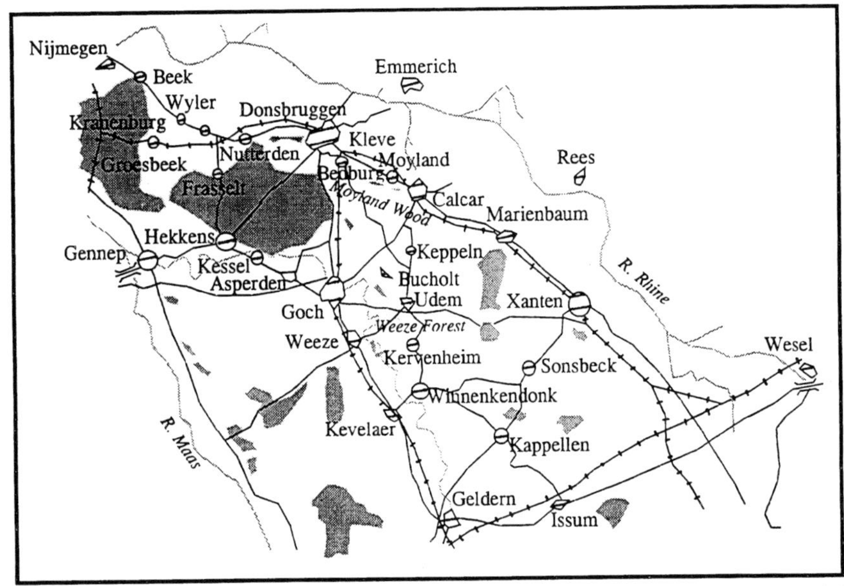

Map 12 *The Rhine Crossing*

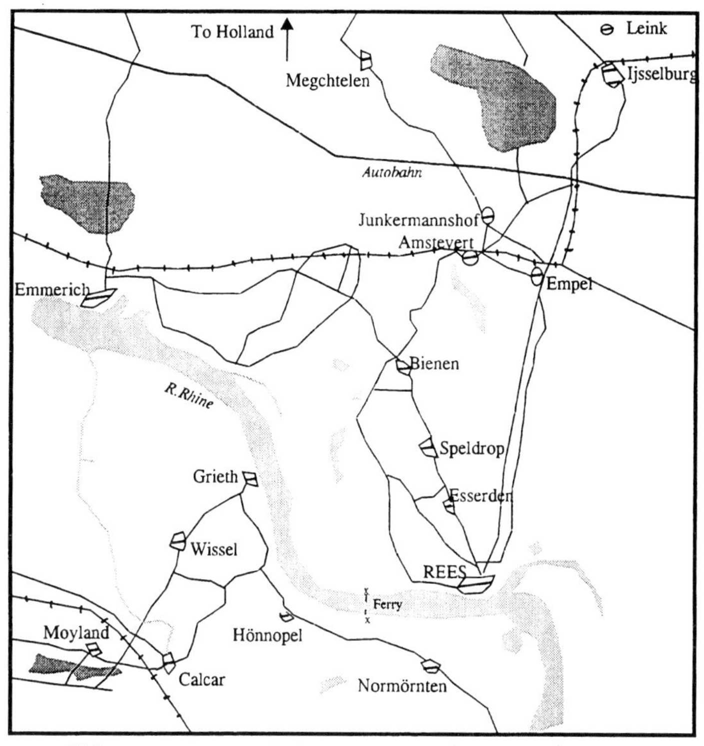

Map 13 *Arnhem West*

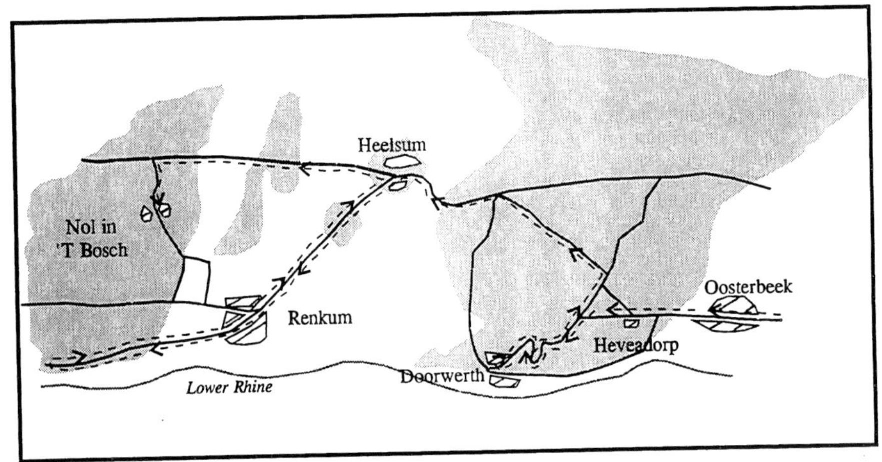